AN ECOLOGICAL APPROACH TO THE STUDY OF CHILD CARE
Family Day Care in Israel

Miriam K. Rosenthal
The Hebrew University of Jerusalem

LAWRENCE ERLBAUM ASSOCIATES, PUBLISHERS
1994   Hillsdale, New Jersey   Hove, UK

Lawrence Erlbaum Associates, Inc., Publishers
365 Broadway
Hillsdale, New Jersey 07642

Library of Congress Cataloging-in-Publication Data

Rosenthal, Miriam K.
An ecological approach to the study of child care : family day
care in Israel / Miriam K. Rosenthal.
p.   cm.
Includes bibliographical references (p.   ) and index.
ISBN 0-8058-1163-X (acid-free paper)
1. Child care--Israel.   2. Child-care services--Israel. 3. Day-
care centers--Israel. I. Title.
HQ778.7.I75R67 1994
362.7'095794--dc20   94-15083
                                                               CIP

Books published by Lawrence Erlbaum Associates are printed on
acid-free paper, and their bindings are chosen for strength and dura-
bility.

Printed in the United States of America
10 9 8 7 6 5 4 3 2 1

This book is dedicated to
the memory of my father, *Aaron*
who left me with a song
about believing in dreams and the human spirit
and the memory of my mother, *Hedva*
whose spirit gave me the strength to sustain these beliefs

Contents

Introduction

In recent years, children in most industrial societies are experiencing a new type of childhood (Dencik, 1989). As a result of social and economic changes, a growing number of infants and toddlers in these societies participate in some form of out-of-home care (Clarke-Stewart & Fein, 1983; Kahn & Kamerman, 1987; Melhuish & Moss, 1991; Rosenthal, 1992). This social trend has been paralleled by an increasing interest in studying the effects of child-care attendance on the development of children.

This interest reflects the growing involvement of developmental and educational researchers in political and social debates and in the attempt to influence social policy that is likely to shape the life and development of young children in their societies (Clarke-Stewart, 1988; Rosenthal, Biderman, & Luppo, 1987; Scarr & Eisenberg, 1993, Scarr, Phillips, & McCartney, 1990).

Most of the North American research into the effects of child care has been based on the assumption that the early experiences of children, either because of their critical nature or because of their cumulative effects, are important for children's development. This premise was the source of the great hopes placed on early child care as "intervention," or compensatory education, for children from disadvantaged families. The same premise was however, also the source of great concern regarding the possible damaging effect of full-day child care on the socioemotional development of the child.

These hopes and concerns were greatly influenced by social and economic changes and the social ideology that prevailed in North American society in the past 30 years. Both hope and concern had a great influence on the outcome measures selected for the investigation of the effects of child care on development. (e.g., Booth, 1992)

Several investigators have employed the metaphor of "waves" to describe the evolving trends in the last 20 years or so of child-care research (Belsky, 1984; Clarke-Stewart, 1987; Holloway & Reichart-Erickson, 1989; Scarr & Eisenberg, 1993). There is a general agreement among these investigators as to the nature of these waves.

The first wave refers to studies carried out mostly in the early 1970s. These studies attempted to answer questions such as "Is child care good or bad for children?", generally assuming that child care attendance implies a homogeneous set of experiences. They focused on the comparison of maternal and nonmaternal care, without considering the quality of care in either setting. This wave led to the growing awareness that the experiences of staying at home or attending child care are more complex. The nature of these experiences seemed determined mostly by the quality of care offered in either setting.

The second wave of studies, conducted mostly during the late 1970s and early 1980s, asked questions such as "What are the effects of different quality of child care?". This research introduced the idea that child care of different kinds and varying quality may have different effects on children's development. It examined the relationship of children's social and intellectual development to the quality and variety of child-care settings.

Generally, these investigations evaluated quality of care by actually observing the structural and process characteristics of the child-care settings (Belsky, 1984) and related them to developmental outcomes for individual children. It is interesting to note that the choice of dimensions defining quality and the choice of outcome measures in these studies were based mostly on earlier findings of what constitutes a "good" home environment, supportive of cognitive development and socioemotional adjustment of individual children. These choices reflect Western values and developmental goals.

These investigations were based on a global concept of quality care and assumed generally that "good things go together" (Phillips & Howes, 1987). Recent studies have suggested, however, that specific aspects of quality may be related to specific developmental outcomes and not to others (Clarke-Stewart, 1987; Kontos & Fiene, 1987; Rosenthal, 1990).

The third wave attempts to integrate characteristics of parents and home settings into child-care research (Clark-Stewart, Gruber, & Fitzgerald, 1994). It poses more complex questions such as "How do child-care qualities combine with family factors to produce effects on children's development?". In this wave of studies, characteristics of both home and child care were considered in relation to various developmental outcomes. The early studies in this wave reflect a methodological concern over the confounding of family and child-care characteristics arising from parental selection of child-care settings. They examined the effects of variations in child care while controlling for family influences.

As a result, these analyses have yielded some data concerning the relative contribution of home and child-care settings to children's developmental outcomes (Kontos, 1987; Phillips et al., 1987). However, the family characteristics examined have often been global and without clear relevance to the developmental outcome measures that were selected.

A more recent research goal within this wave was to explore how elements of the home and child care interact in predicting child development. This new development attempted to map the elements in the home that may modify how children experience child care. Attention has been drawn to parents' beliefs, attitudes, and values and family's life conditions such as stressful events or the availability of support (Holloway & Reichart-Erickson, 1989; Howes & Olenick, 1986; Kontos, 1991).

Studies emerging in other societies (Dencik et al., 1989) have suggested that future research should examine not only long-term developmental outcomes of the joint impact of home and child care, but should shift its focus to how children are negotiating the daily shifts between these two childrearing contexts.

A fourth wave seems to have emerged in the early 1990s. As Scarr, Phillips, and McCartney suggested (1990), including individual differences among children in the same research model together with variations of child-care quality and family characteristics creates a richer picture of the ecology of the child care. Thus, for example, besides their family background, children's child-care history and individual characteristics such as age, temperament, or illness may modify the effects of different qualities of child care on their development (Feagans 1992; Vandell & Corasaniti, 1990).

Most of the studies in the last waves of child-care research followed a strategy by which attempts are made to identify, with the help of multivariate analyses, the "best" predictor, or "best combination" of predictors of developmental outcomes from among a variety of variables defining the characteristics of children, families, and child-care settings.

Recent research has called attention to cultural variations as important aspects of the ecological study of children in child care (Lamb et al., 1992; Tobin et al., 1989). This development is in accordance with current theory and models of the "environment" that emphasize the interface between development and culture as a context for development (Bronfenbrenner, 1979; Super & Harkness, 1986).

Whether or not this will become a new wave of child-care research is yet to be seen. This research trend suggests, however, that child-care policy in different countries reflects basic differences in cultural values and social beliefs and attitudes toward child care (Lamb et al., 1992). This means that out-of-home care may have different goals, and hence different developmental outcomes in different cultures or within the same culture during different periods in its history. Thus, societies undergoing social and cultural changes may alter the goals for their child-care services as the old goals may not match the changed ideology or the changing needs of the population.

This trend suggests, therefore, that the investigation of child-care outcomes in any given society requires an articulation of the relationship between cultural values and beliefs and the definition of the developmental goals set for child care in that society (Sigel, 1992). Differences in developmental goals that are set for child care imply that different definitions of "quality care" may be needed in different societies. What might be "thresholds of quality" (Howes et al., 1992) in one society may be irrelevant to the definition of quality of care in other societies.

The metaphor of waves has been expanded by researchers in the field of child care to warn against the danger of the field becoming engulfed, deluged, and drowned by waves of mixed, ambiguous, inconclusive, and inconsistent results (Clarke-Stewart, 1987a; Scarr & Eisenberg, 1993).

The motivation for much of the research on child care has sprung out of the social involvement of researchers attempting to influence policy so as to facilitate optimal development for children in their societies. The motivation for change and influencing policy decisions should not be confused, however, with the motivation for uncovering basic environmental processes responsible for developmental outcomes among children attending child care.

The present analysis of child-care research, as well as our own data, suggests that researchers should examine their research motivation and its relationship to their chosen research strategy. It is suggested that future research can avert the danger of ambiguous and inconsistent results, by changing from a research strategy that is based on empirically extracting statistically significant relationships between environmental predictors and developmental outcomes to a more theoretically based strategy. Such an alternative strategy will draw on both theory and empirical knowledge available in the general field of developmental psychology as well as that derived from cross-cultural developmental research. This alternative strategy should consist of a careful articulation of the relationship between the developmental goals set for child care, the environmental processes relevant to attaining these goals at home and in child care, and the interaction between these processes and personal characteristics of children.

This approach implies a shift in strategy from attempts to find "the best predictor" or "the best combination of predictors" of certain outcomes to a carefully planned, systematic, and theoretically based, investigation of the interactions and mutual relationships between the relevant child, family, child care, and societal characteristics and the processes through which they influence the development of children in child care.

This does not mean that the empirical search for the relationship between society-specific regulatable and process variables should be dismissed. On the contrary, such research can be a powerful tool in influencing policy decisions. Yet, it is suggested that the cultural and social values that guide our investigation, become part and parcel of research that is "informed by science" (McCartney, 1993).

The historical trends of child-care research led us to an attempt to investigate a specific child-care system, in a given society with its culture, history, values, and beliefs. The aim of this volume is to analyze the daily experiences of infants and toddlers in family day care in the framework of a culture-based ecological approach. The book is based on a conceptual model that suggests that culture and socioeconomic processes in a given society determine the nature of the social policy concerning its child-care services. This policy reflects the goals set by the society for its child care.

The purpose of the book is to present the sponsored family day care system in Israel as a "case study" for the discussion of issues derived from this conceptual model, which are of central concern for the investigation of child care in any society. The book examines the experiences of infants and toddlers in this sponsored family day care system with reference to cultural and social policy issues, family background and parental beliefs, caregivers' background and beliefs, the nature of the child-care environment, as well as the child's personal characteristics. The orientation of the book is both theoretical and applied and as such is addressed, not just to researchers in the field of child development, but also to educators, sociologists, and social workers who are interested in the study of environmental influences on the development of children during the early years of life. It should be of special interest to researchers interested in the study of child development in context, or within an ecological approach and mostly to those interested in the study of out-of-home-care for young children.

The book opens with the social and historical context for the development of child care in Israel and how it is related to the social policy and the goals set for its sponsored FDC. Chapter 2 outlines the unique features of the FDC program, the research goals and research questions, and the methods employed in our investigation.

Cultural values and social policy are likely to determine which families will be using a particular child-care program. Chapter 3 describes the Israeli parents that are using the FDC system, their demographic characteristics as well as their childrearing beliefs and attitudes toward child care. As in the case of parents, cultural values and social policy are likely also to determine who will be the care providers in a given child-care system. Chapter 4 examines the personal and professional background of the caregivers in the sponsored FDC system as well as conditions of their work environment. It then proceeds to explore the relationship of these factors to the caregiver's childrearing beliefs, her spontaneous and planned interactions with the children, and the quality of the physical environment she offers children in her home. This research recognizes the fact that children in most Western societies move back and forth, on a daily basis, between two socializing worlds. Chapter 5 examines therefore, the similarities and differences between these worlds especially in terms of the childrearing beliefs and expectations from the development of children attending the FDC system under investigation.

Chapter 6 focuses on the behaviors of children attending the FDC program. It discusses the conceptual framework of these behavioral outcomes and the rationale for their inclusion in the study. It further examines the effects of the personal characteristics of children and their home background on these behaviors. This analysis is followed, in chapter 7, by an examination of the features of FDC as a child-care environment. This chapter investigates how different aspects of this environment influence the children's behavior, while controlling for the effects of the their personal and family characteristics. Chapter 8 discusses the interface between family, child, and child care. The investigation of this interface follows several steps and addresses a number of issues raised by the third and fourth research waves of child-care research described earlier. The interface is examined in relation to the nature of Israeli society and its child-care policy that may affect this interface.

The last two chapters offer a summary, conclusions, and a discussion of the implications of this study for future child-care research and policy. Chapter 9 summarizes our findings concerning the daily experiences and behaviors of children attending the FDC system under investigation. It examines the overall picture of the factors that were found to influence these behaviors. The chapter then concludes with the implications of our studies and their results for future research in the field of child care.

Chapter 10 examines our findings in the context of the social policy that guided the sponsored FDC system under investigation. The chapter then explores the implication of these findings for child-care policy in general and concludes with an epilogue describing the current developments in Israel's child-care policy in general and its impact on the FDC system in particular, at the cost of ignoring other aspects of development that might be effected by the experience of attending child care.

ACKNOWLEDGMENTS

I would like to acknowledge JDC-Israel for their financial support of this project, as well as their professional help in the attempts to bring about the policy modifications that were suggested by these studies. Further thanks are given for their financial support of the preparation of this book.

I owe a debt of gratitude to my graduate students Nadine Frank-Gorin and Esther Zilkha who helped with many aspects of the project; to Shmuel Broner, who acted as statistical advisor and programmer to these studies; and to Dr. B. Bogush and M. Barash who edited the English of parts of the manuscript.

Thanks are also due to the observers and interviewers who traveled to the various locations of the program; to the caregivers who opened their homes to us; the mothers who opened their hearts and minds; and the children who turned this journey into a delightful experience.

I also would like to acknowledge the editorial help I obtained from my husband, Alan Rosenthal, who assisted me all along the way in crossing the syntactical and grammatical bridges between Hebrew and English.

Last, but not least, I would like to thank my sons, Gil and Tal, for their much needed patience and support over the years of involvement in this project. Finally, a very special acknowledgment to Tomi, my first granddaughter, and Tzofnut, her mother, who made the following discussions and deliberations very real.

Miriam K. Rosenthal

1

The Social and Historical Context for the Development of Child Care

In order to understand the development of out-of-home child care and, in fact, the entire education and child welfare system in Israel (Jaffe, 1982), it is necessary to take a closer look at some of the social ideologies and processes that evolved during the pre-state era.

The cultural context for nonparental care in modern Israel has its roots in the historical tradition of the Jews who struggled to maintain their cultural identity when they were dispersed throughout the world and exiled from their land. This struggle to preserve their identity led to the development of a rich and intricate community life. Community services, as well as educational and welfare institutions were developed to strengthen the links between the individual, the family, and the community. Jewish communities throughout the world always assumed responsibility for the welfare of their members and provided education for their very young. The main goal of these services was to strengthen and maintain the community identity, continuity, and community ties, rather than meet the needs of individuals.

Although Jews have lived in and immigrated to Israel for more than 2,000 years, contemporary Israeli society is generally regarded as dating back to the latter part of the 19th century. Three major historical processes took place during the last hundred years that laid the foundations of modern Israeli society: (a) the persecution of Jews in Europe; (b) the evolution of political Zionism as a national liberation movement in the context of other national movements in Europe; and (c) the establishment of a Jewish homeland as a haven for Jews fleeing a hostile environment wherever they lived.

During the 45 years since its independence, Israel has remained the haven for Jews from all over the world and has done its best to absorb continuous tides of immigrants from a myriad of cultures, including the Jews of Kurdistan, Iran and India, North Africa, South America, Western and Eastern Europe, the English-speaking countries, and recently, Ethiopia. Thus, Israeli society has evolved as a society of immigrants hailing from a wide variety of cultures, with each group contributing its ethos to the emerging new society.

THE PRE-STATE ERA

The first flaw of immigration (1882–1903) brought with it a "revised conception of Judaism" (Bentwich, 1965) that was basically nonreligious. It regarded Jewish national liberation and political autonomy as its new self-identity. One of its major revolutionary achievements was the revitalization of ancient Hebrew as a modern living language.

The newcomers of the second period of immigration (1905–1914) were intensely involved with ideologies of social and cultural revolution. Many of them were intellectuals who had witnessed the revolutionary struggles in Eastern Europe, and who had been disillusioned by the gap between the revolutionary dream and its political reality.

Their goal was to establish a productive, self-sufficient society based on socialist principles. During this period the first kibbutz, the first all-Jewish city, and the first Jewish self-defense force were established. Although Palestine was at that time under Turkish rule, the Jewish community established its own democratically elected institutions, paralleling the structure of a parliament and cabinet. Its central authority (*Vaad Leumi*) developed and supported socioeducational services alongside those developed by the local communities. The Jewish working class organized (1920) into what was to become one of the most powerful institutions in the country, the General Federation of Jewish Labor (*Histadrut*). It established comprehensive mutual aid institutions, including a sick fund, social welfare services, a housing company, day-care centers, and so forth. These early decades were characterized by incessant experimentation with various forms of social organization and ways of life.

In addition to large numbers of *Halutzim* (pioneers) who were motivated to immigrate by social and nationalistic ideals, this wave also included tradesmen and manufacturers who set up commercial and industrial enterprises, and who contributed to the development of urban life (M. Smilansky, Weintraub, & Hanegbi, 1960).

Trade and industry continued to be developed, during the pre-state era, by the subsequent arrivals of immigrants, the last one of which (1933–1948) consisted primarily of Jews who had escaped from Europe following the rise of the Nazis to power, and those dislocated Jews who had survived the Holocaust (M. Smilansky et al., 1960).

At the time of the Declaration of Independence in 1948, the 650,000 members of the Jewish community in Palestine were mostly of European background. Within the next 3 years (1949–1951), this community, while fighting for its physical survival, absorbed 754,000 Jewish refugees from the surrounding Moslem countries, providing them with housing, jobs, health, social, and educational services.

The demographic and ethnic composition of this immigration, its social and economic character and the process of its absorption has changed Israeli society over the past 45 years in ways that cannot yet be fully understood. In contrast to the earlier European waves of immigration, these refugees were generally characterized by traditional, large, and extended families; a high birth rate; and low levels of literacy and vocational training (Gross, 1970). Although the immigration from Europe included both the middle and lower social strata of the Jewish community, it was mainly the less modernized and poorer elements that came to Israel from certain Middle Eastern communities. Many of these immigrants from Arabic-speaking countries, accustomed to an agrarian, pre-industrial society, had difficulty in adjusting to the social and economic patterns in Israel previously established by immigrants from industrialized Western societies. Furthermore, these Jewish communities had not undergone the social and cultural upheavals to which the European Jews had been exposed and were therefore less prepared for the changes in attitudes toward traditional habits and beliefs.

Social Ideology and Its Effect on Early Childhood in the Pre-State Era

The pioneers of the first periods of immigration were mostly young people in their 20s who rebelled against their parents and against the traditions they represented. They had not only left home and country never to return, but also sought to transform the Jewish nation by building an independent society with a "normal" occupational structure and a "modern" social and political outlook (M. Smilansky et al., 1960). Their goal was to develop an alternative culture, based on new beliefs and ideologies, that was as different as possible from the culture of the diaspora (Super & Harkness, 1986). It soon became evident, however, that some of their deep-seated cultural beliefs had not changed at all. In accordance with traditional practice, these immigrants also looked to their children, the future generation, to realize the cultural transformation. These children were expected to become the "New Israelis," strong, healthy, free, and proud Jews, living in their own land, speaking their own language, and adhering to the ideology of equality and fraternity.

Possibly the most extreme but also most representative example of this trend is that of the children's homes in the kibbutzim. Ideology, practical life necessity, and later on a rationale based on psychodynamic theory, resulted in a social system in which, from the first days of their life, children were reared in communal homes and spent only a few hours a day with their parents (Kraft, 1967; Levin, 1985; Neubauer, 1965). This system enabled both parents to work outside the home, which was not only an economic necessity but also an ideological norm. It further enabled the community to provide the housing, hygiene, medical care, and safety facilities needed to ensure the survival of its young. Thus, although their parents lived in tents and were plagued by illness, undernourishment, and fever, the young generation lived in houses, received the best food available, and were raised by carefully chosen caregivers (*metaplot*), trained in both the latest ideas of modern education and the most revered principles of social revolution. The provision of a professional educator was expected to help both child and parent overcome the "bourgeois" past, as well as to avoid the intergenerational psychological strain of nuclear family existence (Levin, 1985). Although in the 1990s the kibbutz movement encompasses only 4% of the population of Israel and its educational ideology concerning early childhood has changed considerably, the child-care and education systems that developed in the kibbutzim in the early years had a great impact on the evolution of overall preschool education in Israel.

A similar trend emerged in the cities and towns. The first priority was to guarantee the survival of children. All over the country, the community's responsibility for the health of its young was expressed through the establishment of a network of mother and child health centers that attended to the needs of pregnant women and their infants. Trained public health nurses instructed mothers in "modern" ideas of pre- and postnatal care, as well as in nutrition and hygiene practices. In later years, these centers also provided the necessary inoculations and other measures of preventive medicine, all free of charge; the cost was covered by public community resources.

Once their health care was secured, the next step was to rid these "new Israeli" children of any traces of the Diaspora Jew mentality for they were to be the foundation on which the new culture and society would be built. In many cases, for this reason the pioneers even disqualified themselves as parents who were competent to rear their own children. After all, they did not know the language that was supposed to be their children's mother tongue and they could not shake off all the old customs and habits.

Just as their forbears had done so often in other times of distress, these pioneers also sought help from community resources. This time, they turned to the professional educator, to provide guidance and models for the cultural socialization of their children.

Half-day nursery schools, run by teachers whose education was similar to that of the kibbutz teachers, were opened throughout the country. It was from their children who attended these nursery schools that parents learned nursery rhymes, new ways of celebrating the Jewish holidays, and in many instances even the Hebrew language. This commitment to preschool education as a major vehicle in the acculturation of the young in a principally immigrant society has remained a central feature of Israel's educational policy. In this context one should note that policymakers in the revolutionary Soviet Union adopted a similar commitment to early childhood education as a vehicle for social and cultural change (Bronfenbrenner, 1970; Lamb, Sternberg, Hwang, & Brogerg, 1992).

1948–1993: 45 YEARS OF CHILD CARE IN ISRAEL

Shared Community Responsibility for Child Care

With the advent of statehood, many institutions that had been organized on a voluntary basis were transferred and adapted to the state authority. The mutual responsibility based on sectional or other small group ties gave way to state laws and bureaucracy and the responsibility of the community became the responsibility of the state. The state adopted the two major national goals relating to the future generation: assuring the survival of the young and integrating the children of new immigrants into a unified Jewish Western society.

In order to meet the first goal, the new government assumed responsibility for the provision of a healthy and safe beginning for infants while they were still at home. This was accomplished in two ways:

First was legislated maternity leave enabling working mothers to receive 70% of their salary while staying home for 12 weeks following delivery. The National Insurance Institute paid for maternity leave and also provided each family with a special grant on the birth of a child. This policy has evolved over the years so that working mothers in the 1990s can take an additional 9 months of unpaid leave while their job is held secure, thus encouraging at-home care by the mother and extending it up to 12 months.

Second, the network of mother and child health centers (better known by its pre-state title *Tipat Halav*, meaning "a drop of milk") became the responsibility of the Ministry of Health. It provided free pre- and postnatal care, emphasizing health (immunization and inoculation), nutrition, and physical care to all mothers and their children up to the age of 3. In recent years, many of these centers have also started screening all infants for early detection of developmental risk, using an abbreviated form of the Bayley Infant Test. In the 1990s, these services are used by over 90% of the population. Together with the general medical care system, this service is probably responsible for the steep decline over the years in infant mortality in Israel (Israel Ministry of Labor and Social Affairs, 1987).

Attempts to meet the second goal continue to this day, partly because Israel continues to absorb waves of immigrants and partly because earlier attempts at social and cultural integration have met with only partial success.

The Commitment to Education

The newly created State of Israel perceived the education system as an integral part of its struggle for social integration and its search for cultural identity. This system was expected to provide the means by which its extraordinarily diverse population of refugees from post-Holocaust Europe, Middle Eastern Arab countries, and Eastern Europe could share equally in the challenges and opportunities of a society rapidly moving toward increased industrialization (Lombard, 1973). The commitment of the new state to education was exemplified by the Compulsory Education Law enacted in September 1949, less than 8 months after the election of the first Israeli Parliament (Kleinberger, 1969). In fact, so important were educational issues that violent political conflicts over education policies led to the resignation of the government and to new elections in 1951.

The Compulsory Education Law of 1949 provided each child with 9 years of education, starting with kindergarten at age 5 and covering 8 years of primary school. Approximately 20 years later, the law was extended to provide free high school education. The inclusion of at least 1 compulsory year of kindergarten was seen as a necessary prerequisite for the later success in school of children whose immigrant parents neither spoke the Hebrew language nor were familiar with a modern educational system (Lombard, 1973). These laws applied to all citizens of Israel, including the 20% non-Jewish minorities.

Lombard (1973) and other researchers (e.g., M. Smilansky & Smilansky, 1967) noted that the evolution of government policy reflected the continuous struggle to find a solution to the problems facing the education system, when more than 50% of the children entering school were described as "educationally disadvantaged," with very poor prognosis of academic achievement. Following the failure of earlier attempts, in 1967 the Ministry of Education decided to put its efforts into a policy that supported intellectual development and skill acquisition necessary to educational success (Lombard, 1973). This policy, combined with an awareness of the importance of the early years to the child's intellectual development, resulted in a selective expansion of free preschool education to 3- and 4-year-old children from disadvantaged homes.

Extended Preschool Education

The 1967 shift in policy was also reflected in the modified curricula for 5-year-olds, which gradually began to put greater emphasis on intellectual development and school readiness, and on more academic orientation and methods for preschool teachers. In addition, educational television programs for preschool children were developed, and in recent years computers were introduced into the preschool classroom.

There has recently been a significant increase in the number of 2- to 4-year-old children attending nursery schools (Israel Ministry of Education and Culture, 1989). Attendance is very close to 100% for 4-year-olds among the Jewish population, even though this is not part of the compulsory and universally free education system.

The prevalence of the Israeli norm of sending very young children to nursery school can be seen in a comparison of changes in the preschool attendance rates of 2-year-old children from Israeli and new immigrant homes over a 10-year period (1976–1986). The gap between the two groups has narrowed considerably during these years, as a growing proportion of new immigrant families accept the norm and send their 2-year-old children to nursery school. The average rate of increase in nursery school attendance for 2-year-olds, 2.1% per year, is identical to the average rate of increase in the number of students registering for university.

The Emergence of Day Care

In contrast to the historical trend that assigned cultural and national priority to preschool education, day care emerged in the 1920s as a service for "needy" families: to meet the needs of disadvantaged mothers and children and the needs of working mothers (Jaffe, 1982). The concept of day care was thus developed outside the educational ideologies of the time. It emerged as a branch of the welfare system, along with orphanages. Its goals were to provide shelter for needy children and a service for working mothers who required all-day care for their children.

Thus, the preschool educational system, which was invested with the goal of creating the "New Israeli," focused on cultural and language input. The day-care system, which was expected to meet family welfare goals defined in terms of individual needs, focused on providing basic custodial care. At the time, neither system exerted any influence on the other.

Until the mid-1960s, even working mothers preferred to send their children to half-day nursery schools and to make afternoon arrangements with relatives and neighbors, rather than send their children to day-care centers.

Social Change and Its Effects on the Day-Care System: Emerging Challenges

Two major social developments led to a rapid increase in the number of day-care centers since the early 1970s. The first was the social unrest during the late 1960s and early 1970s, which was reflected in various grass-root protest movements that worked toward improving conditions for lower income families; the second development was the growing attractiveness of employment to middle-income and upper income young mothers (Jaffe, 1982).

The Effects of Social Unrest

In the wake of widespread social unrest, a special committee on "Children and Youth in Distress," sponsored by the Prime Minister's Office, was established. The committee's report (1973) recommended the development and expansion of day-care centers for children under the age of 3 as a means of providing enrichment for children of disadvantaged families, who would take part in the same programs as the children of working mothers. The committee recommended that "these centers [will] be supervised by the Ministry of Education and Culture, which will take the necessary pedagogic and educational steps ... to promote the progress of young children in all aspects of their development" (p. 20). The committee further recommended that the government "provide education to all children from four years of age by means of a graded tuition, with priority given to depressed areas in which the children should be cared for by educational facilities that begin at age three" (p. 24).

Although day-care centers had existed previously, they were now charged with new responsibilities. The initial goals of providing a hygienic environment and nutrition, and of facilitating absorption of the immigrant families of the 1950s, gave way to educational goals and "enrichment" for the disadvantaged, in order to help close the social gap.

The Prime Minister's Office committee charged the Ministry of Education with the responsibility of improving the educational quality of day care and promoting the development of children below 3 years of age in day care. It is quite clear that the committee's intention was to extend the national priority already given to early education as a vehicle for meeting social and cultural goals, to include education in the first 3 years of life.

TABLE 1.1
Percent of Working Mothers

	Years		
Age of Child	1970	1979	1985
0–1 year	20.6	39.5	45.7
2–4 years	27.0	47.9	56.4

The Effects of the Return of Mothers to the Labor Market

Although social unrest resulted in various attempts to address the educational gap of disadvantaged children in the framework of day care, the return of increasing numbers of mothers of young children to the labor market had a different set of ramifications on the day-care system (Rosenthal, 1992).

Table 1.1 shows a marked increase in women's participation in the work force during the 1970s and a continuation of this trend well into the 1980s.

Thus, day care was assigned a second major social function: to promote and facilitate the participation of mothers in the labor market. Indeed, studies have shown that working mothers were highly represented among the users of day care (Baer & Marcus, 1977). Furthermore, one of the major reasons cited by mothers for not returning to work was the lack of satisfactory day-care arrangements for their children (Bergman, 1979).

In 1970, the Ministry of Labor established a special Division of Women's Rights and Status with a mandate to develop new day-care centers for working mothers by supplying the women's organizations operating day-care centers with funds for building, and by providing subsidies to mothers using day care.

At the same time, even though the quality of care in day-care centers had not changed, middle-class working parents were altering their perceptions of day care, and now regarded it as a fairly adequate environment for their children and as a legitimate form of supplementing home care. This alteration in parental attitudes to day care was most likely triggered by the social and economic changes in Israel at the time that affected childrearing ideologies (Super & Harkness, 1986).

The changed attitudes toward the use of day-care centers has been paralleled by an increasing number of parents who believe that infants, and definitely toddlers, have social needs that can be met only by attending some form of group care.

Meeting the New Challenges: The Current Day-Care System

The most tangible result of the recommendations for day care made by the Committee on Children and Youth in Distress, combined with pressure from the Division of Women's Rights and Status, was the allotment of substantial funds by the Ministry of Finance for the building of new day-care centers (Jaffe, 1982). It should be noted that with limited funds and in a serious attempt to meet the needs of as many families as possible, the immediate objective of both ministries and parents was the opening of more day-care facilities rather than improving the standards of care in the existing ones.

The dilemma of quality versus quantity that faces policymakers becomes even more acute when it concerns the needs of "distressed" families with battered or neglected children. In these cases the placing social worker feels that as long as the child-care setting does not seriously harm the child, he or she is better off in a poor quality child-care setting than at home.

These pressures are familiar dilemmas in the field of social policy relating to child care in many Western societies (Lamb et al., 1992; Melhuish & Moss, 1991). The dilemmas are likely to remain unresolved as long as research data cannot state in clear probabilistic terms the danger accruing to children by the introduction of a 28th child into a day-care toddler group with two untrained caregivers (Howes, Phillips, & Whitebook, 1992). Furthermore, these dilemmas are likely to stay with us as long as the perception of day care by policymakers and society at large remains that of a system designed to meet the needs of individuals rather than to address general cultural or national goals. The effects of the alternating perception can be seen in the day-care systems developed in Denmark or Sweden (Lamb et al., 1992).

The current Israeli day-care system serves children 3 months to 4 years of age, with approximately 87% of these children being under 3 years old (Jaffe, 1982). These day-care programs usually operate 8 hours a day (8 a.m.–4 p.m.), 6 days a week, although some programs now offer half-day arrangements. Priority admission to these programs is given to children whose development is endangered by their parents.

Parents using day-care centers are entitled to a subsidy from the Ministry of Labor and Social Welfare according to a sliding scale based on income level, area of residence, family size, the presence of developmental problems or risk, recency of immigration to the country, type of maternal employment, and number of hours of maternal work. Families that receive subsidies include those that reside in development towns or in poor neighborhoods, whose income is below a given level, who immigrated to Israel less than 3 years ago, who have a child in day care who suffers some developmental arrest or is one of multiple birth infants, and where the mother works in industry or works more than 30 hours a week. Families that do not fulfill any of these criteria tend to pay the *full tuition* (Israel Ministry of Labor and Social Welfare, 1989).

Standards, salaries, budgets, and fees for the subsidized system are set by national committees that include representatives of the Ministry of Labor and Social Welfare, the Finance Ministry, the operating agencies such as the women's voluntary organizations, and representatives of parents.

Previous and current assessments of both structural and process aspects of quality of care in Israeli day-care centers make it clear that the goals of providing enrichment or even care of a satisfactory quality, could not possibly be achieved within the existing system (Howes et al., 1992; M. Rosenthal, 1991b; Rosenthal, Biderman, & Luppo, 1987).

A survey of 90% of all day-care centers in Israel (Livnat, 1971) revealed that 73.3% of the staff, including the directors, were nonprofessional. In the women's organization that cared for the largest number of children in day care, the level of nonprofessional staff was as high as 81.5%. These were women who agreed to work 8 hours a day with 2 weeks annual leave, for one of the lowest salaries in the labor market. Most, in fact, themselves came from a disadvantaged background. Without any formal training in either child development or the principles of education, this staff was obviously unable to meet the challenge of providing enrichment to the disadvantaged children in day care. In recent years several short preservice and periodic in-service training programs were developed for those caregivers with less than high school education. These short programs have been supplemented by educational supervision in the centers. These goals, however, are not clearly defined and there are no set criteria as to what should be taught, how, for how long, and by whom. Although sporadic visits to the centers suggest that here and there one can see some implementation of educational ideas, there is no systematic evaluation of the training and supervision offered currently to some of the caregivers.

Regardless of the education and level of training of the caregivers, the potential of the Israeli day-care system to provide enrichment or even good quality care is further reduced by the large group size, poor adult-to-child ratio and the large size of the centers (Roupp & Travers, 1982). Thus, a typical center has more than 80 children divided into age-homogenous groups. The group sizes and adult–child ratios are described in Table 1.2 (M. Rosenthal et al., 1987).

In order that day care could meet its new challenges, various attempts were made to change the social policy regulating these structural features, but they met with very little success (M. Rosenthal, 1988). Thus, a proposal by the director general of the Ministry of Education and Culture (1974) for training day-care personnel (following the recommendations of the Committee on Children and Youth in Distress) was met with objections from the powerful Teacher's Union, as well as from the Ministry of Welfare. The latter was not prepared to accept the redefinition of the goals set for day care from a service to needy (welfare) families to a program that would address wider national goals, nor was it ready to relinquish control over the existing service. In fact, the rivalry between the ministries has been one of the primary obstacles in the potential development of quality day care in Israel (Dubler, 1974). Similarly, the recommendation by an interministerial committee headed by the Demographic Center of the Prime Minister's Office, to establish a national authority in charge of day care that would coordinate the efforts of the various ministries involved, was turned down by the Ministry of Finance in 1977. Another

TABLE 1.2
Day-Care Centers: Standards of Group Size and Adult-to-Child Ratio

	Age in Months			
	3–18	*18–24*	*24–36*	*36–48*
Number of caregivers	2	2	2	2
Children in a group	15–18	22	27	35

report, prepared by a committee appointed by the director general of the Ministry of Labor and Social Welfare, which set standards for day care, training of staff, and procedures to enforce existing regulatory legislation (M. Rosenthal et al., 1987), was also shelved following objections by the Ministry of Finance.

Sponsored Family Day Care

At the time the Demographic Center of the Prime Minister's Office committed itself to facilitate the implementation of the recommendations of the Committee on Children and Youth in Distress and its repeated failures to change national day-care policy led it to attempt side-stepping the existing system. These activities led to two important developments: The first was the opening in the mid-1970s of a 1-year graduate training program in early childhood (the Schwartz Program) at the Hebrew University to prepare early childhood specialists as leaders and trainers in programs for infants and toddlers. This program was designed to provide the infrastructure for future upgrading of the educational quality of out-of-home care provided for children under the age of 3. To date, more than 300 students have graduated from this program and have made a visible impact on the field of early childhood in Israel. The second development was the creation, in conjunction with the Israeli Community Center Association and through a public Inter-Ministerial Steering Committee, of alternative models of out-of-home care for children under 3 years old, directed and coordinated by graduates of the university-based training program.

These developments were paralleled by a slowly growing awareness of middle-class parents beginning to search for programs that best suited their own and their children's needs.

The most successful of these alternative models is the system of sponsored family day care (FDC) developed by the graduates of the Schwartz Program within the Community Center Association, which has since grown very rapidly (from 25 homes in 1977 to approximately 1,530 in 1990). Following its apparent success and appeal to parents, the model has since been adopted by the Ministry of Labor and Social Welfare, as an additional service they offer to families.

According to this model, groups of FDC homes, where a woman cares for a number of infants and toddlers in her own home, are sponsored either by the local community center or by the local welfare department and are to be supervised regularly by a professional with a graduate academic training in early childhood. This professional is to provide, in addition, regular in-service training to the caregivers under his or her supervision.

The high standards of professionalism of this new system were quickly acknowledged and it was perceived by both parents and experts in the field as the best alternative care for infants and toddlers.

The Inter-Ministerial Steering Committee that guided the development of this model requested that the new FDC program be evaluated, so as to enable policy-makers to assess the extent to which the program follows the set standards and criteria, the quality of care provided and its impact on the behavior of children in this setting. The evaluation was expected also to identify key regulatable conditions that influence the quality of care in these homes.

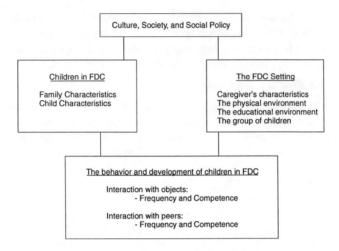

FIG. 1.1. The conceptual model of the present study.

The new model of sponsored family day care carried several messages that challenged the existing day-care system: First, parents and children are entitled to quality services that meet their needs. Second, the developmental needs of infants and toddlers are of special concern to society. These needs require that children should be cared for in small groups where the caregiving is guided by a professional with knowledge in the field of early childhood.

The added evaluation component carried the message of the importance of accountability in terms of effect on children's development. It also highlighted the existing relation between regulatable conditions, quality of care, and developmental outcome.

The challenge in these messages reflects the conflicting perceptions of the goals for child care in the present day Israeli society. The conflict is between the goal of providing large numbers of affordable and safe child-care programs and the goal of providing children with an early start for achieving early academic and social competence. Regardless of the specific goals there exists the expectation that the community at large through its government ministries and other public organizations should make provision for meeting these goals.

This book presents the conceptual model on which the evaluation of the sponsored FDC system was based, as well as the results of this evaluation. The model is based on an ecological, or system, approach to child development (Bronfenbrenner, 1979b).

According to the model presented in Fig. 1.1, culture and socioeconomic processes are related to the nature of the social policy that addresses the needs of children and their families. Standards and criteria set by this policy are likely to determine who will be the children attending child care, their age, their family background, and life history. The policy further influences the characteristics of teachers, or caregivers, in these settings (e.g., education, training) and the quality of care offered in them. The behavior and development of children in child care is therefore related to the social policy of the society in which they are raised.

It should be noted that Fig. 1.1 employs no "arrows" that may suggest direct or linear effect of one aspect of the system on another. A system approach implies that each part of the system is both a mediator of effects and is being mediated by effects of the other parts.

The book discusses the results of the evaluation of the Israeli-sponsored FDC system and their implications for policymaking and the design of early education programs, as well as for theory and research on early development in general.

2

Research Goals
and Methodology

THE SPONSORED FAMILY DAY-CARE PROGRAM

The following description of the FDC program is based on interviews with the members of the National Steering Committee, including the heads of the two agencies sponsoring FDC and with the nine coordinators of all the FDC programs at the time. It is also based on documents gathered from the two sponsoring agencies, the Israeli Association of Community Centers and the Ministry of Labor and Social Affairs, which reveal that the primary social goal set for the sponsored FDC program is similar to that of day-care centers.

The main goal of the FDC program, like that of the other day-care programs, is to meet the needs of families with working mothers and those with social and economic problems. Likewise, it was agreed that FDC was to be subsidized by the government on the same basis as other day-care programs and would serve the same target population.

Three additional major objectives were stated by the Inter-Ministerial Steering Committee of the FDC model: to provide and maintain quality care; to provide a support system for distressed families with very young children; and to meet the unique needs of infants and toddlers by providing stable and continuous care by one caregiver in the intimacy of a small group in a home environment.

The steering committee expected that the collaboration between early childhood specialists and the two sponsoring agencies that regulate and enforce standards set by the same public committee would attain these objectives.

The standards developed for the FDC model that were initially accepted by both sponsoring agencies address criteria for (a) selection of program operators, (b) admission policy and priorities, (c) group composition, (d) physical conditions, and (e) educational program.

Program Operators (Caregivers and Coordinators).   The standards require that a full-time coordinator with special academic training in early childhood and supervision methods, should supervise each program of 10–12 homes. This coordinator should also be responsible for the training and supervision of the caregivers as well as contact with the families and social or health agencies in the community. The standards further require that the caregiver has at least 10 years of formal education and some previous experience in child care, and that her personality and the attitude of her family to her work are appropriate. The caregiver has to participate in a 2-month preservice training course, continue to participate in ongoing training or group supervision, and receive individual supervision in her home on a weekly basis. Although there is no such requirement, all program operators are women.

Program Participants.   The program is expected to serve children from 3 to 36 months of age whose mothers work or children considered "at risk" from families with severe social and economic problems (as defined by the local welfare department). Admission priorities and subsidies are based on the same sliding scale used for day-care centers.

Group Composition.   The maximum number of children allowed per home is five. The ages of the children, limited to the 3–36 months range, are to be moderately mixed, so that the caregiver can better attend to the children's individual needs. The groups are expected to represent a wide range of socioeconomic status (SES) backgrounds in order to avoid a high concentration of children at risk in any one given FDC home.

Physical Conditions.   A detailed list specifies conditions of physical care, health and safety criteria, furniture, indoor space and access to outdoor space, play materials, and equipment. Some financial support is available to new caregivers to help them equip their homes according to the required standards.

Educational Program.   No specific educational program is stipulated by the standards, although the goal of enrichment for children from poor families requires that educational activities should be incorporated into the daily routine. In-service training and individual supervision to be provided to the caregiver by the professional coordinator are the means by which educational activities are introduced into the daily routine.

RESEARCH GOALS AND RESEARCH QUESTIONS

The evaluation of the FDC program is based on an ecological model of child care and presents its research questions on several levels.

Following our analysis of the cultural and social ideology behind the Israeli child-care system and examining the specific social policy derived from this ideology that led to the development of a sponsored FDC system, our ecological model led us to explore the relationship of this policy to the lives of parents, caregivers, and children.

An ecological approach to the study of child care raises questions about the families using child care. Who are they? What are their expectations from child care, from their child? How do they perceive their role vis-à-vis the role of the caregiver? Do their backgrounds and/or expectations influence the behavior of the caregivers and/or the behavior of their children?

It also raises questions concerning the FDC caregivers. Who are they? What is their professional background? How do they perceive their role vis-à-vis the role of the parents? How do they understand the development of children? Are their expectations and beliefs related to their behavior? How do these expectations and behaviors affect children in their care?

One also has to be concerned about the continuity between the home and the child-care environment. Does the different childrearing context lead to different socializing roles and beliefs of mothers and caregivers? How does growing up in two socializing worlds affect the behavior of children?

The ecological approach also brings up issues regarding the children in child care. Who are they? What do they do while in child care? How is what they do influenced by who they are, their life histories, their family background, the social and nonsocial aspects of the FDC environment? Finally how do all these sources of influence on the child's behavior interact with each other?

The following chapters of this book are structured in accordance with these research questions concerning the families, the FDC caregivers, the children and the effects of the two childrearing environments on the behavior of children.

The ecological model enables us to explore some of the intricacies of the lives of children moving back and forth between home and child care. At the same time, it also provides us also with answers related to the goals and objectives defined by policymakers on the macrosystem level. These focus on questions such as:

1.   To what extent does the program adhere to the standards set by the steering committee? Does it serve the population it is supposed to serve? Do the program operators meet their educational standards? Are the groups structured according to the standards? Are the physical conditions and daily routines developmentally appropriate?
2.   Is adherence to these standards set by the policymakers related to the quality of care offered in these sponsored FDC homes? Do any of the standards predict the quality of care better than others?

The final chapter of this volume examines the social policy implications derived from this study and considers them in the context of the recently evolving changes in Israel's policy concerning its very young children.

Because this study applies the ecological approach in a culture that is somewhat different to the United States, where most child-care research has been conducted in the last decades, it enables us to examine definitions and research strategies developed in the United States in a different cultural context.

THE RESEARCH PROJECT

With these goals and questions in mind, a nationwide, ecologically based series of studies of sponsored FDC in Israel was designed.

Study 1 focuses on the key adults who provide care at home and in child care (i.e., mothers and caregivers). Study 2 focuses on the children's experiences generated by their own interactions with the social and nonsocial environment in the child-care setting as well as experiences generated by this environment (the caregiver, the peer context, and the physical environment). Study 3 utilizes the data gathered in Studies 1 and 2 to examine the interface of the effects of the children's personal characteristics, their family background, and the FDC environment on the children's behavior.

Samples and Sampling Procedures

Forty-one FDC homes and their caregivers were sampled out of the 97 FDC homes that operated in 1983 throughout Israel. Due to the growing concern about the effects of out-of-home care on infants, only homes that had at least one infant were included in the sample. Because of ease of access, all homes in Jerusalem that had infants were included in the sample ($N = 30$). In each of the other six locations where FDC functioned, homes were sampled randomly ($N = 11$). These locations were all in rural communities in central Israel. All the caregivers agreed to participate in the study.

In each one of the FDC homes, two children were sampled and the mothers of these children constituted the sample of mothers. The sampling procedure thus enabled us to examine relationships between different aspects of the data collected.

Study 1: Mothers and Caregivers

The sample for this study included caregivers and the mothers of children in the care of these caregivers.

Mothers.   The sample consisted of 71 mothers of the 82 children in the 41 FDC homes sampled. The sample did not include all 82 mothers because 2 participated as caregivers, 2 refused to be interviewed, and 7, by the time they were reached, had moved and could not be traced. As the interviews with the mothers and the FDC records (REC) revealed, 94% of the families were intact. There were more mothers of boys ($n = 45$) than of girls ($n = 26$).

Caregivers.   All FDC homes were run by women who participated willingly in the study, a sample of 41 caregivers. All but one were married mothers.

The demographic characteristics of the sample of mothers and the sample of caregivers such as country of origin, educational level, and age, are described in chapters 3 and 4, respectively.

Study 2: Observations of Children, Caregivers, and Environment in FDC

Observations were conducted in the sample of FDC homes. In each home the caretaker and two children were sampled for observation.

Most homes had five children under the age of 3 and were mostly age hetero-geneous. The age span in each home (the age difference between the youngest and oldest child) ranged from less than 8 months (31.7%) to greater than 17 months (31.7%). The homes also varied in terms of the mean educational level of parents, as well as in the proportion of children from families with social problems.

Of the 82 children sampled, 1 child was always the youngest in the home and the other was selected randomly from among the other children. The sample consisted of 49 boys and 33 girls, most of them were 2 years olds. More than half (57%) were first-born and 22% were third-born or of a higher birth order. More than half had attended FDC for over 10 months. Additional characteristics of the children are described in chapter 6.

Data Collection Procedures and Definitions of Measures

Study 1: Mothers and Caregivers

Data Collection Procedures

Structured interviews (INT) conducted by five trained interviewers took place in the homes of the mothers and caregivers. Information was obtained about the personal and professional background of the interviewees, their life and work circumstances, as well as the interviewees' childrearing beliefs and attitudes to child care. The information obtained in the interviews was supplemented, and whenever possible also verified, by information taken from the FDC registration records (REC) described later.

Measures

Personal and Professional Background, Life, and Work Circumstances. For parents, six measures of mothers' (and three of fathers') personal background were derived from the interviews with mothers (MINT): *education* (Mo, Fa), *ethnic origin* (Mo, Fa), *age* (Mo, Fa), *number of children*, *maternal employment*, and age of child's *placement in child care*. Two additional measures were obtained from the FDC records (REC): the family's use of public *financial support* and *social problems* in the family as reported by the local social worker. Table 3.1 gives details of these measures.

For caregivers, eight measures were derived from the interviews with the caregiver (CINT). Six of them described the caregivers' personal and professional background: *education*, *ethnic origin*, *age*, *number of children*, child-care *experience*, and preservice *training*. The other two measures described aspects of the professional support offered by the sponsoring agency: *supervision* and *autonomy*.

Five additional measures, which described the group of children they worked with, were derived from the FDC records (REC). These measures include: *group size*, the *mean age* of children in the group and its *age mix*, the mean level of *parents' education*, and the proportion of children from *socially distressed* families. Table 4.1 gives details of these measures.

Childrearing Beliefs.   The measures describing the childrearing beliefs of the two socializing agents were derived from their respective interviews (MINT, CINT). We examined two sets of childrearing beliefs: The first were beliefs about development. They included developmental expectations, beliefs concerning conditions that influence development and preferred methods of discipline. The second set referred to beliefs about the role of different socialization agents and included the attribution of influence to mother, father, and caregiver. Both sets are described here in detail as they relate to both mothers and caregivers. We obtained a third set of measures from mothers. This set described their attitudes to child care.

Data reduction procedures of childrearing beliefs:

1. *Beliefs about development* were divided into three subsets:

• *Developmental expectations:* a list of 37 items describing various abilities typical of children under 5 was used to assess the developmental expectations of caregivers and mothers in three developmental areas—cognitive, social, and independence. Alpha factor extraction was used to identify consistent common factors among these items. Five items were eliminated from the final measure due to their low correlations with the other items in all three areas. Each agent was asked to indicate the age at which children are expected to master these abilities. All questions started with the phrase: "At what age, approximately, would you expect a child to...."

The cognitive area included eight items (e.g., "...avoid an object when warned verbally", "...know names of colors"). Cronbach alpha coefficients for these items were .76 and .82 for caregivers and mothers, respectively, suggesting a fairly high reliability of this measure.

The social area included 14 items (e.g., "...comply with adult's requests", "...help a friend", "...share and wait turns"). Cronbach alpha coefficients for these items were fairly reliable. They were .75 and .68 for caregivers and mothers, respectively.

The area of independence included 10 items (e.g., "...stay home alone," "...visits to friends without parents," "...get dressed by him/herself"). Cronbach alphas for these items were also fairly reliable, .68 and .74 for caregivers and mothers, respectively.

Developmental expectation are thus described by three measures: Expectations of *independence, cognitive,* and *social* development.

• *Conditions that influence development:* each interviewee responded to "How do you think a child gets to be able to ...?" The interviewees had to choose one of three possible statements describing their beliefs about the process by which children acquire any one of the 37 abilities previously discussed. One statement described a belief in an internal process of "spontaneous maturation": "It will come by itself. You don't have to teach it or do anything about it." The other two described a belief in external processes that differ according to the part played in the process by socializing agents: "exposure to facilitative experiences" where the adult is relatively passive and "direct instruction" where the adult is active through modeling, explanations, encouragement, and/or reinforcements. The scores on each of the three categories refer to the proportion of items on which each one of the three categories was chosen.

Three interdependent measures were derived from these items: *spontaneous maturation, facilitative experience,* and *direct instruction.* The average Cronbach alpha coefficients for the three measures suggest good reliability. They were .72 for caregivers and .80 for mothers. In addition, a fourth measure of *mean degree of involvement* in facilitating development is based on these three measures; its score ranges from 1 to 3, where "3" indicates a high level of involvement.

- *Preferred method of discipline*: each socialization agent selected one of six possible responses, varying in degree of power assertion, to each of 17 episodes of misconduct and noncompliance. The episodes described incidents such as "child refuses to put toys away" or "child refuses to eat food," "child is biting, hitting, or pushing another child," "child keeps on nagging you even though you asked him/her to stop." The responses were categorized, by three independent judges, as permissive (such as "giving in"), authoritative (such as "insisting"), or authoritarian (such as "scolding, shouting, threatening, and/or hitting"). The score on this measure referred to the proportion of items to which the agent gave these responses.

Three interdependent measures were derived from these items: *permissive, authoritative,* and *authoritarian* disciplinary methods. The average Cronbach alpha coefficients for these three measures were only adequate. They were .65 for caregivers and .60 for mothers. In addition, a fourth measure, *mean level of power assertion* to be employed in controlling misbehavior, is based on these three measures; its score ranged from 1 to 6, where "6" indicates high power assertion.

2. *Beliefs about the roles of socializing agents: attribution of influence.* Both mothers and caregivers ranked the relative influence of three adults on a 3-point scale (3 = high): their own, the other agent's, and the father's. Each adult was ranked with reference to 11 items describing two domains in the child's development: The first domain, emotional maturity, contained five items such as "clearly asserts wishes," "controls impulses" (e.g., anger, or wish for bottle); the second, social development, contained six items, such as "child is friendly," "child is sensitive to others," and "child shares or takes turns."

We thus obtained four separate measures from each of the two socializing agents: attribution of influence to two individuals in two domains: to *mother*—in *emotional maturity* and *social development*; and to *caregiver*—in *emotional matu-*

rity and *social development*. The average Cronbach alphas for these measures were .61 for mothers and .70 for caregivers.

3. *Attitudes to child care (MINT - mothers only).* The study examined mothers' attitudes as reflected in their responses as consumers of child care: (a) the reasons given by mothers for their decision and preference to place their child in a given child-care setting; (b) mothers' satisfaction with their child care; and (c) the effect that child care has on their behavior and lives.

• Choosing child care—the reasons given by mothers for (a) placing their child in out-of-home care and (b) their particular preference for the FDC setting were divided into two major categories: reasons reflecting their own needs (e.g., the need to work or study) and reasons reflecting a concern for the child's needs (e.g., misses the company of peers, the FDC offers good quality care). Each category was scored each time it was mentioned by the mother (*Yes* = 1; *No* = 0). Two measures were derived from the reasons given by mothers: *out-of-home care: mother's needs* and *preference for FDC: child's needs.*

• Satisfaction with child care—several items in the interview were used as indicators of the mother's satisfaction with child care. They included her satisfaction with her relationship with the caregiver, with how the caregiver interacts with the children, and with the child's willingness to go to the caregiver every morning. Satisfaction is also expressed indirectly in the mother's readiness (Yes/No) to seek out the advice of the FDC staff (caregiver, coordinator), rather than the advice of family or friends, regarding childrearing issues or a child behavior problem.

Five measures were derived from the answers given by mothers: satisfaction with *communication with caregiver*, with *caregiver's play with child*, with *child's willingness to go to FDC*; and seek consultation with *FDC staff*, or with *family and friends*.

• Effects of using child care—mothers rated the extent of the effects of using child care on 5-point scales ranging from *very little* (1) to *very high* (5). Two measures were derived from these ratings: effects on the *mothers' behavior towards their children* and effects on the *mothers' quality of life*.

Tables 3.3, 3.4, and 4.2 give the descriptive statistics of the belief systems of mothers and caregivers.

Study 2: Observations of Children, Caregivers, and Environment in FDC

Data Collection Procedure

The observations were conducted by four trained observers, who used the following data collection procedures:

1. *A time-sampling observation of the children's and the caregiver's behavior* (OBS). The time-sampling procedure utilized predefined recording sheets and followed a prescribed routine and recording rules. During an observation day, six time-sample periods of 5 minutes each were taken of the behavior of the caregiver

and each target child, in a fixed sequence of Target Child A–Target Child B–Caregiver. Behavior was observed for 10 seconds and then recorded for 10 seconds, yielding altogether 90 time-sampling units of behavior for each target subject. Each observation unit also provided information on the context of behavior. At the end of each 5- minute period, the observer filled in a short questionnaire describing that period and then shifted to the next target subject.

2. *A daily log (DL)*. Throughout the day, the DL continuously recorded the activities of the group and the duration of each group activity. These activities were categorized as the proportion of the total daily activities given to "directed educational activities" initiated by the caregiver and are expected to contribute to development (e.g., painting, playing with puzzles, concept games, singing, storytelling, playing music) to "free play" and to "routine physical care."

3. *An environment rating questionnaire (ERQ)* that was adapted from the Day Care Environment Inventory (Prescott, Kritchevsky, & Jones, 1972) and the Family Day Care Rating Scale (Harms & Clifford, 1984) to the Israeli setting. It was completed by the observer at the end of the observation day.

4. *The FDC registration records (REC)*. The records were kept by the caregivers yielded most of the demographic information about the children in the group and their families.

Measures

The measures in this study were conceptualized in terms of two major sources of daily experiences of children: (a) those generated by the physical, social, and educational environment, and (b) those generated by the child's own behavior while interacting with the environment.

FDC Physical, Social, and Educational Environments. The ERQ used several categories to describe the physical environment in the FDC home, including: ratings (from *high* [5] to *low* [1]) of physical care conditions, amount and organization of toys and play materials, and amount and organization of indoor and outdoor space available for free movement of children.

We derived three measures from these categories: One measure is a rating of the amount and organization of *play materials*. The second measure is a rating of space organization in terms of the availability of *space to be alone* ("private corners" or "shelter corners"). These corners are usually created by hanging curtains that close off a small space such as a corner of the room or the space underneath the high infant cots. The child is free to enter and leave these corners at any time. They differ from the "time out" space used by teachers to remove a child from the group. The third measure is a ratio of the rating of the available space to the number of children in the group yielding a measure of *crowdedness*.

In addition, a composite measure that provides an overall assessment of the educational quality of the physical environment is presented in the following section as an aspect of the quality of care offered by the caregiver.

This study used four of these measures to describe the peer group context of the daily experiences of children in FDC. These included its age composition: *mean age* and *age mix* (in terms of age standard deviation and age span); its sex composition: the proportions of boys and girls presented as *mean sex*, and the *mean level of parental education* in the group.

The measures describing the caregiver's behavior are based on observations (OBS), DL, and ratings (ERQ).

Quality of care in the FDC was defined in this study by two dimensions of the caregiver's behavior: (a) the quality of her spontaneous interaction with the children; and (b) the quality of the educational program she provided, which refers to her planned, rather than spontaneous, behavior.

The caregiver's spontaneous interaction was composed of three measures: *restrictions*, a measure of the frequency of the caregiver's attempts to control the children's behavior (i.e., diverting attention, warning, or scolding [OBS]); *group interaction*, a measure of the frequency of caregiver's interactions with the entire group (OBS), and the third, *positive interaction*, a composite measure of the ratings of positive affect (ERQ); the frequency of positive responsiveness to children, the frequency of one-to-one interaction, the positive use of language (not including language used to restrict children), the overall involvement with the children (i.e., not engaged in preparations) and encouragement (OBS). Cronbach standardized item Alpha for the composite score is .66.

The caregiver's planned behaviors, designed to provide the children with developmentally appropriate experiences, included two measures: *educational activity* which is a composite measure based on: (a) the frequency of behaviors categorized as "directed educational activities" (DL) and (b) the rating of the use by the caregivers of various routine care activities for educational purposes (ERQ). The other measure, *educational quality of the physical environment*, overlaps some of the measures described under the section on measures of the physical environment. This is a composite measure derived from the ratings of the following aspects of the physical environment (ERQ): physical care conditions, the amount of indoor and outdoor space, and the amount and organization of toys and play materials. Cronbach standardized item Alpha for the composite score is .71. The components of the composite measure were assigned equal weights.

The Children's Behavior.   All measures of the children's behavior were based on data gathered during observations in the FDC home (OBS). The child's engagement with the physical and social environment refers to the quality and type of interaction as well as its competence level.

Active engagement with the physical environment includes two frequency measures and one measure assessing competence:

1. *Fine motor interaction with objects* refers to an activity that requires hand–eye coordination, such as playing with puzzles, threading objects onto a string or a stick, joining Lego pieces, and so on.
2. *Gross motor play* refers to large muscle activity, meaning practice of physical skills or a challenge to the child's developing skills, such as crawling or walking for infants, and climbing, running, riding a bike, pushing–pulling, and throwing a ball for toddlers.

3. *Mean level of play with objects* rates the competence of the child's interaction with objects on a scale devised by Rubenstein and Howes (1979). The 5-point scale rates increasing complexity of play with objects, from *oral contact* (1) through *active manipulation* (3) to the *exploitation of the object's properties in a creative way* (5). The rating was recorded at the end of each 5-minute observation period.

Active engagement with the social environment includes five frequency measures and three measures of social competence.

1. *Positive interaction with peers* refers to the frequency of social exchanges such as smiling, sharing toys, imitating, and showing concern.
2. *Agonistic interaction* refers to the frequency of social exchanges such as struggling with or attacking another child.
3. *Joint peer play* refers to those episodes when the child initiates, or joins into, a play activity constructed by the children themselves. The children engage in repetitive, usually rhythmic, activity that typically involves vocal exchanges, smiles, or laughter (Budwig, Strage, & Bamberg, 1986). For example, an activity where two or more children spontaneously join a child sitting on a mat, banging small wooden blocks in a repetitive rhythmic manner, while exchanging looks and smiles, would be coded as joint peer play. The occurrence of this activity was recorded once at the end of each 5-minute observation period, thus yielding a maximum score of 6.
4. *Solitary context* refers to the frequency of occasions when the child is seen alone. The child could be engaged in interaction with the physical environment or observing a social interaction intently from a distance.
5. *Group context* refers to the frequency of occasions when the child is seen in a context of group activity, engaged in either social or nonsocial exchanges with the environment. Social competence is assessed in this study on the basis of the child's competence in playing with peers and the frequency with which he or she uses language to communicate with others. The level of play with peers is rated on a 5-point peer-play scale (Howes, 1980). Level of peer play as well as verbal communication were recorded during each 10-second unit of observa-tion. The measures refer therefore to the number of 10-second units during which these behaviors were observed.
6. *Peer play: Level 1* refers to occasions when a child plays next to another child but with no mutual awareness.
7. *Peer play: Levels 2–5* refer to social play with turn-taking structure, complementary, and reciprocal play.
8. *Verbal communication* refers to the frequency of the child's talking and verbalizing.

The minimal engagement with the environment category refers to those behaviors that suggest that the child is not exploring, investigating, or otherwise actively

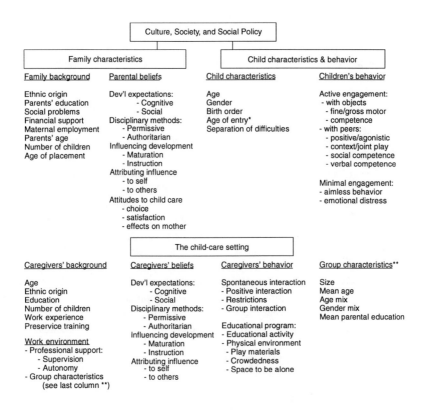

FIG. 2.1. Children in FDC: An ecological research model.

interacting with the environment. They cannot be seen as contributing to his or her
either current positive experience or developing competence. These behaviors were
categorized as follows:

1. *Aimless behavior* refers to the frequency of occasions when the child is seen
   passing time doing nothing and staring into space, unoccupied, nonpurpose-
   ful or uninvolved wandering, or looking around without focusing attention
   on any particular object.
2. *Emotional distress* refers to occasions when the child is observed either
   crying or showing other signs of distress.

The descriptive statistics of the measures of children's behavior are presented
in Table 6.1.[1]

---

[1]Reliability: The interobserver agreement was calculated as the percent of agreement between a
criterion-observer and the three other observers. It ranged for all observation measures from 69% to
90%.

Summary of the Research Model

Figure 2.1 presents the different dimensions explored by our ecologically based research model.

Data Analysis

In order to answer the questions raised in this study, various levels of statistical analyses were applied to the data. They included procedures such as Pearson correlations, *t* tests, analyses of variance, and different multivariate procedures such as multiple regression analyses and MANOVA.

As the sample sizes are not large, the results of the statistical analyses should be interpreted with great caution. Also, because many multiple comparisons are carried out on the same data there is always the possibility of obtaining spurious "significant" differences. Statistically significant relationships can therefore be seen as empirically significant only when they are part of a consistent pattern of results and are supported by underlying conceptual arguments.

Furthermore, as the samples are drawn from the population of families, children and child-care setting in Israel the statistical relationships found in these studies can on the whole be generalized to this population only. However, because these relationships are drawn from a conceptual framework that allows for social and cultural variations, one could expect that with appropriate modifications the conclusions would be applicable to many other societies raising similar questions.

3

Parents of Children in Family Day Care

Child care has frequently been studied as an independent socialization environment, separate from the influences of the child's home. An ecological approach to the study of child care highlights the fact that children in child care move back and forth between (at least) two socialization milieus. This approach implies that a better understanding of all aspects of child care and its effects on children will be reached by examining it in the context of the child's family (Bronfenbrenner, 1979a).

Although previous studies on the effects of schooling on children have highlighted the importance of family influences (Jencks, 1972), it is only since the mid-1980s that studies of child care started paying attention to family factors and how they may add to or interact with the effects of child care (Clarke-Stewart & Gruber, 1984; Cochran & Robinson, 1983; Everson, Sarnat, & Ambron, 1984; Goelman & Pence, 1987; Howes & Stewart, 1987; Kontos & Fiene, 1987; Phillips, McCartney, & Scarr, 1987). Although earlier studies were mostly concerned with the effects of child care while controlling for the influences of global family characteristics such as socioeconomic status (SES), recent investigations have examined how specific elements of the home and the child-care setting interact in influencing specific dimensions of child development (Clarke-Stewart, 1987b; Holloway & Reichart-Erickson, 1989; Howes & Olenick, 1986; Kontos, 1991).

Our research (Study 1) investigates some family characteristics that are likely to be related to the fact that these parents are using child care and to the effect child care, as another socialization context, may have on their child. This chapter examines, therefore, several family factors that have been shown in previous research to have an effect on the child's development and are likely to interact with the influence of child care. They include the parents' sociodemographic character-

istics, their childrearing beliefs, as well as their attitudes to child care. The chapter
further explores the interrelationship between these family factors.

CHARACTERISTICS OF PARENTS' BACKGROUNDS

Three dimensions of the characteristics of parents' backgrounds are considered of
special relevance to the interface between home and child care: parents' sociocul-
tural background, such as ethnic origin and education; their life experience and
circumstances, such as age, maternal employment, social and economic difficulties; and their parental experience, such as number of children, and age of the child's
placement in child care. These are considered important sources of influence not
only on parents' interactions with their children, but also on their childrearing
beliefs (Goodnow, 1988). They are also likely to influence parents' attitudes toward
the use of child care and the selection of a specific child-care program (Scarr &
Eisenberg, 1993).

The six measures of mothers' personal background derived from the interviews
with mothers (MINT) included ethnic origin (country of birth), years of education,
age and number of children as well as maternal employment status (number of work
hours outside the home), and age of the child's placement in child care (months).
The father measures derived from these interviews (MINT) included ethnic origin,
age, and years of education. An average of the years of education of mother and
father generated a measure of parental education level.

The additional measures derived from the FDC records (REC) concerned the
family's use of financial support (rated as 1 = none, 2 = child-care subsidy, and 3
= full welfare dependence) and social problems in the family based on reports by
the local social worker (husband in prison, one of the parents frequently hospital-
ized, one of the parents mentally ill, 1 = no, 2 = yes). A composite index of the
family's SES was generated from the two measures: parental education level and
family social problems.

The data gathered in Study 1 concerning the family's background are presented
in Table 3.1.

TABLE 3.1
Demographic Characteristics of Families: Descriptive Statistics

	Means	SD	Minimum	Maximum	N
Education (years): Mothers	13.37	2.99	8	20	70
Fathers	13.26	3.58	8	21	69
Age: Mothers	28.27	4.99	20	40	70
Fathers	31.79	7.77	18	67	67
Family social problems (1 = none)	1.25	.43	1	2	80
Financial support (1 = none)	1.52	.67	1	3	71
Maternal employment (hours)	6.32	1.64	4	9	63
Number of children	2.01	1.42	1	8	71
Age of placement in child care (mo)	13.04	6.12	3	30	70

Ethnic and Educational Background

Mothers were predominantly Israeli-born (69%); 19% of Western and only 12% of Middle Eastern origin. Only half of the fathers (51%) were Israeli born; 21% of Western and 27% of Middle Eastern origin. There were twice as many fathers of Middle Eastern origin as there were mothers. As can be seen in Table 3.1, both mothers and fathers on average have a high school education. There was, however, a considerable range of differences in parental education (i.e., although 24% of the mothers did not finish high school, 41% had more than 15 years of education). An ANOVA using the three categories of parents' origin as an independent variable and the other background variables as dependent variables showed that although the father's ethnic origin was significantly related to a large number of other demographic characteristics (education level of both parents, social and economic problems, number of children, and hours of maternal employment), the mother's origin was related only to her age and number of children. However, an ANCOVA done on these variables, with parents' education level as a covariate, showed that none of the relationships just mentioned were statistically significant, with one exception: Regardless of their education level, mothers married to men of Middle Eastern origin worked less hours, suggesting that the objection of these fathers to maternal employment outside the home is rooted in their more traditional cultural background. This relationship remained significant even when controlling for number of children in the family.

The overall pattern suggests, however, that the relationship between parents' ethnic origin and their life and parental experiences is largely mediated by their education level. The intercorrelation matrix in Table 3.2 shows that, in addition, mothers with a higher education level have better educated spouses, tend to be older, have fewer children, and their families are less likely to be burdened by social or economic difficulties.

TABLE 3.2
Intercorrelations of Parents' Background Characteristics

	Educ. Fa	Age Mo	Age Fa	Social Problem	Finan Supp.	Mo Empl.	No. Child.	Age of Entry
Education: Mother	.77***	.33**	.22*	−.41***	−.36***		−.21[a]	
Father		.27*[b]		−.44***	−.41***		−.26*[b]	
Age: Mother			.60***			−.26*[c]	.52***	
Father							.35**	
Social problems					.54***		.30*	.24*
Financial supp.								
Maternal employment (hours)							−.38**	
Number of children								
Age of placement in child care								

[a]This correlation is −.45*** when mother's age is partialled out.
[b]This correlation is .04 when mother's education is partialled out.
[c]This correlation is −.06 when number of children is partialled out.
*$p < .05$. **$p < .01$. ***$p < .001$.

The Amount of Life and Parental Experiences

Typical parents in this study were in their mid- to late 20s, both working and with one to two young children who had been in child care from infancy.

As may be expected, older mothers tended to be married to older men, and had a higher level of education and more children. Yet, in general, mothers with more children had a lower level of education. They worked less hours a day and were more likely to have families with social problems.

Even though none of the parents was under 18 years of age and the majority were in their late 20s to early 30s, their parental experience was rather limited: 70.4% had only one to two children and only 8.5% had four or more children. Parental experience was further curtailed by the early entrance of their children into child care. Eighty-two percent of the children entered child care as infants below the age of 18 months, regardless of their parents' level of education or mothers' employment status. The latter reflects a general trend in Israeli society discussed in chapter 1. Mothers in families with serious "social problems" tend to send their children to child care on average about 3 months later than other mothers (15.5 as opposed to 12.2 months on the average). It seems that these mothers only send their children following a referral by the Welfare Department.

It seems, therefore, that number of children as well as age of entry are characteristics that reflects much more than just the amount of parental experience.

Life Circumstances: Maternal Employment

The information gathered in Study 1 shows that although 85% of the children were registered in child care because their mothers were working, only 53% of these mothers worked more than 7 hours a day. Contrary to expectation, Table 3.2 suggests that the mothers' working hours were not related to their education or social or economic circumstances but only to the number of children. In order to evaluate the separate effect of number of children and maternal education on their employment, a two-way ANOVA was carried out. Both main effects were significant with no interaction effect: mothers with less than high school education worked an average of 6.96 hours per day, whereas mothers with higher education worked only 5.88 hours per day [$F(1,55) = 4.95, p < .05$]. A similar difference was found between mothers with one child who worked an average of 6.69 hours per day, and mothers with more children who worked only 5.77 hours per day [$F(1,55) = 5.41, p < .05$]. Thus, the number of maternal employment hours seems to be related to either education level or size of the family. One should note, however, that although better educated mothers, or those with a larger family, chose to work less hours, both groups still sent their very young children to child care. It is likely that the two groups used the time their children were in child care for different purposes.

Life Circumstances: Social and Economic Hardship

Of the mothers, 25% were reported by the local social worker as having serious "social problems" (e.g., father imprisoned, one parent mentally ill, or a known drug addict). Of the families, 32% received some subsidy to cover part or most of the child-care cost, and an additional 10% were living on welfare. Families with economic difficulties were more often identified as also having social problems (Table 3.2) and, as was already mentioned, parents in these families had a lower educational level. It is interesting to note that although families with social problems tended to have more children and send their children to child care at an older age, those receiving financial aid did not. These parental characteristics reflect two aspects of the government policy described in chapter 1: (a) there is a quota of places in public child care for children of at-risk families, and (b) Israeli parents using child care are entitled to a subsidy, according to a sliding scale based on several demographic criteria.

The analysis of parents' characteristics suggests, therefore, that this sample is highly representative of families in all sponsored FDC homes in Israel, and to a great extent of young parents in Israel in general. The data show that parents using child care vary in their educational background, parental experiences, and life circumstances. The analysis further indicated that background characteristics were interrelated. As is commonly found in other Western societies, parents' education level was related, both directly and indirectly, to much of their life circumstances and parental experiences: Although better educated parents had less children, they were older and worked less hours and they also had less social and economic difficulties. Fathers' background was similar to that of mothers and even more strongly related to their families' life circumstances. Although highly correlated, life circumstances of families with social problems seem somewhat more difficult than those in need of financial support. As is commonly found in studies done in Israel, parents' education was related to their ethnic origin and their life experiences (Ninio, 1979). A partial correlation analysis suggested that parents' life circumstances were related to their education level rather than to their ethnic origin.

PARENTAL BELIEF SYSTEM

Recent studies have shown that parents' preference for childrearing practices (e.g., nurturing or restrictive) and values concerning prosocial skills or child learning and development may interact with the effects of child care (Howes & Stewart, 1987; Kontos, 1991; Phillips et al., 1987). The pattern of these interactions may vary depending on the nature of the population of parents and child-care settings from which the sample under investigation is drawn (Phillips & Howes, 1987). Furthermore, a child who is moving back and forth between home and child care may need to negotiate and adjust to the different expectations and beliefs of the socializing agents in each of these environments.

An ecological approach to the study of child care must, therefore, take into account the belief system of parents. Furthermore, a comparative analysis of the beliefs of the socializing agents in the two childrearing environments is another important component of the ecological study of child care (Holloway, Gorman, & Fuller, 1988). A comparison of the beliefs of different socializing agents and their relationship to the child's behavior is examined in later sections of this book. This chapter focuses on a description of the mothers' beliefs and their relationship to background on one hand and attitudes to child care on the other.

Recent years have seen a revived interest in the social cognitions of parents (Goodnow, 1984; Goodnow & Collins, 1990; Miller, 1988; Sigel, 1985), as a social phenomenon worthy of its own study and as a cognitive model of parental functioning (Maccoby & Martin, 1983).

Much of the research presented here dwells on the question of how parents perceive and interpret the behavior and development of their children and the perception of their own role in influencing this development. These include the parents' goal for their children's development, their perception of the course of development and the conditions that influence it, as well as the particular influence and responsibilities of parents and what they view as optimal or reasonable childrearing methods (Goodnow & Collins, 1990). Some of these studies suggest that beliefs vary in accordance with the contextual differences between home and child care (Bronfenbrenner, 1979a; Hess, Price, Dickson, & Conroy, 1981; Holloway et al., 1988; Rubenstein & Howes, 1979; Winetsky, 1978).

Study 1 examines two important aspects of the childrearing belief system that have been shown to be sensitive to such contextual differences: (a) beliefs about how children develop, such as timing and the process of development; and (b) beliefs about the role of different socializing agents in influencing this development. The first aspect consists of three subsets of beliefs: developmental expectations, belief in conditions that influence development, and preferred disciplinary techniques. The second aspect deals with the mothers' perceptions of their influence over the child's development, as compared with the influence attributed to other socializing agents.

The first subset of beliefs of developmental expectations relate to the ages at which a child is expected to master certain developmental tasks. Such expectations are associated with the ages at which parents provide their children with developmentally facilitating experiences (Ninio, 1979). These expectations are also the basis for the agent's pressure for the acquisition of skills and more mature behavior in children (Hess et al., 1981). Because parental expectations have been found to vary according to specific areas of development (Knight & Goodnow, 1988), this study focuses on expectations in three such areas: independence, cognitive, and social development.

The second subset of beliefs about development describes explanations offered by the mother for the conditions that influence development. These can be categorized as *internal* (maturation) or *external* (environmental) processes that are responsible for the developmental progression of children. These beliefs are related to the parents' behavior (McGillicuddy-DeLisi, 1980, 1982; Sigel, 1985). Beliefs in external influences allow for greater involvement of the socialization agent in shaping the child's development. This study examines three such explanations offered by the parents: maturation, exposure to experience, and direct instruction.

The third subset deals with the preferred disciplinary techniques believed by parents to be effective in dealing with children's misconduct. "Discipline encounters" (Hoffman, 1975) are a significant part of adult–child interactions in the early years, thus the parents' preference for different degrees of power assertion or permissiveness has important implications for the children's development (Baumrind, 1967, 1971). This study examines parents' preference for permissive, authoritative, and authoritarian methods of control.

We examined beliefs concerning the role of different socializing agents by studying the mothers' perception of their influence over the children's development relative to the influence attributed to caregivers and to fathers (Feldman & Yirmiya, 1986; M. Rosenthal & Zilkha, 1987). Believing that what one does makes a difference is likely to be related to one's interactions with the child (Bugental & Shennum, 1984). The attribution of influence to self as compared with influence attributed to other agents is of particular interest in the case of joint socialization, especially because some research suggests that parents perceive their influence as declining when their child enters an educational setting (Newson & Newson, 1976).

Mothers' Childrearing Beliefs

Beliefs About Development

Table 3.3 presents mothers' developmental expectations in three areas of development. The differences between the mean age of expectation in the different areas

TABLE 3.3
Mothers' Childrearing Beliefs: Descriptive Statistics

	Mean	SD	Minimum	Maximum	N
Beliefs about development					
Developmental expectation (months):					
Cognitive	25.51	5.96	13.17	42.00	69
Social	27.17	5.27	14.27	44.57	70
Independence	35.75	7.73	20.89	55.80	65
Conditions influencing development:					
Maturation	.22	.13	.03	.68	71
Facilitative experience	.29	.14	.05	.78	71
Direct instruction	.49	.16	.03	.89	71
Mean degree of involvement (1–3)	2.31	.22	1.49	2.86	71
Preferred disciplinary method:					
Permissive	.34	.13	.07	.64	71
Authoritative	.48	.18	.14	.88	71
Authoritarian	.18	.14	.00	.53	71
Mean level power assertion (1–6)	3.11	.42	2.25	4.00	71
Beliefs about roles of socializing agents					
Attribution of influence to:					
Mother: social	2.28	.43	1.00	3.00	70
Mother: emotion, maturity	2.34	.45	1.00	3.00	64
Father: social	1.76	.62	1.00	3.00	68
Father: emotion, maturity	1.81	.60	1.00	3.00	63
Caregiver: social	2.32	.50	1.00	3.00	70
Caregiver: emotion, maturity	2.28	.46	1.00	3.00	63

reflects mostly differences in the items included rather than any difference in importance ascribed to the different areas.

The three interdependent measures derived from the mothers' descriptions of conditions that influence development were spontaneous maturation, facilitative experience, and direct instruction. In addition, a fourth measure of *mean degree of involvement* in facilitating development was based on these three measures. The data gathered in Study 1 suggest that a relatively small number of mothers believed that children develop mainly through spontaneous maturation (Table 3.3). The majority believed that developmental goals were achieved mostly through direct instruction by an adult who demonstrated, explained, and encouraged.

The three interdependent measures derived from the mothers' descriptions of their preferred disciplinary techniques were permissive, authoritative, and authoritarian disciplinary methods. In addition, a fourth measure, *mean level of power assertion* to be employed in controlling misbehavior, was based on these three measures.

Most mothers described themselves as preferring either authoritative or permissive disciplinary techniques. A few, however, described themselves as authoritarian.

Beliefs About the Roles of Socializing Agents

As Table 3.3 shows, mothers attribute the same degree of influence to themselves and to the caregivers, which is significantly higher than influence attributed to fathers in either domain (the T levels are 5.42 and 7.15 for mothers and caregivers respectively; $p < .001$).

Although mothers make no distinction between domains in the degree of influence they attribute to themselves or to the fathers, they do tend to attribute more influence to caregivers in the social domain than in the domain of emotional maturity ($t = 1.87; p = .07$).

Interrelations Between Mothers' Childrearing Beliefs

Mothers were consistent in their ideas concerning the developmental timetable and attribution of influence. Those who expected early mastery in one area of development expected it in other areas as well and those who attributed significant influence to an agent in one domain tended to do so in other domains as well. Pearson correlation values range from .43 to .84 with $p < .001$.

Less marked, yet statistically significant relationships were found among all subsystems of maternal beliefs: Mothers who expected early development of independence (as well as cognitive abilities) attributed significant influence to themselves. Mothers who expected early development were also less likely to believe in spontaneous maturation as a process underlying development and less likely to prefer power assertive disciplinary methods. In general, mothers who believed direct instruction to be an important process that facilitates development preferred less power assertive disciplinary methods.

The data concerning the parental belief system suggest, therefore, that mothers perceive themselves as responsible for their child's development. Even though they accept that this responsibility is shared with the caregiver, they differentiate between the domains of development and the influence they attribute to the caregiver is greater in the domain most relevant to the context of her role. They also attribute greater impact to direct instruction, suggesting a belief in the importance of the caregiving adult's involvement with the child.

Furthermore, mothers' beliefs are fairly consistent and coherent. The patterns of mothers' beliefs can be interpreted as expressions of mothers' locus of control (Rotter, 1966). Parents with internal locus of control were found to attribute considerable influence to themselves over the child's behavior (Bugental & Shennum, 1984) and react with less power assertion to their child's transgression than parents with external locus of control (Loeb, 1975; Patterson, 1979). Thus, the data show that mothers who expect early development are more likely to perceive themselves as influential and tend to believe in environmental influences on development and in the effectiveness of less coercive disciplinary methods.

Mothers' Attitudes Toward Child Care

Child-care research to date has not yet defined the theoretical grounds on which parents' attitudes to child care should be investigated. We would like to propose that these attitudes reflect two major cognitions: The first relates to parents' perception and understanding of the mothers' role and the second to their perception of the child-care setting. Perceptions of the mothers' role can include that of mother as homemaker and main caregiver for her child, or that of mother-and-professional who shares with others the responsibility for the child's socialization. Another dimension is the perception of an effective and competent mother or that of an ineffective, dependent, and insecure mother. Perceptions of child care may refer to its function as a support system to the parents, to the quality of care it offers, or to its relationship with the care provided at home. Several types of attitudes have been examined in previous research, most of which were found to be related to the effects of child care on children as well as on parents. The mothers' positive or negative disposition to use child care was seen to have an influence on the child's adjustment to child care. When the mothers' decision concerning the use of child care was inconsistent with their attitudes, the child was more easily upset, distressed, and noncompliant (Everson et al., 1984). Hock (1984) argued that mothers' attitudes about separation from their children (resulting from choosing to work outside the home) are associated with the different types of child care they use. These studies focus mostly on the mothers' attitudes toward their maternal role rather than toward the specific characteristics of child care. Other studies highlight the mothers' different responses to different types of child care. Thus, Steinberg and Green (1979) reported that although mothers using FDC felt the most congruence between their values and practices and those of the caregiver, those using center care felt that child care had improved their relationship with their children and improved their lives.

Study 1 examines the attitudes reflected in parents' behavior and their responses as consumers of child care: (a) the reasons given by parents for their decision and preference for placing their child in a given child-care setting, (b) parental satisfaction with their child care, and (c) the effect child care has on their behavior and lives.

Choosing Child Care

Two measures were derived from the reasons given by mothers for (a) placing their child in out-of-home care, and (b) their particular preference for a given type of child care: the first is "out-of-home care: mother's needs" and the second is "preference to FDC: child's needs."

The most common reason (48%) given by mothers in this study for placing their infant in child care concerned their need, or wish, to be part of the day outside the home (Table 3.4). Other reasons, which do not necessarily exclude the former, were less frequent and included references mostly to the child's social needs.

TABLE 3.4
Parents' Attitudes to Child Care: Descriptive Statistics

	Mean	*SD*	*Minimum*	*Maximum*	*N*
Reasons for choosing child care					
Out-of-home care: mother's needs	.48	.50	0	1	71
Preference for FDC: child's needs	.17	.38	0	1	71
Satisfation with child care					
Satisfied with:					
–Communication with caregiver	3.49	.68	1	4	70
–Caregiver's play with children	3.31	.63	1	4	67
–Child happy to go to FDC	3.29	.81	1	4	69
Seeks consultation with FDC staff	.47	.50	0	1	71
Consults with family or friends	.38	.49	0	1	71
Effects of using child care on:					
Mother's behavior with child	1.83	.85	1	4	70
Mother's quality of life	2.17	1.06	1	4	70

Although only half the mothers reported that they had a choice of alternative types of child care, 88% stated that even if there were alternatives, FDC would have been their first choice. Most mothers (61%) explained their preference in terms of the quality of care offered (e.g., the small group of children or the availability of professional supervision) that best met the needs of their child.

It should be noted that no data is available on parents' selection of specific FDC homes. According to the child placement policy of the Israeli FDC system children are assigned to the specific homes according to predetermined criteria of SES heterogeneity. Parents in this sample, therefore, do not select the FDC home which their child attends.

Satisfaction With Child Care

Study 1 documented several indicators of the mothers' satisfaction with child care: satisfaction with their relationship with the caregiver, with how the caregiver interacts with the children, and with the child's willingness to go to the caregiver every morning. The scores on these measures are mothers' ratings of their satisfaction on a 5-point scale ranging from *very low* (1) to *very high* (5) satisfaction. Satisfaction was also expressed indirectly in the mothers' readiness to seek out the advice of the caregiver or the FDC coordinator regarding childrearing issues or behavioral problems.

The nature of the mothers' relationship and communication with the caregiver was reported as mostly informal. Most of them (89%) had regular "chats" with the caregiver, usually while delivering or picking up the child. Only one third attended the occasional group discussions which were offered, and even less (27%) spent some time visiting their child in the FDC.

Most mothers (91%) were either "satisfied" or "most satisfied" with the nature of their relationship and communication with the caregiver. Most of them (89%) were likewise satisfied with the amount of time the caregiver devoted to playing with the children, and as many as 87% rated their children as "happy" or "very happy" to go to the FDC in the morning. This rate of satisfaction has been reported by researchers in other countries as well (Moss, 1987).

Table 3.4 further shows that more mothers turned to the FDC staff than to their own families, husbands, or close friends. The rest turned to professionals such as a doctor, a nurse, or a psychologist. An ANOVA with a repeated measure design showed these differences to be statistically significant [$F(2,140) = 3.27; p < .05$].

The Effects of Child Care on Mothers

Mothers vary in the extent of support they attribute to child care. Some largely perceive it as a facility that allows them to do other things during the day, whereas others see it as having a considerable effect on their life and/or the socialization of their child. The data of Study 1 show that quite a large number of mothers found that that having their child in child care had no effect on their life (37.1%), or on their behavior toward the child (44.3%). Table 3.4 suggests that mothers observed more changes in their life in general than specific changes in their behavior toward the child ($t = 2.74; p < .01$).

It is interesting to note that among the mothers who reported specific changes in their behavior, most quoted "more patience and attention" to the child (56%), whereas others mentioned more "spoiling" (26%) or "negative" changes. Among those who reported changes in their life, only 33% mentioned the freedom to go to work. Other changes were having free time to run errands (22%), "feeling better" (19%), or "other changes" (26%).

Interrelations Between Mothers' Attitudes to Child Care

Mothers' attitudes seem to be consistent within each of the three categories described. Thus, those mothers who gave priority to their own needs when deciding to use out-of-home care were less likely to emphasize their child's needs in choosing from among different types of care.

Mothers were consistent in the pattern of their satisfaction with the various aspects of the FDC. Those who were happy with the amount of time the caregiver played with the children were also happy with the nature of their relationship and communication with her, saw their child as happy in the FDC, and tended to seek the advice of the FDC staff. On the other hand, those who thought their child was less happy about going to FDC were instead more likely to seek the advice of their families and friends rather than consult the FDC staff. Pearson correlations for these relationships were all significant and ranged from -.20 to .58.

Similarly, mothers who perceived the use of child care as affecting their life tended also to report more changes how they behaved with their child ($r = .47$; $p < .001$).

The three categories of maternal attitudes to child care rarely related to each other. The only exception to this generalization is that mothers who reported more changes in their behavior toward their child were more likely to consult the FDC staff than those who reported less changes ($r = .36$; $p < .01$).

Altogether, the data show that although the mothers' initial decision to use out-of-home care for their child was designed mostly to meet their own needs, their preference for FDC mostly reflects considerations regarding the quality of care offered and the child's needs. Mothers were indeed satisfied and happy with their decision, appreciating not only the quality of care offered and the child's happiness in going to FDC, but also their ability to communicate with the staff and seek advice or guidance in matters of childrearing. For most of them, their quality of life improved as a result of using child care. Those who observed changes in their behavior toward the child were not always very happy with these changes.

The findings concerning mothers' attitudes to child care suggest that the basic attitudes of the majority of mothers in this study toward child care is acceptance and satisfaction with (a) the quality of the child-care setting, and (b) the idea that their responsibility for childrearing is shared with the FDC staff. Many see child care as a source of support in terms of improving their quality of life but not necessarily as influencing their mothering behavior.

The Relations Between Attitudes to Child Care and Childrearing Beliefs

Maternal childrearing beliefs and attitudes to child care can be seen as different aspects of the same cognitive structure mothers have of their role as parents. It was expected, therefore, that mothers' attitudes to child care should be related to their more general belief about childrearing. The Pearson correlations reported in Table 3.5 generally support this contention.

Choosing Child Care. Mothers who said that they decided to place their infant in child care because of their own needs or wishes tended to prefer either a permissive or authoritarian control method and were less likely to choose authoritative techniques. It seems that pragmatic considerations of the mothers' own "convenience" underlie both preferences. On the other hand, the mothers' preference for FDC (over other types of care) because of their child's social needs reflects a more general awareness of the child's developing needs, which can be seen in the early developmental expectations of these mothers in all areas of development.

TABLE 3.5
The Relation of Parents' Beliefs and Their Attitudes to Child Care[a]

	Choosing Child Care			Satisfaction With Child Care				Child-Care Effects	
	Care:Mo Need	FDC:Ch Need	Comm. w Cg	Cg's Play	Ch is Happy	Consult Staff	Consult Family	Mo Behavior	Mo Life
Developmental beliefs									
Developmental expectation:									
Cognitive		-.30*						.40**	.26*
Social		-.24*						.26*	.32**
Independence		-.43***							
Condition of development									
Maturation									
Experience							.20*		
Instruction									
Control method:									
Permissive	.23*								
Authoritative	-.33**						.22*	-.24*	-.25*
Authoritarian	.24*						-.20*	.27*	.22*
Socializing roles									
Attribution of influence:									
Mo: social			.36**				.43***		
Mo: emot. maturity							.29*	-.23*	
Fa: social		.25*					.24*		
Fa: emot. maturity		.27*							
Cg: social			.32**	.21*	.25*	.19*	-.44***		
Cg: emot. maturity				.26*	.23*		-.22*		

[a]Only statistically significant correlations are presented.
*p < .05. **p < .01. ***p < .001.

Satisfaction With Child Care. This consistently related to mothers' attribution of influence to the caregivers: Mothers who were highly satisfied with the play interaction between caregiver and children and with their own relationship with the caregiver, who tended to consult with the caregiver and felt their child was happy in the FDC, tended to attribute greater influence to the caregiver than did those who were less satisfied. It should be noted, however, that attributing considerable influence to the caregiver does not necessarily imply attributing little influence to the mother. Thus, mothers who expressed satisfaction with the relationship between themselves and the caregivers also attributed considerable influence to themselves.

It is interesting to note in this context the pattern displayed by mothers who chose to seek the advice of family and friends instead of consulting with the FDC staff. These mothers tend to attribute considerable influence to themselves and to the father and little influence to the caregiver, in both domains. They preferred authoritative over authoritarian disciplinary techniques and believed that facilitative experiences promote development.

These mothers presented themselves as knowledgeable of quality mothering and were unwilling to share responsibility with the child-care setting. It should be noted, however, that in spite of this attitude and even though they did not think their child was very happy going to FDC, these mothers continued sending the child to child care.

The Effect of Child Care on Mothers. It is interesting to note the way in which this is related to the childrearing beliefs of mothers. The mothers who view themselves as influenced by the use of child care consider themselves to have little influence over their child's development. They also tend to prefer more power assertive control methods and expect later achievement of competence both in the cognitive and social areas. These findings suggest that it is the less effective mothers who view child care as influencing them. The pattern is reminiscent of that of parents with external locus of control (Patterson, 1979).

Overall, the findings lend some support to the assumption that both childrearing beliefs and attitudes to child care are derived from the same cognitive structure. They suggest that mothers who are aware of their child's early development tend to select child care on the basis of the child's developmental needs. They further suggest subtle differences in the mothers' willingness to share the responsibility for childrearing, differences that are related to the mothers' perceptions and feelings concerning the child-care environment. They can also be interpreted to indicate that it might be the mothers' locus of control that underlies their view of themselves as being influenced by the use of child care.

THE RELATION OF THE MOTHER'S
BACKGROUND TO HER BELIEFS AND ATTITUDES

In their various reviews of the literature, Goodnow (1988) and Goodnow and Collins (1990) suggested two major processes through which parents' beliefs are formed: cultural transmission and the personal construction of beliefs that transforms personal experience into knowledge (Sigel, 1985).

Cultural transmission is reflected in the differences found in the beliefs (e.g., developmental expectations) of socializing agents in different cultures (Hess, Kashiwagi, Azuma, Park, & Dickson, 1980) or in different immigrant communities in a given culture (Frankel & Roer-Bornstein, 1982; Goodnow, Cashmore, Cotton, & Knight, 1984; Rosenthal, 1984). The process takes place through exposure to prepackaged cultural norms of development and parenting. Cultural norms can also be transmitted through education as can be seen in the relationship between education or SES and parents' modern or Western childrearing norms and values (Miller, 1988).

Israeli society consists of immigrants who represent a very wide variety of ethnic origins (M. Rosenthal, 1992). These are usually grouped as Middle Eastern, Western, and Israeli-born. This classification tends to be highly correlated with educational level (Ninio, 1979). Both educational level and country of origin are therefore expected to be related to the degree of Western influences on the parents' childrearing beliefs, as well as their attitudes to child care.

It has been proposed that childrearing beliefs are acquired through construction from direct personal experiences as well as by cultural transmission. Despite the consensus that parents' beliefs are constructed from their childrearing experiences (Sigel, 1985), reviews of the research literature lend relatively little support to the importance of parental experience in the construction of their beliefs (Goodnow, 1988; Miller, 1988). It has been suggested that the failure to find differences between parents with varying amounts and types of parental experiences might be partly due to the fact that parents' experiences with their children are not as critical for the construction of such beliefs as their more general life experiences. Parents, as individuals, acquire constructs of social norms through various social encounters in their families, with their peers, in their work places, and dealing with various social institutions (Goodnow & Collins, 1990). These constructs are likely to be closely linked to their constructs related to child development and parenting (Goodnow, 1988). Furthermore, Knight and Goodnow (1988) argued, that the study of nonnormative experiences that fall outside the normal course of parenting may be of special relevance to the understanding of the construction of beliefs from experience.

These arguments suggest that a more appropriate investigation of the constructivist view should examine a wider range of parents' life experiences than that defined by their age or number of children. For example, maternal employment, or living under stressful conditions such as social and economic hardship, may involve certain everyday experiences and routines that are likely to influence the parents' view of their children's development and their own responsibility in influencing it (Emiliani, Zani, & Carugati, 1981; Greenberger & O'Neil, 1992; Kochanska, Radke-Yarrow, Kuczynski, & Friedman, 1987).

The following analyses examine these major sources of parental beliefs.

The Effects of Cultural Transmission

A two-step hierarchical regression was used to examine the relative contribution of ethnic origin and level of education to maternal beliefs and attitudes to child care. The three classifications of ethnic origin were compared using dummy coding where in GP1 1 = Middle Eastern and 0 = all others and in GP2 1 = Western and 0 = all others. The two ethnic origin variables were entered in the first step and maternal years of education in the second.

Our analysis shows that the ethnic origin of mothers contributed relatively little to the childrearing beliefs under examination, and fathers' ethnic origin did not contribute at all to mothers' childrearing beliefs.

One should not, however, interpret these results as suggesting that ethnic origin is not a source of cultural transmission. These findings are understood in terms of the limitations set by the characteristics of the sample that included mothers of a wide variety of ethnic origins. Subsuming all of them under the traditional categories of Western and Middle Eastern may be misleading for studying cultural influences on parental beliefs and attitudes. Frankel and Roer-Bornstein (1982), for instance, pointed out the considerable differences in childrearing beliefs between Kurdish and Yemenite Jews who are usually included in the same Middle Eastern category. Likewise, little uniformity of cultural transmission can be expected in the Western origin category when it includes, as it does in this sample, mothers from different East European and South American countries, from England, South Africa, Australia, and the north and south of the United States as well as Canada. The category of Israeli origin in an immigrant society such as Israel is not very informative either, as most of these are only first-generation Israelis, possibly adhering to some of the childrearing beliefs held by their parents (Frankel & Roer-Bornstein, 1982). The fact that some of the spouses of these mothers have come from different countries further complicates the picture.

It seems, therefore, that in order to examine cultural transmission of childrearing beliefs in different ethnic groups a more careful method of classification into culturally different groups must be employed.

Maternal education seems to be a better predictor of mothers' beliefs and attitudes than their country of origin. Our data suggest that three processes are involved in mediating the effects of mothers' education.

First, mothers with higher education levels are more likely to hold beliefs characteristic of parents in modern or Western cultures. Better educated mothers expect earlier development of both cognitive and social skills (βs = -.43; $p < .001$ and -.27; $p < .05$, respectively). They are also more likely to prefer authoritative over authoritarian methods of discipline than less educated mothers ($\beta = -.40$; $p < .001$). This relationship of maternal education to her expectations and preferred methods of discipline has been reported by others as well (Martin, 1975; Ninio, 1979; Tulkin & Cohler, 1973). Both beliefs reflect values and norms of educated socialization agents in a modern or Western culture.

Second, the data suggest that besides directly transmitting specific childrearing beliefs, parents' education may affect their beliefs indirectly through its influence on their locus of control (Rotter, 1966). Better educated mothers are more likely to have an internal, rather than external, locus of control. This is expressed in the educated mothers' greater attribution of influence over the child's emotional maturity to themselves and in the belief that child development is a result of environmental influences such as direct instruction rather than of a maturation process outside their control ($\beta = .33$ and $-.34$, respectively; $p < .01$). Similar results concerning the relationship of maternal attributions to her level of education have been reported in other studies (Bugental & Shennum, 1984; McGillicuddy-DeLisi, 1980, 1982). This process is also evident in the attitude of the better educated mothers that credits child care with very little effect on their own behavior or life ($\beta = -.34$ and $-.49$, respectively; $p < .01$).

Third, the fact that educated mothers attribute to themselves great influence in the domain that is considered their primary responsibility (i.e., emotional maturity) reflects, in addition, a pragmatic process. In other words, if these mothers are to continue effective socialization in the domains for which they perceive themselves responsible, they need to believe that they have a great deal of influence in these domains (Knight & Goodnow, 1988). One could argue that these mothers are responding to the fact that the caregivers have a lower educational level than their own. However, if this was so, we should have found that better educated mothers attribute to caregivers less influence than mothers with lower educational level (Kontos, 1984). This, however, was not found.

Our data shows that maternal education is clearly a vehicle of cultural transmission. Through their education mothers integrate Western norms into their belief system. These norms relate to the childrearing beliefs in both a direct and indirect manner. Developmental expectations and preferred disciplinary methods are transmitted directly. The indirect aspects of the cultural transmission concern the person's attitudes to their locus of control and their perceived effectiveness in influencing their own life as well as the life of their children.

Construction of Beliefs From Personal Experiences

The construction of beliefs from personal experiences was investigated in two stages, by means of regression analyses. The first stage examined the effects of mothers' general life experiences and the second examined the more specific effect of their parental experience while controlling for the effects of life experiences.

The first regression analysis explored the relationship of mothers' beliefs and attitudes to child care, to their life experience, and circumstances. Because the mothers' age, hours of employment, as well as social and economic problems were all related to their education level, a two-step multiple regression analysis was used, controlling for education in the first step. Information on maternal employment was missing for some of the mothers, thus the sample size for this analysis has been reduced to $N = 56$.

The results of the regression analysis presented in Table 3.6 suggest that maternal life experiences are indeed related to maternal beliefs concerning their own influence and that of the caregivers, their preferred disciplinary methods, as well as their attitudes to child care.

The data led us to several conclusions: First, as the beta values of the final equations (Table 3.6) suggest, maternal life experiences associated with the

TABLE 3.6
The Regression of Maternal Beliefs and Attitudes on Mothers' Background

| | Step 1 | Step 2[a] | | | | | |
	Δ Mo Educ	Mo Age	Mo Empl.	Social Problem	Finan Supp.	Δ	R^2
Childrearing beliefs							
Developmental expectation:							
Cognitive	.08*	.24	−.08	.10	.02	.07	.15
Social	.06[†]	.22	.15	−.12	.19	.08	.14
Independence	.00	.05	.14	−.03	.09	.02	.02
Conditions of development:							
Maturation	.14**	.08	.00	.22	−.06	.04	.18[†]
Control methods:							
Authoritarian	.14**	−.22	−.08	.32*	−.02	.13	.27**
Attribute influence to:							
Mo: social	.00	−.16	−.19	.00	.00	.05	.05
Mo: emot. maturity	.02	−.15	−.15	.35*	−.15	.13	.15
Cg: social	.00	−.12	−.23	.00	.04	.06	.06
Cg: emot. maturity	.00	−.29*	−.33*	−.16	.38**	.30**	.30**
Attitudes to child care							
Reasons for choosing ch care:							
Care: mo needs	.04	−.06	−.05	−.13	.05	.02	.06
FDC: ch needs	.02	−.24	.06	.20	.01	.09	.11
Satisfaction with:							
−Comm. with caregiver	.01	−.19	−.04	.07	.18	.07	.08
−Caregiver play w child	.03	.09	.04	.11	−.08	.02	.05
−Ch happy at FDC	.02	−.23	−.19	.33*	−.05	.16	.18[†]
Consult w FDC staff	.02	−.03	.15	−.05	.03	.03	.05
Consult w family	.00	−.17	.01	.05	.03	.03	.03
Ch-care effects on:							
Mo's behavior	.05[†]	−.05	−.31*	−.08	−.01	.10	.15
Mo's life	.21***	−.09	−.14	−.10	.16	.05	.26**

[a]The table presents R^2 increments for each step and the beta values of the final equation.
[†]$p < .10$. *$p < .05$. **$p < .01$. ***$p < .001$.

family's social problems contributed more to the variance in their beliefs and attitudes than did any other of the variables describing different life experiences.

Mothers in socially distressed families believed they have more influence on the child's development than mothers in less distressed families. Although these mothers attributed considerable influence to themselves, their preference for more authoritarian control methods was closer to that of mothers with external locus of control (Loeb, 1975; Patterson, 1979). This may suggest that their attribution of influence to themselves was based on a pragmatic process, rather than on a construct of internal locus of control.

The attribution seemed to reflect their need to believe that they could influence their child's development (Knight & Goodnow, 1988). These mothers, more than those who made their own decision to send their child to child care, may feel threatened by the development of a close relationship between child and caregiver. This interpretation is supported by the finding that these mothers tended to send their child to child care at a later age than other mothers. Presumably they placed their child with a caregiver only following a referral by the local social worker. This interpretation is further supported by the fact that these mothers were more likely than others to think that their child was "very happy" and went willingly to the FDC.

Their preference for power-assertive disciplinary techniques seemed to provide these mothers with a cognitive framework that may be functional in as much as it helped justify their punitive disciplinary behavior. Such behavior was likely to result from their emotional distress and impatience related to the task of parenting, and the same pragmatic process may have been at the base of their attitude that their child was happy in FDC. It is interesting to note the similarity between our findings and those reported for depressed mothers (Kochanska et al., 1987). The same pragmatic process may be operating in this group of mothers as well.

However, two alternative interpretations could be offered to the one just cited. The first can suggest that these mothers have acquired a preference for authoritarian techniques through experiencing power assertive models in a hierarchical family relationship throughout their life. The second could argue that this is a case of cultural transmission, rather than construction from personal experience. Such an interpretation may stress the possibility that these mothers have been reared in a traditional culture that emphasized the values of the maternal role in rearing the child and of family hierarchy and obedience (Holloway et al., 1988). The fact that this finding emerged after controlling for maternal education, and was not related to mothers' ethnic origin, suggests that this result is best understood in terms of mothers' construction from their personal experience.

A second major conclusion from this analysis concerns a group of what might be described as *dependent* mothers. These are young mothers, who were dependent on financial support from the Welfare Department and worked only part time. These mothers attributed a high degree of influence to caregivers in the domain of emotional maturity. It should be noted that this domain is considered to be the major responsibility of mothers rather than caregivers. These mothers do not seem to have an internal locus of control. This construct is also evident in the fact that it was these mothers who worked fewer hours who tended to report that child care considerably affected their own behavior with their children.

The second stage of our analysis examined the relationship between amount of parental experience (i.e., number of children) and mothers' beliefs and attitudes to child care. The age of the child's placement in child care was disqualified as an assessment of parental experience because 82% of the parents sent their child to the FDC within the first 18 months. A preliminary analysis, in fact, showed no relationship between this measure and any of the mothers' beliefs and attitudes.

A two-step multiple regression analysis was used, controlling in the first step for maternal education, employment status and social problems, all of which were found to be related to number of children.

Two major findings emerged from this analysis. First, like mothers who had social problems, mothers with more children also preferred more power-assertive techniques ($\beta = .39$; $p < .05$). The second finding is that even though these mothers are not satisfied with their communication with the caregiver ($\beta = -.42$; $p < .05$), nor with the caregiver's interactions with the children ($\beta = -.33$; $p < .05$), they do report changes in their behavior toward their children as a result of using child care ($\beta = .42$; $p < .05$). In addition, these mothers with more children are less likely to consult with family or friends regarding various childrearing problems, than mothers with fewer children ($\beta = -.44$; $p < .05$).

It could be that on the basis of their experience with many children mothers construct the belief that power-assertive techniques are a more effective way of controlling their children's misbehavior. An alternative interpretation is that coping with a large number of children, like with other hardships, is stressful for mothers and that the mothers' preference has a pragmatic basis, reflecting the need to justify their punitive behavior within a cognitive framework. Furthermore, these experienced mothers seem to feel they know enough about childrearing and have no need to consult with family or friends. They also seem quite critical of the FDC caregiver, although they feel that using FDC for their child has led to changes in their own interactions with their child.

Our analysis of the construction of childrearing beliefs from the mothers' personal experience suggest that this process is modified by pragmatic motivation. Distressed mothers, as well as mothers with many children, construct a cognitive framework that enables them to enhance their sense of value as mothers by attributing to themselves high influence over their child's development, or by criticizing the caregiver. Another aspect of this cognitive framework enables them to justify their punitive disciplinary behavior.

In summary, our discussion of the relationship of mothers' background to their belief system shows that the mothers' childrearing beliefs and attitudes to child care are indeed related to their educational background and life experiences. This relationship reflects processes of cultural transmission as well as personal construction. It has been suggested that in their construction of beliefs people do not always operate in a scientific mode (Goodnow & Collins, 1990) and that the process is rather invested with feelings and motivation. The findings of this study support the contention that mothers seem to hold to certain attitudes and beliefs in order to make life with their children more meaningful or more rewarding (Knight & Goodnow, 1988).

This chapter has discussed various aspects of the parents' background and their beliefs and attitudes that are likely to be related to their own and their child's experiences in child care. These relationships are analyzed in chapter 8, which examines the interface between home and child care.

4

FDC Caregivers

One important dimension of a childrearing context, which has been shown to influence development, is the quality of care it provides (Clarke-Stewart & Gruber, 1984; Howes, 1988a; Howes & Olenick, 1986; Lamb, Bookstein, Broberg, Hult, & Frodi, 1988; Phillips et al., 1987; Roupp, Travers, Glantz, & Coelen, 1979; Vandell, Henderson, & Wilson, 1988). In most settings, but especially in FDC, it is the caregiver who defines the child-care context and its quality. Children's experiences in child care have been shown by both theory and research to be mediated by their interaction with the caregiving adult (e.g., Phillips, 1987; Roupp et al., 1979).

The centrality of the caregiver to the definition of quality of care draws attention to the fact that relatively little is known about caregivers and their role. It is generally agreed among researchers that from both a theoretical and an empirical point of view, one needs a better understanding of the role of the caregiver in child-care settings (Pettygrove, Whitebook, & Weir, 1984; Phillips & Whitebook, 1986).

Recent research has begun to provide descriptive data regarding the caregivers in child care. It has also examined a number of factors in the caregivers' background, professional socialization, and work environment that may influence their behavior with children as well as their cognitions concerning child development and their role (Whitebook, Howes, & Phillips, 1990).

Individual differences in caregivers' behavior and the quality of care they provide may result from processes occurring on different levels. First, as in the case of parents, it has been suggested that the way caregivers interact with children is partly determined by their childrearing beliefs (Miller, 1988; M. Rosenthal, 1991a; Sigel, 1985) Thus, for example, findings show that caregivers' child-oriented attitudes are related to caregivers' behaviors such as responsive encouragement and restrictions (Berk, 1985). More specifically, other studies showed that caregivers' attributions regarding child misbehavior were related to their responses to the children (Scott-Little & Holloway, 1991).

47

Second, individual differences between caregivers, in both their childrearing beliefs and interactions with children, were found to be related to differences in their level of education and professional training as well as to some characteristics of their work environment, such as group size or work hours (e.g., Arnett, 1989; Berk, 1985; Howes, 1983; Kontos & Stremmel, 1988; Pence & Goelman, 1987; Roupp et al., 1979; Whitebook et al., 1990).

Although many research findings have documented the relationship between the caregivers' behavior and these background and work environment factors, relatively little is known about how their behavior or background are related to their childrearing beliefs. Furthermore, although there are some data available concerning the belief system of professionally trained educators working in educational institutions such as nursery schools or day-care centers (Hess et al., 1981; Holloway et al., 1988; Winetsky, 1978), very little is known about the childrearing beliefs of caregivers with less training who work in less formal settings such as FDC.

This chapter examines data gathered in our studies of the personal and professional backgrounds and work environments of caregivers in sponsored FDC in Israel. It examines the behavior of these caregivers, which defines the quality of care provided in their homes, and the relationship of this behavior to the caregivers' childrearing belief system. The chapter also investigates the relation between this behavior and these beliefs and the caregivers' personal and professional background. It further investigates the relation between the caregivers' beliefs and behavior and some characteristics of their work environment.

CAREGIVERS AND THEIR WORK ENVIRONMENT

The dimensions of personal background examined in this study are the caregivers' level of education, ethnic origin, age, and number of children.

The dimensions of professional background include the length of the caregivers' training (months) and professional experience in working with children other than their own.

Two major categories were used to characterize the context in which the caregivers interact with children or their work environment. The first category includes five dimensions describing the characteristics of the group in care, characteristics that are likely to define important dimensions of the caregivers' working conditions. It included the following: group size, mean age, and age mix. Age mix was defined by two alternative measures: the first the *age SD* around the group mean age; the second the *age span* defined in terms of the age difference between the youngest and oldest child in the group (1 = a difference of 0–8 months, 2 = 9–16 months, and 3 = 17 months or more). It also included the *mean SES* of the group (an index based on a composite of the group's mean parental education and the percentage of families with social problems [$r = .55$]), as well as the presence of the caregivers' *own child* in the group (1 = is present). The second category describes the professional support offered by the sponsoring agency. It includes a measure of the frequency of in-service professional supervision provided by the sponsoring agencies. The frequency of individual and group supervision was averaged yielding a measure of *supervision*, which ranged from *once a week* (3) to *once a month or less* (1). It also included an assessment of the degree of *autonomy* given the caregiver by the agency on the daily routine and the choice of equipment, materials, and space organization. Scores are ratings on a 3-point scale, from *decides with supervisor* (1) to *decides with peers* (2), and *decides alone without consulting anyone* (3).

Professional support can be seen in terms of a process of "empowerment" described by Cochran (1985). This process builds on the strengths rather than the weaknesses of the socializing agent. Professional support has two dimensions: the frequency of professional supervision that aims at preserving the existing strength of the caregivers and the degree of autonomy in decision making concerning the program offered to the children in their care. A high degree of autonomy acts as validation of the caregivers' existing practices. According to Cochran (1988), such validation is a supportive factor contributing to the process of empowerment.

The data gathered in Study 1 on the caregivers' backgrounds and work environments are presented in Table 4.1.

Personal Background

Most caregivers were either Israeli born (41.5%) or of Middle Eastern background (53.6%). Only two caregivers (4.9%) were of Western origin. As Table 4.1 shows, their level of education was almost uniformly low: 70.7% did not finish high school and only one caregiver had more than 15 years of education. It seems that because of the uniformity of caregivers' level of education, no relation was found between education level and ethnic origin, or any other personal or professional characteristic of the caregivers.

TABLE 4.1
Personal and Professional Backgrounds of Caregivers

	M	SD	Minimum	Maximum
Personal background:				
Education (years)	10.41	1.92	6	16
Age	35.10	7.27	25	56
Number of children	3.50	1.36	1	7
Professional background:				
Child care experience (years)	2.66	1.64	1	7
Preservice training (months)	2.27	0.98	1	4
Work environment: group characteristics				
Mean age (months)	25.57	5.45	13	36
Age mix (SD)	5.52	3.56	0.43	14.31
Group size	5.17	.83	3	7
Mean parental eduation (years)	12.37	2.63	8.2	17.8
Mean social problems (proportion)	0.21	0.27	0	1
Work environment: professional support				
In-service supervision[a] (3 = freq)	2.28	0.47	1	3
Autonomy (equipment) (3 = hi)	1.54	0.87	1	3

[a]This is an average frequency of individual and group supervision.

Professional Background

As indicated by the data shown in Table 4.1, caregivers had relatively little experience in caring for children other than their own and very little preservice training. On average they did not have any preservice training other than that offered by the sponsoring agency.

Work Environment

Group Characteristics

Caregivers usually worked with groups of five children, ranging in age from 1 to 3 years old (Table 4.1). Although 89% of the children were under the age of 3, some caregivers had fairly homogenous groups (i.e., less than a 6-month age difference between the youngest and oldest child), whereas others had to cope with extensive age heterogeneity (i.e., more than 2 years between the youngest and oldest child). The groups were quite heterogeneous in terms of the socioeconomic background of the children. This heterogeity reflects the child placement policy of the FDC system discussed in chapter 3 that does not allow parents to choose the specific home their child attends.

Only 20% of the caregivers ($N = 8$) included their own child in the child-care group. These caregivers tended to be older ($r = .32$; $p < .05$) and of Middle Eastern origin ($r = .40$; $p < .01$); they also tended to have less training ($r = -.31$; $p < .05$).

Professional Support: Supervision and Autonomy

Table 4.1 shows that caregivers in this study received support from their sponsoring organizations. Our distributions show that most caregivers (92.5%) received some professional supervision (individually and/or in a group) at least every other week. Of the caregivers 58.5% ($N = 24$) reported receiving individual supervision (usually in the form of a home visit) and 66.7% received it at least once a week.

Caregivers were fairly autonomous in their planning of the daily routine and activities and less so in their decisions on the choice of equipment, furniture, toys, and the adaptation of their apartment to the children's needs. Although 71% planned the daily program on their own, only 24% decided alone on choice of equipment.

In general, Table 4.1 suggests that the typical caregiver in this FDC system was a middle-aged mother, with two to five children of her own, and with less than high school education. Older caregivers tended to be of Middle Eastern origin ($r = .33$; $p < .05$) and had more children ($r = .61$; $p < .001$).

The caregivers had about 2 months of training and relatively little experience in child care. They cared for five children under the age of 3 who came from a fairly heterogeneous SES background. All caregivers had some professional support in the form of bimonthly supervision as well as a fair level of autonomy in decisions concerning their program.

Although the various aspects of the caregivers' work environments and their professional and personal backgrounds were not interrelated, the group characteristics were. Heterogeneous age groups tended to be larger ($r = .32$, $p < .05$), with older children ($r = .36$, $p < .01$) who came from lower SES homes ($r = -.50$, $p <$

.001), and had caregivers with more preservice training ($r = .39; p < .01$). Caregivers working with older children, as well as those working with children who were predominantly of lower SES background, tended to receive more frequent supervision ($r = .29$ and $-.35$, respectively, with $p < .05$). Older caregivers tended to care for smaller groups ($r = -.39; p < .01$).

The results suggest that the general characteristics and qualifications of Israeli FDC caregivers were similar to those found in North America and among caregivers in Britain. In contrast to standards in these countries, Israeli standards allowed for as many as five children, below 3 years of age in each home. The caregivers' work environment and low wages tend to be similar to those in other countries (Clarke-Stewart & Gruber, 1984; Goelman, Rosenthal, & Pence, 1990; Howes, 1983; Moss, 1987; Stallings & Porter, 1980).

THE CAREGIVERS' BELIEFS AND BEHAVIORS

Caregivers' Childrearing Beliefs

As with mothers, the caregivers' beliefs concerning child development, as well as their perception of their role in influencing it, are of special interest. These cognitions supposedly reflect the knowledge base of the caregivers' professional interactions with the children in their care. They are expected to reflect the caregivers' knowledge of the developmental needs of children and how best to interact with them so as to meet these needs in the most adequate way. On the basis of the research literature available, one might expect that caregivers who believe in the earlier attainment of developmental competence, in the influence of environmental factors on development, and in their own influence over the children's development may invest more in facilitative interaction and creating an environment that supports this development (Hess et al., 1981). Similarly, one might expect that caregivers who prefer less power-assertive disciplinary methods will respond in a less authoritarian way to children's misbehavior.

The same two aspects of the childrearing belief system that were described for parents were also examined for caregivers (Study 1): beliefs about how children develop, and beliefs about the role of different socializing agents in influencing development.

An examination of the childrearing beliefs presented in Table 4.2 shows that caregivers tended to believe in environmental (rather than maturational) influences on development and preferred either permissive or authoritative methods of control.

Caregivers attributed more influence to themselves than to mothers, especially in the domain of social development (T pairs $= 4.69; p < .001$). Significant differences were found between the degrees of influence caregivers attributed to themselves in the different developmental domains: Caregivers believed they had greater influence over social development than over emotional maturity ($T = 3.07; p < .004$). Although altogether very little influence was attributed to fathers, more influence was ascribed to them in emotional maturity than in the social development domain ($T = 2.51; p < .02$).

TABLE 4.2
Caregivers' Childrearing Beliefs

	M	SD	Minimum	Maximum
Developmental expectation (months):				
Cognitive	25.93	4.96	15.8	40.4
Social	25.80	4.29	19.1	35.7
Independence	37.55	8.48	21.3	51.8
Conditions influencing development[a]:				
Maturation	.20	.11	0	1
Facilitative experience	.26	.11	0	1
Direct instruction	.53	.11	0	1
Mean degree of involvement (1–3)	2.33	.20	2.0	2.8
Preferred disciplinary method[b]:				
Permissive	.41	.14	0	1
Authoritative	.48	.14	0	1
Authoritarian	.11	.08	0	1
Mean level power assertion (1–6)	2.80	.34	2.0	3.4
Attribution of influence to[c]:				
Mother: social	2.23	.32	1	3
Mother: emotion. maturity	2.30	.41	1	3
Caregiver: social	2.66	.37	1	3
Caregiver: emotion. maturity	2.50	.50	1	3
Father: social	1.37	.45	1	3
Father: emotion. maturity	1.49	.49	1	3

[a]Proportion choosing one of the following three measures, averaged across 37 items.
[b]Proportion choosing one of six responses (categorized into groups), averaged across 17 episodes.
[c]Mean rankings of influence for three adults (child's mother and father, FDC caregiver), averaged across 11 items in two domains.

Interrelation Between Caregivers' Beliefs

Caregivers were consistent in their ideas concerning "developmental timetable" and attribution of influence. That is, those who expected early mastery in one area of development expected it in other areas as well. Those who attributed considerable influence to an agent in one domain tended to do so in other domains as well. Pearson correlation values ranged from .43 to .81 with $p < .001$.

Less marked relationships were found between caregivers' developmental expectations, beliefs in conditions that influence development, and attribution of influence. Pearson correlations for these relationships ranged from .26 to .39 with $p < .05$.

The data suggest that caregivers tend to perceive themselves as influential over children's development. More influence was perceived in the domain of social development that presumably is more relevant to the group context of their interaction with the children. They also attribute greater influence over development to environmental rather than maturational factors.

The correlation patterns suggest that caregivers' beliefs were fairly consistent and coherent. Thus, caregivers who believe that environmental rather than maturational factors influence development are more likely to see themselves as influential. These caregivers expect early development and believe in the effectiveness of less coercive disciplinary techniques. As in the case of mothers, these findings can be interpreted as expressions of the caregivers' locus of control (Bugental & Shennum, 1984; Loeb, 1975; Patterson, 1979; Rotter, 1966).

The Caregivers' Behavior and Quality of Care

It could be suggested that two dimensions of the FDC caregivers' behavior are relevant to the quality of care they offer: (a) their spontaneous interaction with the children, and (b) the educational program they create to facilitate the children's development (M. Rosenthal, 1990, 1991a). A factor analysis done recently by Howes, Phillips, and Whitebook (1992) on their Harms scale data revealed two sub scales (Appropriate Caregiving and Developmentally Appropriate Activities) that are not unlike the dimensions proposed by our studies. Both dimensions have been shown by previous research to affect the development of infants and toddlers (e.g., McCartney, Scarr, Phillips, & Grajek, 1985); they are affected by the caregivers' level of education and training in child development (e.g., Kaplan & Conn, 1984) and other structural aspects of the child care environment (Howes, Phillips, & Whitebook, 1992).

This distinction is of particular interest in the case of FDC, which contains both homelike and institutional elements in its childrearing environment and where the caregivers' professionalism may be less clearly defined.

Some researchers view the quality of the physical setting and daily program not as aspects of the caregivers' functioning but rather as factors in the work environment that influence the caregivers' interactions with the children (Whitebook et al., 1990). Thus, caregivers in centers with higher quality yards were found to be more sensitive and friendly (Prescott, 1981). Similarly, FDC caregivers in homes with child-designed space expressed more positive (rather than negative) affect and were less restrictive (Howes, 1983). Beecause an FDC caregiver working in her own home is reasonably autonomous in her decisions regarding the daily program as well as how to arrange the space and equipment, we prefer to view these decisions as yet another dimension in the quality of care offered by the FDC caregivers.

In this study we assessed the quality of the caregivers' spontaneous and direct interaction with the children using three measures based on the FDC observations: a composite score of positive interaction (including the frequency of direct involvement, facilitative encouragement, responsiveness and a rating of affectionate expressiveness), the frequency of restrictions, and the frequency of the caregivers' engagement in group rather than individual interaction.

The educational program and environment provided by the caregivers generally requires some planning and possibly some articulation of educational goals. Their quality was assessed by two measures: the first, a composite measure describing the educational quality of the physical environment, such as space available for play and accessibility of toys; the second, a composite measure based on the frequency of educational activities stimulated by the caregivers and a rating of the caregivers' utilization of routine care activities for educational purposes.

Spontaneous Interaction

Data suggest that, on the average, caregivers in these settings tended to engage in positive interactions with the children. Examining some of the specific measures making up the composite score of "positive interaction," we find that caregivers spent 32.6% of the observation time in facilitative and encouraging interactions. Only 27% of the time was spent in preparation work not involving the children. Caregivers spent an average of 23.2% ($SD = 9.03$; range = 7%–43%) of the time in group interaction with the children. They spent an average of 11.2% ($SD = 6.6$; range 2%–24%) of the observation time restricting and controlling the children's behavior.

Educational Program

The ratings of the components of the composite score of the educational quality of the physical environment indicate that caregivers generally offered sufficient play space in their homes with adequately varied play materials and equipment and a reasonable amount of time was devoted to educational activities. The caregivers, for instance, initiated educational activities during an average of 26% ($SD = 18$; range = 0%–70%) of the time of the daily program. The rest of the time was given to other activities, such as care of physical needs or free play.

Interrelation of Caregivers' Behaviors

There is a significant correlation between the composite measure of the educational quality of the physical environment and the measure of educational activities ($r = .66$, $p < .001$). No other significant correlations were found between the various behaviors of the caregivers.

The data suggest that although these caregivers restrict the behavior of children just as often as U.S. FDC caregivers (Howes, 1983), they offer a fair quality of care. Furthermore, these caregivers spend more time teaching and playing with their groups of children than the sponsored FDC providers in the NHDC study in the U.S. (Stallings & Porter, 1980). Although the educationally minded caregivers are likely to provide a daily routine and a physical environment that are educationally suitable for children, these patterns of caregivers' behavior, although consistent, are not related to their spontaneous interactions with the children. One should also note that the caregivers' tendency to engage in positive interactions is unrelated to their use of restrictions. We suggest, therefore, that although the findings generally support the conclusion that "good things go together" (Phillips & Howes, 1987), these various behaviors do not necessarily belong to a single dimension of "quality of care."

The Relation Between Quality of Care and Caregivers' Beliefs

Table 4.3 clearly suggests that different aspects of the quality of care as measured by the caregivers' behavior are related to somewhat different beliefs. Three major patterns seem to emerge: In the first pattern, the caregivers who engage more frequently in spontaneous positive interactions with the children attribute considerable influence to themselves, and little to the mother, in both the social and

TABLE 4.3
The Relationship Between Quality of Care and Caregivers' Beliefs

Childrearing Beliefs	Spontaneous Interaction			Educational Program	
	Positive Inter'	Restrictions	Group Inter'	Educat'l Activity	Physical Environment
Developm'l expectation:					
Cognitive	− .17	.29	.25	− .17	− .09
Social	− .21	.23	.36*	− .07	− .02
Independence	− .26	.46**	.38*	− .31*	− .32*
Conditions of developm:					
Maturation	− .03	.37*	.26	− .09	− .21
Control methods:					
Authoritarian	.06	.38**	.06	− .25	− .36*
Attribute influence to:					
Mo: social	− .27†	.13	.16	− .12	.13
Mo: emot. maturity	− .47**	.19	.07	− .28	− .12
Cg: social	.49***	− .24	− .37*	.17	.02
Cg: emot. maturity	.48**	− .37*	− .28	.29	.11

emotional maturity domains. There is, likewise, a slight tendency among those who initiate more educational activities to attribute considerable influence to themselves and little influence to the mothers, but only in the emotional maturity domain.

In the second pattern, spontaneous positive interactions and the more planned educational aspects of the program are related to somewhat different beliefs. Thus, although spontaneous positive interaction is not related to any of the beliefs concerning child development, caregivers who initiate more frequent educational activities and provide a better physical environment tend to expect early achievement of independence and are less likely to prefer power-assertive disciplinary techniques.

In contrast with these behaviors, which are generally associated with good quality care, we find a third pattern in which caregivers impose frequent restrictions on the children, spend more time interacting with the children as a group, and tend to expect late achievement of competence. They are also less likely to attribute great influence to themselves, or for that matter to the environment in general, as they tend to believe that maturation is the main process at the basis of development. Furthermore, caregivers who exercise more restrictions are those who indeed prefer more power-assertive disciplinary methods. Also, caregivers who offer a poorer quality physical environment tend to prefer more power-assertive methods.

The data concerning the relationship between caregivers' beliefs and behavior suggest that like parents with internal locus of control (Rotter, 1966), the caregivers in this study who attribute considerable influence to themselves over the children's development, provide frequent positive interactions with the children and are less likely to restrict their behavior or interact with them as a group. In contrast, those caregivers who believe that maturation is the main determinant of development do not perceive themselves as influencing children's development. These caregivers often expect children to achieve control over their behavior (independence) at a later age. They prefer power-assertive disciplinary methods and use more frequent restrictions when interacting with the children.

Altogether it seems that the caregivers' behavior and the quality of care they offer are generally consistent with the cognitive structure of their beliefs.

THE RELATION OF CAREGIVERS' BACKGROUNDS AND WORK ENVIRONMENTS TO THEIR BEHAVIORS AND BELIEFS

One expects the personal and professional backgrounds of caregivers, as well as factors characterizing their work environments, to be related to their childrearing beliefs and the quality of their behavior with the children in their care. It therefore seems worthwhile to investigate the relation of these beliefs and behaviors to several factors that included (a) the personal backgrounds of the caregivers (ethnicity, education, age, and number of children), (b) their professional backgrounds (training and child-care experience), and (c) their work environment (the availability of in-service supervision and degree of autonomy in decision making as well as characteristics of the group of children, such as group size, age mean and mix, children's SES, and the presence of the caregivers' own children).

Three sets of regression analyses were carried out examining the relationship of caregivers' beliefs and behavior to the factors just cited. Each model was computed separately for the different measures of caregivers' behavior and beliefs. As was done in the analysis of maternal beliefs, only one variable of a set of interdependent beliefs was included in the analysis. Table 4.4 summarizes the results of these regression analyses.

Personal Background

Previous studies found that the caregivers' education level is related both to the caregivers' childrearing beliefs and their interactions with the children. Thus, for instance, it was found that caregivers with more education tended to have more "child-oriented" attitudes and greater job satisfaction (Berk, 1985; Peters & Sutton, 1984). They also tended to spend more time in social interaction and cognitive/language stimulation (Roupp et al., 1979). Findings from the National Child Care Staffing Study suggest that caregivers with higher levels of formal education (BA or higher) were more sensitive and offer better quality care (Howes, Whitebook, & Phillips, 1992). Various studies suggest that possible effects of other dimensions of personal background (such as ethnic origin, age, and number of children) on their behavior or beliefs are generally overshadowed by the effects of their education and professional training (Roupp et al., 1979; Winetsky, 1978).

A two-step multiple hierarchical regression analysis was employed to examine the relation between caregivers' personal background and their beliefs and behavior. Country of birth and level of education were entered in the first step, caregivers' age and number of children in the second. This model enables us to examine both cultural and experiential factors in the caregivers' personal background.

TABLE 4.4
A Summary Table of the Regression Analyses

	Childrearing Beliefs	*Caregivers' Behaviors*
Personal background		
Ethnic origin	None	None
Education	Attribute influence—self	less group inter'
	Environment → Maturation	less restrictions
Age	None	None
Number of children	None	None
Professional background		
Training	Expect late development:	more group inter'
	Social & independence	
Experience	Expect early development:	None
	Independence	
Work environment:		
Autonomy	Direct instruction → Maturation	Positive inter';
		less group inter'
		better phys. env.
Supervision	None	Positive inter'
Work environment: group		
Size	None	None
Mean age	None	Older: more group int
		more educ'l activity
		better phys. env
Mean SES	None	High SES: more
		educ'l activity
Own child present	Attribute influence to mother	None
	Expect late dev.: social	

An examination of the beta values of the equation revealed that although education level explained some of the variance in a number of beliefs and behavior, the caregivers' country of birth (Middle Eastern vs. non-Middle Eastern), age, and number of children contributed very little, if anything, to the understanding of their behavior or beliefs.

The caregivers with a few more years of education attributed considerable influence to themselves and little influence to the mothers, but only in the social domain (βs = -.45 and -.44, respectively; $p < .01$). They were also more likely to perceive developmental changes as resulting from environmental rather than maturational processes (β = -.27 ; $p < .09$).

In addition to the effect of education on their beliefs, we find that caregivers with less education were more likely to restrict the children's behavior and engage in group (rather than individual) interaction with them, than those with higher levels of education (β = -.29; $p < .08$, and β = -.39; $p < .01$, respectively).

Our data is in agreement, therefore, with other research in this area. It suggests that among the different characteristics of the caregivers', education had the most significant effect on both their beliefs and behavior. The lack of significant effect of the caregivers' age and number of children is congruent with findings of other researchers (Goodnow & Collins, 1990; Roupp et al., 1979). The fact that ethnicity did not explain any of the caregivers' childrearing beliefs or behavior can be understood in terms of the inadequacy of its definition. As was already mentioned in the earlier discussion of parents' beliefs, the classifications used in this study can be very misleading as each category incorporates cultures that vary greatly in their childrearing beliefs and practices (Frankel & Roer-Bornstein, 1982).

One should note that although the caregivers' education was almost uniformly low, the small differences in their level of education did contribute to the variance in their beliefs and behavior. It seems that their education may have shifted their more basic perception of locus of control from external, which is to be expected among Middle Eastern women with a low level of education, to a more internal one. This finding confirms Bugental and Shennum's (1984) contention that agents' locus of control is expressed in how much influence over a child's development they attribute to themselves. Furthermore, the better educated caregivers believed that child development is a result of environmental factors rather than maturational ones (McGillicuddy-DeLisi, 1980, 1982). As might be expected from the earlier analysis of the correlation between beliefs and behaviors, these better educated caregivers are less restrictive and prefer individualized over group interaction with young children.

Professional Background

Studies have shown that the caregivers' specialized early childhood education, or training in child development, is the most consistent predictor of the quality of care offered in a child-care setting. Caregivers with more child-related training provide better quality interactions with the children and a better physical environment (Arnett, 1989; Berk, 1985; Clarke-Stewart & Gruber, 1984; Howes, 1983; Kaplan & Conn, 1984; Roupp et al., 1979; Stallings & Porter, 1980). It has been suggested recently, however, that only very high levels of specialized training is likely to be as effective as formal academic education in securing high quality of care (Howes, Whitebook, & Phillips, 1992).

Training has proved to be of great importance in modifying caregivers' beliefs as well. Holloway et al. (1988) reported, for example, that Mexican caregivers whose training was based on U.S. textbooks adhered to more Western educational values and norms than Mexican mothers. Caregivers with more training were more child-oriented and less authoritarian in their childrearing attitudes (Arnett, 1989; Berk, 1985).

It has been suggested that norms and beliefs transmitted through socialization to a role, as in the case of professional training, may override those transmitted by the trainees' culture of origin (Arnett, 1989; Holloway et al., 1988). Winetsky

(1978) used this argument to explain her finding that, unlike those of parents, teachers' expectations did not differ by social class or ethnicity.

Other studies suggest that a cultural transmission of beliefs and values may take place not only through knowledge acquired in training but also through formal and informal role definitions provided by society at large, or by the social institution in which the person is reared (Hess et al., 1981).

Some researchers argued, however, that for the FDC caregiver, whose role resembles more that of a mother than a professional teacher, training may be less important and the role definition more ambiguous (Howes, 1983).

In contrast to the clear effects of training on all aspects of the caregivers' functioning, experience in working with children seems to have a differential effect on different dimensions of the quality of care. Thus, it was found that caregivers with more experience spent less time on educational activities that promote development (Roupp et al., 1979) but were more responsive in their spontaneous interactions with children (Howes, 1983). Others found no relationship between the caregivers' experience in the field of early childhood and their behavior (Howes, Whitebook, & Phillips, 1992; Stallings & Porter, 1980).

The second set of multiple regression analyses examined the relationship of caregivers' behavior and beliefs to their professional training and experience. Given the uniformly short preservice training and experience of these caregivers, it is not surprising that with the exception of caregiver's developmental expectations and group interaction, this equation did not explain any other belief or behavior: Caregivers with more preservice training expected social skills and independence to develop later (βs were .37 and .29, respectively, with $p < .05$). They tended to engage more frequently in group interaction with children than caregivers with less training ($\beta = .31; p < .06$). In contrast, the more experienced caregivers expected earlier, rather than later, achievement of independence ($\beta = -.32; p < .05$), possibly reflecting greater pressure toward independence among these caregivers.

Our findings suggest that even little training succeeded in passing on a message of "lower the pressure of expectations for achievement" in the area of independence and social skills, but not in the area of cognitive development. This meant that the trained caregiver expected infants and toddlers to be able to share, play cooperatively, or be independent later than caregivers with less training, or those with more experience. This finding indeed reflects values emphasized in their training, that highlight early cognitive achievements and the lowering of pressure on social development. At the same time, however, it seems that caregivers with more training have adopted a self-image, or a role model, of a professional educator or school teacher leading them to more frequent group (rather than individual) interactions with the children.

This finding calls for caution in our understanding of the effects of training. Not all training is effective in improving the quality of care provided by the caregiver. When the goals and content of training are not connected to each other or clearly articulated, or when the process of training assumes a "cookbook" approach and/or is too short, training may result in negative effects on the quality of caregiving.

Consistent with other studies, and with the exception of the tendency of more experienced caregivers to pressure children toward early achievement of independence, we found very little difference between caregivers with varied amount of experience.

Work Environment

The work environment has direct and indirect effects on the quality of interaction between caregivers and children. Some of its features have been described as the structural characteristics of child care, especially when the discussion focused on the implications of research for policy and licensing issues (e.g., Howes, 1986). It was shown, for example, that caregivers who worked fewer hours were more responsive, engaged in more facilitative interactions, and were less restrictive than those working longer hours (Howes, 1983). Dimensions of the work environment were found to be related to the professional orientation of caregivers (Jorde-Bloom, 1989).

Group composition is one of the dominant features of the work environment that affected caregiver–child interaction. Thus, it was found that caregivers who worked with smaller groups were more responsive, engaged in more facilitative interactions, provided more cognitive/language stimulation, and were less restrictive. They provided more appropriate caregiving and more developmentally appropriate activities (Howes, 1983; Howes, Phillips, & Whitebook, 1992; Roupp et al., 1979). Stallings and Porter (1980) found that the age mix of the group affected the amount of time the caregiver spent with different age children and the type of activity she engaged in (e.g., more controlling and less developmental activities with a high proportion of toddlers and more language activity with preschoolers). Relatively little is known about the effect of the presence of her own children in the group on the caregiver's behavior and beliefs. Following the work of Kontos (1984) and Kontos and Wells (1986), one would expect the caregivers' perception of mothers to be affected by the SES characteristics of the group in their care. Thus, one may expect that caregivers working with mothers of lower SES background (lower education, welfare referrals) will attribute less influence to these mothers (and more to themselves) than caregivers working with higher SES families.

There is relatively little research demonstrating that professional support in the form of consultation, supervision, or simple home visiting can improve the quality of care in FDC homes. Such supportive supervision may even be more effective than short-term training course in changing caregivers' attitudes and role perception and behavior (Jackson & Jackson, 1979; M. Rosenthal, 1990; Shinman, 1981). Similarly, it was found that participation in a short series of meetings based on an empowerment model introduced changes in the perceptions and behavior of FDC caregivers (Henry, 1992). Other research has indicated that caregivers who were more autonomous in decisions concerning their program provided more verbal interactions with their children by asking questions and offering choices. These strategies lead to the enhancement of language development in young children (Tizard, 1974). Our expectation, therefore, is that caregivers who had a higher degree of autonomy and more frequent supportive supervision will both perceive themselves as having more influence over children's development and provide better quality care.

The third set of analyses employed a stepwise multiple regression analysis that examined the relationship between caregivers' beliefs and behavior and their work environment. A preliminary analysis revealed that age mix and level of autonomy in decisions concerning the daily routine (which was uniformly high among caregivers) were not related to caregivers' beliefs or behaviors. The equation included, therefore, the frequency of supervision and the degree of caregivers' autonomy in their choice of equipment, which were entered in the first step. Group size, mean age, and mean SES level were the group characteristics that were entered in the second step.

Altogether, although this equation explained relatively little of the variance of caregivers' beliefs, it was quite useful in explaining their behavior (with R^2 ranging from 24% to 47%).

Group Composition. Considering the relative uniformity of group size, it is not surprising that it explained very little of the variance in caregivers' behaviors or beliefs. Caregivers who cared for children of higher SES families also provided more frequent educational activities ($\beta = .39, p < .03$). Caregivers who cared for older children engaged more frequently in group interaction, offered more frequent educational activities and provided a better quality physical environment ($\beta = .46, p < .01; .48, p < .004;$ and $.35, p < .04$). Because it was anticipated that the effect of the group's age mix on the caregiver's functioning may be curvilinear and may be related to the age of the children involved, a 2×3 ANOVA was used with child's age and level of age heterogeneity as main effects and caregiver's behavior as dependent variables.

The findings show that caregivers working either with very homogeneous or very heterogeneous groups were less likely to interact with the five children as a group. Caregivers were found to be more restrictive when the groups were either very homogeneous, and had very young children in them, or when the groups were very heterogeneous and had older toddlers in them. Homogeneous groups, with mostly babies in them, were offered the least frequent educational activities and homogeneous groups, with mostly older toddlers, were offered most. Age mix is also related to the quality of the physical environment in the FDC home. The best quality is offered in the homes with the most heterogeneous groups and the worst in the most homogeneous groups, and this is independent of the effect of the groups mean age reported previously. The overall pattern of results suggest that when young children are in age-homogeneous groups the caregivers tend to excersize more control, engage in little group interaction, and offer a poorer physical environment with fewer educational activities.

The beliefs and behavior of caregivers with and without their own children in their group were compared by means of a t-test. The former group responded more like mothers: They expected later development of social competence (29.11 vs. 25.07 months; $T = 2.53; p < .04$) than the latter group. They also attributed a higher degree of influence to mothers in the domain of emotional maturity (2.48 vs. 2.25;

T = 2.20; p < .04) than caregivers who did not care for their own children in the group. No differences between these two groups were found in the caregivers' behavior. One could expect from the research literature on the effects of experience, the specific experiences relating to working with a group of given characteristics (e.g., size, mean age) did not modify the caregivers' beliefs. Contrary to our expectations, the experiences related to working with children of different SES background were unrelated to caregivers' perceptions of mothers (Kontos & Wells, 1986) The nature of the group in their care did have an effect, however, on the caregivers' behavior: More educational activities (usually in the context of the whole group, rather than individually) were provided when the group consisted of older children or children from higher SES families. The effect of the children's age and age mix was not unlike the one reported by Stallings and Porter (1980). This may have been in response to the children's behavior or in response to what the caregiver believed their needs might be, or was expected of her with these children. The uniformity of adherence to the regulation of group size resulted in no statistically significant effects of this group characteristic.

An interesting subgroup of caregivers are those eight women who cared for one of their own children as a member of the group. The presence of their child did not affect any of the observed behaviors but it did have an effect on some of their beliefs. These effects seem to be linked to some of the better known conflicts of these women in trying to fulfill two different roles at the same time. Unlike the other mothers, or caregivers, they attributed greater influence to mothers, presumably as a result of a pragmatic process reflecting the need to boost their self-image as good mothers to their children. Their expectation of later achievement of social skills (such as sharing toys) presumably reflects their need to explain their children's difficulties in sharing their toys or mother's attention with the other children in the group. Obviously, one should be very cautious in interpreting findings based on such a small group (N = 8).

Professional Support: Autonomy and Supervision. The degree of the caregivers' autonomy in making decisions about equipment, space arrangement, and so forth, and the mean age of children in the group were the best predictors of the quality of care they offered. Caregivers who were more autonomous in their choice of equipment tended to interact more positively with the children (β =.48; p < .01), provided better physical environment (β = .32; p < .06) and were less likely to interact with the children as a group (β = -.32; p < .05). They also tended to expect early achievement of independence (β = -.28; p < .09) and were more likely to believe in the effect of direct instruction on development (β = .37; p < .05). The professional support provided to the caregivers, in the form of individual and/or group supervision, contributed significantly to the caregivers' positive interaction with the children (β = .42; p < .01). It was related to some extent to later expectations of independence (β = .30; p < .07), but did not explain much of the variance of any other behavior or belief.

The more autonomous caregivers did not attribute greater influence to themselves than the less autonomous caregivers. However, their belief in the effect of direct instruction on development, their frequent positive spontaneous and more individualized interaction with the children, as well as the better quality physical environment and educational program, suggest a greater acceptance of professional responsibility and reflect values more typical of a Western professional educator who has had more extensive training. Our results lend some support to the effectiveness of an empowerment model of professional support, as compared with that of a short training program (Cochran, 1985; Henry, 1992). The degree of autonomy was unrelated to any background characteristics of the caregiver, thus it seems rather evident that the provision of autonomy is an administrative decision of some of the FDC operators. This argument has been supported by findings in the study of policy issues presented in chapter 1.

It was found that professional support in the form of individual and group supervision is related to an increased frequency of positive interaction between caregivers and children, yet it is unrelated to any other aspects of the quality of care provided by the caregivers (M. Rosenthal, 1990). This finding suggests that these meetings were indeed used as a support system rather than as an in-service training framework to teach caregivers either educational skills or how to organize the environment.

CULTURAL TRANSMISSION AND CONSTRUCTION FROM EXPERIENCE

In our earlier chapter on parents' beliefs we followed a distinction offered by Goodnow (1988) and Goodnow and Collins (1990), who suggested two processes, or sources, through which parents' beliefs are formed: cultural transmission and the personal construction of beliefs that transforms personal experience into knowledge (Sigel, 1985).

Although education, training, and other forms of professional support are expected to be vehicles for cultural transmission of childrearing values and beliefs, accumulated life, parental, and child-care experiences are expected to provide the experiential basis for the caregiver's personal construction of such beliefs.

As a by-product of our analysis, it is possible to examine the relative contribution of these processes of cultural transmission and construction from personal experience to the formation of the child rearing beliefs of caregivers in FDC.

With the exception of the effects of the caregivers' experience working with children on their expectation of early achievement of independence, none of the measures used in this study that reflect the process of construction from personal experience (i.e., age and parental experience or the specific experiences of a caregiver with her specific group of children) were related to any of the childrearing beliefs under investigation. This finding may support a contention that personal experience is less likely to have an impact on childrearing beliefs than cultural transmission (Goodnow & Collins, 1990; Miller, 1988; Winetsky, 1978). One could argue, however, that the measures used in this study, as in other studies, do not tap the most meaningful personal experiences that may have an effect on the construction of childrearing beliefs.

The assumption that some childrearing beliefs are culturally transmitted was explored by examining the relationship of these beliefs to the ethnic origin of caregivers, their level of education, training, and other forms of professional support.

There is a basic Western assumption that what one does has an influence over events in general and over child development in particular. This assumption is reflected in the beliefs of the better educated caregivers. They attribute a high degree of influence to socialization agents, including themselves, and do not regard maturation as a main process underlying development.

Their training acts as a vehicle for the transmission of yet another Western educational norm, that of lowering pressure for achievement in the area of social development. In addition, the fact that the level of these caregivers' education is rather low, their training fairly short, and their in-service supervision not very effective in influencing their beliefs, suggests that much of their childrearing beliefs may have been acquired through informal exposure to the cultural norms that define the role of a professional caregiver, rather than through accumulated knowledge.

DIMENSIONS DEFINING QUALITY OF CARE

The definition of *quality of care* employed in this study refers to process dimensions only. Structural aspects are seen as conditions that may facilitate or hinder the expression of caregivers' behaviors that relate to these processes. Furthermore, our work argues against a monistic view of quality of care for children, and suggests that different dimensions that define quality of care might be relatively independent of each other. Although there is a fairly high and positive correlation between the variables that describe the dimension of planned educational program, the relation of this dimension to the more spontaneous aspects of the caregivers' interactions with the children is rather ambiguous. Furthermore, the two dimensions are related differently to the caregivers' belief system. Attributing to herself influence over the children's development is related both to positive spontaneous interactions and to educational activities. The latter are highly correlated with early developmental expectation, whereas the former are not related to any beliefs concerning child development. In addition, each dimension is related to somewhat different factors in the caregivers' background and work environment. Thus, as can be seen in Table 4.4, although both dimensions of the quality of care are related to the support offered by the sponsoring organization (supervision and autonomy), spontaneous interaction by caregivers is related mostly to the her personal (education) and professional background (training) and planned educational activities and environment aspects of her care are mostly related to the characteristics of the group in her care.

It should be borne in mind, nonetheless, that cultural differences may lead to some modifications in the dimensions defining quality of care, such as "group interaction." Psychologists and early childhood education specialists in many Western societies tend to view a prevalence of one-to-one interaction with infants and toddlers as an indicator of a better quality of care than interacting with such young children mostly as a group. Research has shown that cultural values in societies such as Japan or China may lead educators to a different perspective on the issue of individual versus group interaction (Lamb et al., 1992; Tobin, Vu, & Davidson, 1989). Israeli caregivers of infants and toddlers may be caught between different cultural values as to how an educator is supposed to interact with children. We have seen that the autonomous, better educated caregivers as well as those who attributed to themselves considerable influence tended to interact with the children more individually, although those who had had a little more preservice training, or those who worked with older children tended to interact with them more as a group. The former group seemed to hold to Western norms of child care, although the latter seemed to see themselves more like the typical Israeli school teacher, associating more serious educational interventions with group activities. It seems, therefore, that any investigation of the effects of different quality of care on children's behavior and development should address the issue of a multidimensional definition of quality care.

5

Growing Up in Two Socializing Worlds

Bronfenbrenner (1979b) pointed out that most data in studies of environmental influence on development consist of information about mostly the characteristics of the children rather than about the settings in which they grow. The data focus on differences among children growing up in different contexts rather than on the dimensions along which these contexts differ from each other. Thus, for example, the infant day-care debate focuses on attachment as a developmental outcome of children growing up in different settings instead of focusing on different dimensions or characteristics of the settings in which a child develops different quality attachments (e.g., quality of care, stability of care arrangements). Bronfenbrenner pointed to the absence of a theoretical framework appropriate for analyzing childrearing environments and the need to define transcontextual parameters for such an analysis.

Coming from an anthropological perspective on human development, Super and Harkness (1986) proposed a model made up of a set of concepts that define a number of dimensions for a transcontextual analysis. Their "developmental niche" seems to be useful not only in research on culture and child development but also in other attempts to define and describe different child development contexts or settings.

Modern childhood, as experienced by children in Western societies in the 1990s, is strikingly different from that of their parents (Dencik, 1989). Researchers can, therefore, benefit from an anthropological perspective while investigating child development in their own culture. One of the most striking features of childhood in the 1990s is that a majority of very young children are reared in at least two socializing worlds: home and child care. Dencik (1989), like Bronfenbrenner a decade earlier, pointed out how little is known, over and beyond a very limited range of developmental outcome measures, about the life and daily experiences of children moving back and forth between these two worlds. The Scandinavian BASUN project has been collecting very extensive data on the life of children in "postmodern Nordic society" at home and in their child care setting in an attempt to understand how these two worlds affect children (Dencik, Langsted, & Sommer, 1989).

One of the three major subsystems or components in Super and Harkness' (1986) "developmental niche" is what they call "the psychology of the caretaker," which refers to the expectations, values, and general belief systems of socializing agents. The developmental niche of children moving between home and child care includes the expectations and values of at least two important caretakers. The beliefs of these two socialization agents may be similar or different, resulting in continuity, discontinuity, or even conflict as the case may be.

Relatively little is known about the continuity or discontinuity between the developmental expectations, values, and other childrearing beliefs of the socializing agents at home and in child care. Even less is known about the effects of continuity or discontinuity between childrearing belief systems of the two settings on the behavior and development of children. The research reviewed in chapters 3 and 4 showed that cognitions such as childrearing beliefs appear to play an important role in shaping interactions between the socializing agent and the children and may have long-term consequences for a child's development (Kontos & Wells, 1986; Miller, 1988; M. Rosenthal, 1991a; Scott-Little & Holloway, 1991; Sigel, 1985). It is suggested, therefore, that the study of similarities and differences between the childrearing beliefs of socializing agents at home and child care is of crucial importance for a more comprehensive understanding of the impact of child care on children's development. The similarities, or alternatively the clear distinctions, between the belief systems of the socializing agents at home and in child care, are likely to determine the quality of the child's daily transitions between the two childrearing settings, as well as the effects of these settings on the child's behavior and development.

This chapter discusses the potential sources of difference between the beliefs of mothers and caregivers as socializing agents caring for children in different contexts. The beliefs of these agents are then compared. The possible effects of continuity and discontinuity on these beliefs are examined in chapter 8.

Research studies that compare mothers and out-of-home caregivers point out the differences in their childrearing context and role definition as important determinants of the behavior and beliefs of these socializing agents. The differences between these developmental contexts relate to the physical and social setting, activities and time frame for interaction, as well as to the type of involvement and the nature of the emotional relationship between the socializing agent and the child.

Thus, although the child-care environment is mostly designed to meet the needs of children, the home also has to meet the needs of the whole family once the children in child care return home at the end of the day. Childrearing contexts are generally short term, public, and group-oriented and are based on the principle of equal division of attention and on objective and uniform norms for every child (Hess, Dickson, Price, & Leong, 1979; Hess et al., 1981; Lightfoot, 1975).

In contrast, the interactions in the home tend to be intimate and individual; the mothers' involvement is around the clock and based on a long interpersonal history. It involves different interactive contexts and therefore carries more complex emotional meanings (Dix & Grusec, 1985; Hess et al., 1979, 1981).

Although the normal emotional relationship between mother and child is fairly intense and based on mutual attachment, the relationship with the caregiver who is paid for her interactions with the child is of a lesser emotional intensity. The relationship is usually somewhat detached, maintaining an impartial attitude to the children (Bronfenbrenner, 1979a; Katz, 1980; Newson & Newson, 1976). Hess et al. (1981) further suggested that teachers may deliberately reduce the level of intimacy in their relationship with children in order to deal more comfortably with the whole group and in order to protect themselves and the children from emotional commitment.

In addition, caregiving in a child-care setting is usually defined as a *professional* or *semiprofessional* role (Spodek, Saracho, & Peters, 1988) and as such further modifies the developmental context of this setting, influencing its physical, social, and relational components.

The recognition of these very basic contextual differences between home and child care has recently led to studies of the congruence of parents' and caregivers childrearing practices and their perception of continuity in their child care (Kontos, 1984). Although mothers and caregivers are aware of the differences in their childrearing behaviors, they consider themselves to be essentially in agreement regarding childrearing values (Long & Garduque, 1987; Nelson & Garduque, 1991). This recognition of contextual differences led to some serious questions concerning the feasibility, or possibly even the desirability, of the attempt to maintain continuity between home and child care (Long, Peters, & Garduque, 1985; Powell, 1980).

Studies comparing the childrearing beliefs and practices of mothers and caregivers in child care suggest that these vary in accordance with the contextual differences between home and child care (Bronfenbrenner, 1979a; Hess et al., 1981; Holloway et al., 1988; Rubenstein & Howes, 1979; Winetsky, 1978). Such differences in contexts of interaction seem to be related to beliefs concerning the nature of development and the nature of processes that effect this development as well as to the agent's role perception. In other words, mothers and caregivers in child care are expected to embrace somewhat different "theories" of how children develop, how one can influence their development, and who is influencing what in this development.

The data available up to now mostly deal with the comparison of mothers and professionally trained educators working in educational institutions such as nursery school, day-care centers, or kibbutz (Feldman & Yirmiya, 1986; Hess et al., 1981; Holloway et al., 1988; Winetsky, 1978). Although less formal settings such as FDC are a much more common form of child care, very little is known about the similarities and differences in the childrearing beliefs of mothers and caregivers in these settings.

Family day care has been regarded by some investigators as a homelike environment, mostly due to the physical and noninstitutional nature of its environment and the lack of training of the caregivers (Cochran, 1977; Howes, 1983). In other words, caregivers in FDC were observed as behaving more like mothers than like professional preschool teachers. Their role definition is usually that of a "mother substitute," meaning that they are expected to be like mothers but they are not as important as mothers.

Nevertheless, in spite of these similarities, the childrearing context of FDC is rather different from the home context both in terms of the social setting, the activities, the time frame of interpersonal interaction and the nature of the emotional relationship between the socializing agent and the child. Furthermore, sponsored FDC homes tend to belong to a wider organization that usually provides the caregivers with some training or professional supervision, as well as setting limits, standards, and requirements for equipment and play materials. It seems that although FDC caregivers appear to resemble teachers in terms of the nature of their relationship and involvement with the children, they really fall somewhere between mothers and day-care center-based teachers regarding two major dimensions: the degree of institutional organization of the context in which interaction with the child takes place and the extent of formal socialization to the role of a socializing agent.

The earlier discussion of the belief systems of mothers and caregivers (chapters 3 and 4) focused on two aspects of their childrearing beliefs: (a) beliefs about how children develop, such as timing and process of development; and (b) beliefs about the role of different socializing agents in influencing this development. These two aspects have been shown by previous research to be sensitive to the contextual differences between home and child care (Feldman & Yirmiya, 1986; Hess et al., 1981; Holloway et al., 1988; Rubenstein & Howes, 1979; Winetsky, 1978), thus this study analyses the differences in the beliefs held by mothers and FDC caregivers. It is expected that in spite of the similarities between home and FDC, and the very limited amount of training caregivers in these settings usually receive, the beliefs of caregivers in these settings differ from those of the mothers of the same children.

A COMPARISON OF THE BELIEF SYSTEMS OF MOTHERS AND CAREGIVERS

Whose Child is it Anyway?

One important aspect of the beliefs about the roles of socializing agents is the perception of the relative influence different agents have over the child's development. Mothers and teachers differ in the relative influence over child development they attribute to themselves and to other socialization agents. Cognizant of their long-term relationship with their child, as well as their emotional involvement, mothers tend to attribute more influence to themselves than to caregivers and teachers (Feldman & Yirmiya, 1986). They attribute influence to caregivers and teachers mostly in domains that are of special relevance to the school or child-care

70

Chapter 5

context, such as acquiring cognitive skills or social competence in peer interaction (Bronfenbrenner, 1970; Knight & Goodnow, 1988). Caregivers in Israeli kibbutzim and day-care centers, on the other hand, tend to attribute more influence to themselves than do the mothers, presumably because of a need to boost the importance of their role (Feldman & Yirmiya, 1986).

In view of this, we expected that both mothers and caregivers would attribute greater influence to themselves than to the other agent. We further expected that both agents would perceive mothers' influence as similar in both domains of development, and that both mothers and caregivers would attribute to caregivers greater influence in the domain of social development than in the domain of emotional maturity.

In order to explore the differences in the attribution of influence of mothers and caregivers to themselves and to each other, in the domains of social development and emotional maturity, we carried out a two-way ANOVA with a repeated measures design (Fig. 5.1). The two groups of attributing agents (mothers and caregivers) constituted one factor and the four repeated measures (of influence attributed to each agent in the two domains of development) constituted a within-subject factor.

Significant main effects were found for the factor of the attributing agent [F $(1,102) = 4.62, p < .03$] and for the factor of the repeated measures [$F (3,306) = 6.86, p < .001$]. In addition, we found a significant interaction was found between the attributing agent and the factor of the repeated measures [$F (3,306) = 4.32, p < .005$). In other words, differences were found between mothers and caregivers

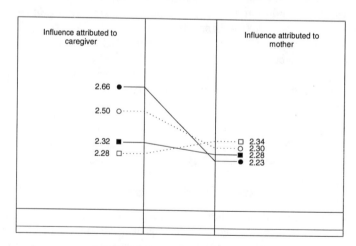

FIG. 5.1. Attribution of influence by mother and caregiver to the two agents in two developmental domains.

in their attribution of influence in the two domains of development to themselves and to the other agent. In order to control for the possible influence of the statistically significant differences in the demographic characteristics of caregivers and mothers, these variables (agent's age, country of origin, and level of education) were introduced as covariates into the same design. All the effects reported here remained significant.

In order to discover the specific pattern of these significant relationships, we also carried out a series of t tests on the attribution scores of mothers and caregivers (see Tables 3.2 and 4.1, respectively).

The analyses show (Fig. 5.1) that mothers generally attributed the same amount of influence to themselves and to caregivers. They do tend, however, to attribute to caregivers more influence in the domain of social development than in the domain of emotional maturity ($t = 1.87$; $p = .07$).

No difference was found between caregivers and mothers in the influence they attributed to the mothers in either domain and no interaction effect was found between domain and attributing agent. However, caregivers attribute more influence to themselves than to the mothers in both domains ($t = 3.37$; $p < .001$). The caregivers attribute to themselves even greater influence in the domain of social development than in the domain of emotional maturity ($t = 3.07$; $p < .004$).

The data support our expectations that the agents' attributions will reflect their awareness of the differences in their respective contexts of interaction with the children. Thus, both mothers and caregivers perceive the mothers' influence as similar in the two domains of development while both attributed to caregivers greater influence in the domain of social development than in the domain of emotional maturity. Although, as expected, the caregivers did indeed attribute greater influence to themselves than to mothers, the mothers in this study, unlike mothers of children in kibbutzim and day-care centers (Feldman & Yirmiya, 1986), did not perceive themselves as more influential than caregivers. It could be that mothers of very young children in FDC respond to the homelike environment of this particular setting and perceive the caregivers' role more like their own, hence the similar degree of influence.

Beliefs About Child Development

Do mothers and FDC caregivers have similar theories on how children develop, when they achieve certain developmental goals, and what is the role of the environment in shaping the child's development? Do they believe in the effectiveness of similar methods of getting children to comply with adult demands?

Previous research has only addressed a few of these questions. Some studies found that differences in childrearing contexts are related to differences in pressure for mastery of developmental skills and compliance with adults' demands. Mothers were found to press for mastery at an earlier age than teachers, to be more direct and demanding, to prefer more structured programs, and to use more authoritarian disciplinary methods than caregivers. These differences are usually explained by differences between the two childrearing contexts related to the nature of involvement and emotional relationships. The training of caregivers in these studies is assumed to partially contribute to the fact that they pressed less for achievement (Hess et al., 1981; Holloway et al., 1988; Rubenstein & Howes, 1979; Winetsky, 1978).

Because caregivers in this study were operating in a more homelike context and they had much less socialization into their professional role than other caregivers, we expected them to respond somewhat more like mothers than like the teachers or highly trained caregivers in day care centers in the earlier studies.

A MANOVA was used to compare caregivers' and mothers' beliefs in the pressure required as expressed in their beliefs about development.

The three measures of developmental expectation (cognitive, social, and independence) and the two average measures of (a) belief in the degree of agent's involvement in facilitating the developmental process and (b) preferred degree of power assertion in controlling misbehavior, were entered in this analysis as the dependent variables. The role of the socializing agent (caregiver or mother) was the independent variable.

The means and standard deviations of the dependent variables were presented in Tables 3.2 and 4.1. The MANOVA, using Wilks statistics, reveals an overall significant effect of the role of the socializing agent [$F(5,99) = 5.53, p < .001$). In order to control for the possible influence of the differences in the demographic characteristics of caregivers and mothers, we did a MANCOVA analysis on the same dependent variables with the agent's age, country of origin, and level of education as the covariates. The effect of the role of the socializing agent remained significant, at the $p < .001$ level.

In order to explore the specific beliefs that contribute to this difference between caregivers and mothers, a series of t tests were carried out comparing their specific beliefs.

Developmental Expectations

A comparison of Tables 3.2 and 4.1, shows no difference was found between the mothers and caregivers in their expectations for achievement in the areas of independence and cognitive development. Caregivers, however, expected children to acquire social skills such as waiting their turn, communicating clearly or helping a friend, at an earlier age than mothers ($t = 2.16$; $p < .05$). Considering the correlations reported in chapter 4 between the caregivers' expectations of early development and the influence they attribute to themselves over the children's development, and considering the fact that caregivers attribute to themselves greater influence in the domain of social development, it is not surprising that they are found to have early expectations in this area of development. It seems that the caregivers have to believe that a child is capable of achieving certain social skills if they are to influence this development.

Conditions That Influence Development

The data in Tables 3.3 and 4.2 suggest that both mothers and caregivers tended to believe that developmental goals were achieved mainly through direct instruction by an adult who demonstrates, explains, and encourages rather than through other conditions in which there is less involvement of a socializing agent, such as spontaneous maturation or sheer exposure to experiences. No significant differences were found between the two agents in these beliefs.

It seems from our data that this belief is related more to the educational background of the agents and their perception of their locus of control, than to the specific context in which they interact with the children.

Preferred Method of Discipline

Although most mothers and caregivers seem to prefer moderate levels of power assertion, the two groups differed in their attitude to the extremities of this dimension (Tables 3.3 and 4.2). Although, as might be expected, more mothers than caregivers gave preference to authoritarian methods ($t = 3.59$; $p < .001$), more caregivers than mothers preferred permissive (rather than authoritative) methods ($t = 2.55$; $p < .01$).

The latter suggests that caregivers had enough socialization to their role to know that they are not supposed to prefer power-assertive methods, but had not had sufficient training to know about the greater effectiveness of authoritative techniques.

Our earlier analyses of the belief systems of mothers and caregivers (chapters 3 and 4) highlighted factors of personal background, such as education level, and their influence on the beliefs of these socializing agents. We found that the beliefs of both socializing agents were fairly consistent and seemed to be organized in accordance with the agents' locus of control. It is suggested that socialization agents with an internal locus of control were those who believed that environment influences development and were more likely to see themselves as influential. They expected early development and believed in the effectiveness of less coercive disciplinary techniques (Loeb, 1975).

The present analysis leads one to assume that beyond this consistency common to both groups of socializing agents, the beliefs of mothers and caregivers are affected by differences in the contexts in which they interact with children, and that some of their beliefs should be understood in terms of the unique homelike nature of the FDC context.

Some of the childrearing beliefs of caregivers in this study resemble those of mothers and some resemble those reported for professionally trained teachers working with preschoolers in more formal institutional settings (Hess et al., 1981). This finding suggests that these caregivers with very little training, working in their own homes, do indeed occupy some middle point between mothers at home and fully trained professional teachers in more formal child-care settings.

Like professional teachers and unlike mothers, they do not believe in power-assertive control methods. Unlike these teachers, however, and more like the mothers in this study they (a) expect early developmental competence in general, particularly in the social domain; and (b) believe in the importance of direct instruction in influencing development.

It should be noted, however, that because the education level of the caregivers in this study is lower than that of mothers, their beliefs as a group should have resembled more those of the less educated mothers in this sample. This, however, was not the case.

Our analysis on the effects of education level on the belief system of mothers (chapter 3) showed that, quite unlike these caregivers with low level of education, the less educated mothers expected later (rather than earlier) achievement of competence both in the cognitive and the social domain. They were more likely to believe that development is a function of maturation (rather than of direct instruction), and were more likely to prefer authoritarian (rather than permissive) control methods.

These differences between the caregivers with low education level and the mothers with a similar personal background support Winetsky's (1978) argument that socialization into a professional role may modify the effects of personal background on caregivers' childrearing beliefs. Furthermore, the data presented in chapters 3 and 4 show that although variations in the education level of mothers are associated with their beliefs about development, these variations in the caregivers' group are related to their role perception, or perception of influence (Rosenthal & Zilkha, 1987).

How does this socialization into the professional role take place? We have seen in chapter 4 that the only effect their short training had on these caregivers, as in the case of the better trained teachers in other studies, was to lower their expectations in the area of social development.

The findings of this study suggest that both the unique characteristics of the context in which they interact with the children and the very definition of their caregiving role as "professional" may be responsible for the differences in the childrearing beliefs of mothers and caregivers (Hess et al., 1981). Thus, for example, the fact that caregivers expect earlier achievement than mothers in the social domain and that both attribute to the caregiver, rather than to the mother, a greater influence in this domain, may be explained by the caregivers' context of interaction with a group of infants and toddlers. This context defines their responsibility as well as sensitizes them to the early social development of the children. The group care context may also have increased the caregivers' motivation to assume such early development so as to allow for smooth functioning of the group's daily life (Hess et al., 1981). The training of these caregivers seems in fact to have counteracted these contextual effects.

The requirements, however, of minimal training that awards the caregivers with a certificate, as well as the regular professional in-service supervision, define their role as *professional caregivers* rather than *mother substitutes*. This definition may prevent conflicts associated with ambiguities in the relationship between mothers and caregivers but, possibly due to the briefness of training, seems to lead to other conflicts. The caregivers receive the message that they are expected to behave differently from mothers and hold beliefs that are different from those acquired through their personal and cultural background, but at the same time they are not very clear as to what their beliefs and behavior should be. The struggle to boost this professional image by attributing greater importance to their own role rather than to the role of the mother is one indication of the weakness of this image (Spodek et al., 1988).

The results of this study highlight the importance of a more specific definition of the concept of a childrearing context beyond the dichotomous distinction between home and child care. FDC provides a unique context that falls somewhere between home and a formal child-care setting both in terms of the degree of institutional organization of the context in which interaction with the child takes place and the extent of formal socialization of the main caregiver to the role of a socializing agent. It seems, therefore, that a comparison of beliefs of different socialization agents must take into account the specific characteristics of the context of their interaction with children, as well as the exact role definition of the socializing agent, rather than be generalized according to preconceived contrasts of home versus child care.

Future studies should address the question of how infants and toddlers are affected by the daily shift between these two childrearing settings with their somewhat different, yet similar, expectations and socialization beliefs. The effects of similarities and differences in the beliefs of mothers and caregivers (continuity) on the behavior of children in FDC are examined in the analyses of the interface between home and child care in chapter 8.

6

The Behavior of Infants and Toddlers in FDC

Research on the effects of child care on children has dealt mostly with the developmental outcomes of day-care attendance. As the various reviews of this work demonstrate (Belsky, 1984; Phillips & Howes, 1987), this research examines the relation of different aspects of child-care attendance, such as age of entry, length of stay, and type or quality of care to developmental outcomes such as general intellectual development, academic functioning, social competence, or the quality of relationship with the mother (e.g., Golden et al., 1978; Ramey & Campbell, 1977; Rogozin, 1980; Roupp et al., 1979; Vandell et al., 1988).

A limited number of studies have examined the effects of child care on the children's behavior or activities (such as aggressiveness, interaction with adults, or solitary and unoccupied behavior) while in the child-care setting. Previous research has highlighted the relationship of these activities to subsequent important developmental outcomes (Rohe & Patterson, 1974; Vandell & Powers, 1983).

An extensive research project completed recently in the Scandinavian countries has drawn attention to the importance of studying children's experiences in child care from the point of view of its intrinsic value for the child itself, regardless of whether or not these experiences have a decisive influence on later functioning. Its emphasis is on examination of the child's activity and well-being as a child, rather than study of the child as a potential adult or as a "calculated investment" (Dencik, 1989).

The analysis of the full range of children's experiences in child care suggests, however, that the activities and experiences that seem to have intrinsic value for the child as a child are also likely to be developmentally valuable. This study focuses, therefore, on the experiences generated by the child's own behavior so as to provide a comprehensive picture of what it is that infants and toddlers do in this child-care setting. The child's interactions with the caregiver in FDC were discussed earlier (chapter 4) and are not included in this discussion primarily because many of these interactions are "adult-driven" and are less under the child's control than the interactions with objects and peers.

76

Our assumption is that the children's active engagement, exploration, and investigation of the environment contribute to their current feelings of pleasure resulting from self-perception of competence, as well as to their developing disposition and ability to negotiate the environment (Carew, 1980; Cassidy, 1986; Ruff, Lawson, Parrinello, & Weissberg, 1990; White, 1959)

In contrast to the children's active engagement, the time the children spend in emotional distress, or in aimless, nonpurposive, or unfocused activity does not contribute to developing competence, nor is it associated with feelings of well-being or other current positive experiences (Vandell et al., 1988).

An examination of the type and degree of the child's involvement with the social and nonsocial environment, the emotional tone, and the level of competence demonstrated in this involvement yields a fairly comprehensive range of children's performance in child care.

Research suggests that different aspects of children's development may be differentially sensitive to different types of child care. Thus, it has been proposed that although FDC children have been found to perform more poorly on intellectual tasks than children in day-care centers, they obtained better scores on social interaction (Golden et al., 1978). Other studies show that family and child-care settings may have differential influences on these two aspects of development (Phillips, McCartney, & Scarr, 1987; Kontos, 1991; Kontos & Dunn, 1989).

On the basis of these findings and the "specificity hypothesis" that suggests that different aspects of the children's behavior and development are likely to be related to different environmental experiences (Wachs & Chan, 1986; Wachs & Gruen, 1982), the analysis here examines separately two categories of interaction with the environment; the first, the children's interaction with objects, the physical, or nonsocial environment, and the second the children's social interactions with peers.

Active engagement with the physical environment such as interactions or play with objects is likely to facilitate the acquisition of fine and gross motor skills, contribute to the acquisition of language and of concepts of space and time relationships, and contribute to knowledge about the physical characteristics of objects. Research has indeed shown that these interactions have a strong effect on the children's intellectual development (e.g., Carew, 1980; Clarke-Stewart, 1973; Cochran, 1977; Elardo, Bradley, & Caldwell, 1977; Roupp & Travers, 1982). Different levels of competence are demonstrated in children's play with objects (Rubenstein & Howes, 1979).

Specific social interactions and social play with peers may facilitate the development of social skills that are important in later life (Garvey, 1977; Howes, 1987). Furthermore, in recent years there has been a growing interest in the effect of out-of-home rearing on the child's social development. The research relevant to this debate draws attention to the fact that although children reared in child care are likely to become more aggressive, they also demonstrate higher social competence (Belsky, 1986; Clarke-Stewart, 1989). These conflicting findings highlight the need for a better understanding of the relationship between social competence and peer conflicts. There is also a need to document and analyze the type and quality of children's daily social experiences in child-care settings, which in addition to home experiences may be the precursors of their social adjustment in school.

We distinguish between the type and/or quality of interaction and the level of competence in each category of interaction in our analysis of the child's active engagement with the environment. The study further explores the degree of children's involvement with the environment by distinguishing between active and minimal engagement with the environment. Minimal engagement is observed when a child wanders aimlessly or engages in unfocused activity or displays emotional distress.

The examination of the type of engagement with the physical environment compares the child's fine motor and gross motor interactions with objects. It further assesses the level of competence the child demonstrates in these interactions (Rubenstein & Howes, 1979).

Our investigation of children's involvement with peers also focuses on the quality of peer interaction. The quality of social exchanges documented in this study refers to positive peer interaction, such as smiling and sharing, or agonistic interaction, such as hitting and biting (Vandell & Powers, 1983). The type of interaction may refer to the social context of the child's play such as solitary or group play, or to unique characteristics of toddler peer interaction such as a form of play described as *joint peer play*. Joint peer play is generated by the children themselves. It is characterized by "action identity" (Brenner & Mueller, 1982) in which whole sequences of behavior are copied by a group of children in some form of rhythmic repetition or in the performance of similar actions in turn. In this way, the children have, on their own, organized a mutual frame of reference, in which the performance of a similar action glues the interaction together. Several researchers of social play among toddlers called attention to shared themes or meanings that organize their interactions (Brenner & Mueller, 1982; Garvey, 1977). Brenner and Mueller demonstrated that toddlers can successfully generate mutually understood themes by means of nonverbal communication. Others highlighted the ways in which toddlers themselves construct play activities through the use of their growing sense of shared understanding (Budwig et al., 1986).

These different social interactions can demonstrate varying degrees of "social competence" reflected in the children's level of peer play (Howes, 1980) and their verbal communicative skills.

It should be noted that, based on previous research, it is not clear what relationship should be expected between the frequency of the children's interaction with peers and their social competence. Studies on the relationship between "social experience" and "social competence" would suggest a positive relationship, yet others have suggested that frequent engagement in peer interaction among young children (presumably at the expense of interaction with adults) lead to lower social competence (Clarke-Stewart, 1987b).

Our study focuses, therefore, on the children's degree, quality, and type of engagement with the environment as developmentally valuable activities, which both theory and research have suggested have a potential contribution to children's future development and are indicators of the children's current feelings of well-being.

Children's engagement with their environment is known to be affected by personal characteristics such as age, gender, or temperament, by their life experiences with siblings and in child care. They are further influenced by family characteristics such as parents' education or childrearing values, as well as by the quality and nature of their child-care environment.

Following the presentation of the results of the observations of the children in our sample of FDC homes, this chapter examines the relationship of the children's performance and their personal and family background. An analysis of the impact of the child-care setting on these behaviors is presented in chapter 7 and is followed by an analysis of the interface of all these factors in chapter 8.

NATURE OF BEHAVIORS OF FDC CHILDREN

As Table 6.1 shows the children spent significantly more time in fine motor interaction with objects than in gross motor activity. Most children played with toys at the manipulative level (Level 3 on the Rubenstein & Howes, 1979, scale), with a relatively narrow distribution around this mean.

TABLE 6.1
Behaviors of Children in FDC ($N = 82$)

	Observed		
	Mean	SD	Range
Active engagement			
Interaction with objects/space			
Type of interaction:			
Fine motor	19.13	11.26	0–46
Gross motor	6.61	6.65	0–24
Competence:			
Mean level of play[a]	3.00	.75	1.5–5
Interaction with peers			
Type/context of interaction:			
Positive interaction	29.60	11.41	1–61
Agonistic interaction	2.02	2.31	0–13
Joint play[a]	2.59	1.96	0–6
Solitary context	14.34	9.69	0–47
Group context	30.60	14.84	2–62
Social competence:			
Level play 1	44.57	32.32	9–90
Levels play 2–5	6.89	7.47	0–34
Verbal communication	15.43	10.67	0–52
Minimal engagement			
Aimless behavior	32.61	12.34	11–67
Motional distress	1.90	2.82	0–13

[a]The possible range for all scores is 0–90 with the exception of "mean level of play with objects" (range = 1–5) and Joint Play (range = 0–6).

Children spent significantly more time in social interaction than in fine motor interaction with the physical environment. Contrary to some frequent descriptions of the nature of toddlers' peer interaction (Bronson, 1975), children in this study spent much more time in positive than in agonistic interaction. They smiled, shared, and imitated for nearly 33% of the observation time (a mean observation period score of 29.6 observation units out of 90 units), and were seen to be in conflict, struggle, or other aggressive exchanges only 2.2% of the time. Furthermore, as children were observed in emotional distress only 2.1% of the time, one may conclude that the overall emotional tone of the daily experiences of these children was not negative. One should note that although the children in this sample entered child care at a very young age and attended it on a full-time basis, the incidence of observed aggressive behavior is rather low. It could be that elevated levels of aggression among children attending full day care, appear only a few years later (Haskins, 1985). Our finding, however, is in agreement with Field, Masi, Goldstein, Perry, and Parl (1988) who reported that although caregivers rated full-time children higher on aggression, the observational ratings of children's behavior found no difference in the rates of aggression between children attending child care on a full-time rather than a part-time basis.

Children spent twice as much time in a group rather than a solitary context. Although some spent as much as 52.2% of the observation time by themselves, most of them spent relatively little time alone. Children were observed, on average, during half of the observation periods to be engaged in episodes of joint peer play.

There were greater individual differences between children's competence in social interaction than in their competence interacting with objects: As could be expected of infants and toddlers, most children played most of the time next to each other with similar or different toys, without appearing to be aware of each other (Level 1 on the Howes, 1980, scale). Some children, however, played with their peers on a higher level of competence (Levels 2–5 on the same scale) as often as 37.8% of the time. Children also varied greatly in their verbal communicative ability. Some did not use language even once, others did so 57.8% of the time.

Although this overall description of the activity and experiences of the "average child" in FDC seems to suggest a rather positive picture, the fact that children spent on average 36.2% of the time in aimless, unoccupied behavior and some were observed doing it as much as 75% of the time, is of some concern. The factors that are likely to explain these individual differences are examined later.

The Interrelation Between Different Behaviors of Children

The data presented in Table 6.2 suggest that the children's level of competence explains much of their performance. Children who played competently with objects and peers, used language frequently, and engaged more frequently in fine motor interaction with objects as well as in positive peer interactions and joint play. These children were less likely to be seen in a solitary context or engaged in aimless activity.

TABLE 6.2
Relations Between Children's Behaviors ($N = 82$)[a]

	2	3	4	5	6	7	8	9	10	11	12	13
Active engagement												
Inter' w objects												
1. Fine Motor	-.22*	.29**			-.18*			.17			-.44***	.17
2. Gross Motor	x									-.28**	-.35***	
3. Mean Level		x	.29**			-.45***	.40***	-.29**	.19*	.20*	-.25**	-.16
Inter' w peers												
4. Positive Inter'			x	-.17	.40***	-.51***	.57***	.34***	.41***	.60***	-.36***	
5. Agonistic Inter'				x		.37***	-.31**	.25**	.18*	.31**	.17	
6. Joint Play					x	-.19*	.27**				.28**	
7. Solitary context						x	-.86***	.45***	-.41***	-.41***	-.16	
8. Group context							x	-.38***	.43***	.51***	.22*	.17
9. Level 1								x	-.41***	-.27**		-.19
10. Level 2-5									x	.61***	-.20	-.20
11. Verbal communication										x		.23*
Minimal engagement												
12. Aimless behavior											x	-.16
13. Emotional distress												x

[a]Only r > .16 are presented.

*p < .05. **p < .01. ***p < .00.

Children who spent much of the time in aimless activity not only were observed more often in a solitary context and spent less time in active engagement with the physical environment, but also functioned at a lower level of competence in their interaction with both peers and objects. They were, however, just as verbally competent as the other children. There was no relation between the frequency of interaction with objects and with peers. Contrary to what one might expect, children who spent more time in aimless wandering were not necessarily more emotionally distressed. Although children's distress was unrelated to the frequency of either their positive or agonistic interactions with peers, or most other behaviors, those children observed to be emotionally distressed interacted more frequently with peers on a higher level. It could be that children's tendency to be distressed reflects a certain emotional sensitivity that predisposes them to more competent peer interaction (Howes & Farver, 1987).

More positive things happened to children who spent more time in a group rather than solitary context: They were more likely to be seen in positive social interactions with peers, in joint play, and less in agonistic peer interaction.

It is interesting to note the behavior pattern of children who tend to engage frequently in joint play with a group of other children. One tends to see them more in a group context; they show frequent positive peer interaction and a high level of verbal competence. These children, however, may show different levels of competence in their play with peers, are less likely to engage in fine motor and more in aimless activity. The results suggest that this form of social play may not require high social competence, yet may be contributing to such competence and may be offering a simpler and an easy to join-in social activity to children whose interest is not captured by interaction with the physical environment.

It is interesting to note that positive and agonistic interactions were independent of each other (i.e., children who spent more time in positive interactions did not necessarily spend less time in agonistic interactions).

THE BACKGROUND CHARACTERISTICS
OF CHILDREN AND THEIR FAMILIES

This chapter concentrates on the relation of children's behavior to their intraindividual life experience and family characteristics.

Child Characteristics

Many studies have found that child characteristics such as age and gender are related to the frequency, type, and competence of engagement with the environment. Older infants and toddlers, for instance, have more frequent and more competent interactions with both objects and peers (Howes & Stewart, 1987). The children's gender at this age seems mostly related to their social interactions. Thus, 18- to 36- month-old boys were reported as playing in a more aggressive manner than girls of the same age (Fagot, 1980; Maccoby & Jacklin, 1974). Some studies reported differences in social competence and cognitive development of children in child care to be associated with the child's gender (Howes, 1988b). Others, however, found no difference in the experiences or behavior of boys and girls in child care (Howes & Hamilton, 1992).

In addition to the effects of these child characteristics, research has shown that the children's life history (such as the nature of their relationship with their mothers and their experience with siblings), and their child-care history are both related to their competence and behavior. Thus, the security of attachment to their parents is related to their competence (Cassidy, 1986; Lieberman, 1977; Pastor, 1981; Waters, Wippman, & Sroute, 1979) and the amount of social experience with other children, such as gained by children with more siblings and early entrance into child care, is related to their social interactions and competence, as well as school functioning (Howes, 1980; Mueller & Brenner, 1977; Sarafino, 1985; Schindler & Frank, 1987; Vandell & Corasaniti, 1990). However, several researchers contend that the effects of children's child-care history overrides birth order effects on measures of social development (Howes, 1988b; Phillips, McCartney, & Scarr, 1987).

The characteristics investigated in our study include the child's age, gender, age of entry into child care, birth order, and difficulties in separating from mother. The latter was rated by the mothers in response to the question "How is it for your child to separate from you in the morning?" as *extremely upset* (1), *a little bit upset but settles down quickly* (2), and *could not care less* (3).

Table 6.3 presents the characteristics of children in this study. Information concerning the family background and the nature of mothers' beliefs is presented in chapter 3. As Table 6.3 shows, most children were firstborn, about 2 years old, and entered FDC when they were about 1 year old. Most (64%) of the children had stayed in FDC for longer than 10 months at the time of the study. Separation difficulties were reported for only 22% of the children; 69% were somewhat sad at separation but settled down into the daily activities very quickly.

Family Background

Family background such as parental education and life conditions, or parental values and beliefs, can have both direct and indirect effects on children's experiences in a child-care setting. Several studies have reported direct effects of family background on social development and level of play with objects in young children (Clarke-Stewart & Gruber, 1984; Howes & Stewart, 1987; Lamb et al., 1988; McCartney et al., 1985; Phillips, McCartney, & Scarr, 1987; Smilansky, 1968). However, some recent work on the differential effects of home background and

TABLE 6.3
The Personal Characteristics of Children in FDC

	Mean	SD	Minimum	Maximum	N
Age (months)	23.63	4.53	14	39	82
Birth order	1.76	1.14	1	5	71
Age of entry to childcare (month)	13.04	6.12	3	30	70
Separation difficulties (1 = diff.)	1.91	.59	1	3	69

child care on the child's development suggests that family background variables are significant predictors primarily of cognitive and language development, rather than of social development (Kontos, 1991). Family SES, as well as parents' childrearing beliefs and attitudes to child care can also have indirect effects on the experiences of children in FDC through processes such as the parental child-care selection process. These are discussed in more detail in chapter 8. This chapter examines the relation of the children's behavior to their parents' education level; social and economic difficulties; and mother's age and employment as well as her childrearing beliefs and attitudes to child care.

The Interrelations Between Child Characteristics and Family Background

With the exception of the somewhat obvious correlation between age of child and age of entry into child care ($r = .47$; $p < .001$), child characteristics were not interrelated. Children of higher birth order were more likely to have older mothers ($r = .59$; $p < .01$), who worked fewer hours ($r = -.41$; $p < .01$) and their families were more likely to be burdened with social problems ($r = -.26$; $p < .05$).

These findings reflect a well-known demographic relation between family size and social difficulties in the family. The fewer hours of employment of these mothers reflects the placement policy concerning their children. This group of children is placed in child care because of the social problems in the family and not because their mothers need to go to work.

Mothers with lower education level reported more frequent separation difficulties ($r = .25$, $p < .05$). We have no explanation for this relation, unless mothers' level of education indicates some other family processes that have an effect on the child's ease of separation form the mother.

FACTORS RELATED TO CHILDREN'S BEHAVIOR

The Influence of Family Background

A series of regression analyses was employed to determine the relative contribution of different family characteristics to the children's behavior.

As our correlation analysis showed (Table 6.2), solitary and group contexts of interaction were almost mutually exclusive, thus only the solitary context appears in the following analyses. Similarly, as Level 1 and Levels 2–5 of competence in peer play are complementary, only the latter was used as an assessment of the child's social competence with peers. Following a preliminary analysis that showed that maternal employment was not related to any of the children's activities, it was not included in any future analysis.

The first analysis in the series examined the contribution of parents' education level, social and economic difficulties, and mother's age. Our analysis shows that mothers' age and the family's dependence on financial support contributed very little if at all to our understanding of these behaviors. Similarly, children of families with social problems did not behave much differently from other children. They tended, however, to use verbal communication less often ($\beta = .30$; $p < .06$) but to engage more frequently in fine motor interaction with objects ($\beta = -.29$; $p < .10$).

Parents' level of education was shown by this equation to be the best predictor of children's performance. Contrary to expectations, children of parents with higher levels of education tend to engage more in aimless behavior and less in gross motor play with the physical environment (βs $= .33$ and $-.39$, respectively; $p < .01$). When they do engage in interaction with objects they tend do it less competently than children of parents with less education ($\beta = -.27$; $p < .08$). The following analyses investigated this pattern of results in the context of other family characteristics.

A second two-step hierarchical regression analysis examines the impact of the mothers' expectations, preferred disciplinary techniques or the degree to which they perceive themselves as influential over the child's development, while controlling for mothers' education level in the first step. The results suggest that maternal childrearing beliefs contribute very little to the explanation of children's activity beyond the already reported impact of the mothers' education. None of the R-square change values of the second step that examined the contribution of mothers' beliefs were statistically significant.

The examination of the beta values of the specific beliefs in the final equation, however, reveals an interesting pattern. Compared with all other beliefs, mothers' developmental expectations had the greatest influence over the child's performance. This relation, however, is contrary to common expectations. The children of mothers who expected early achievement in the cognitive domain spent more time in positive social interactions with their peers and in joint peer play (βs $= -.41$ and $-.37$, respectively; $p < .05$). The children of mothers with expectations of early achievements in the social domain spent more time on the other hand in fine motor engagement with objects ($\beta = -.42$; $p < .05$), and tended to engage less often in positive peer interaction or joint play ($\beta = .32$; $p < .07$, for both).

In addition, children whose mothers prefer power-assertive disciplinary techniques or attributed considerable influence to themselves tended to express more frequent emotional distress (βs $= .23$; $p < .07$ and $.31$; $p < .01$).

A third analysis was then carried out to examine the contribution of mothers' attitudes to child care to the explanation of children's behavior, while similarly controlling for mothers' education. With one exception, none of the mothers' attitudes was related to the children's behavior. The children of mothers who felt that their children were going happily to the FDC home were engaged more frequently in fine motor interaction with objects ($\beta = .40$; $p < .01$). We cannot suggest a clear cause and effect relationship for this result.

Our analysis of the family's influence on children's experiences in FDC highlighted a number of points. First, from all the social and economic characteristics of the family, parental education emerged as the best predictor of children's behavior. It revealed a consistent but somewhat puzzling relationship in that children of better educated parents seemed to find the FDC environment less challenging than those of less educated parents; they played with objects at a lower level of competence and spent more time in aimless activity. This finding is contrary to what would have been expected from previous research that shows that children of educated parents generally perform at a higher level of competence. Our interpretation matches some recent data published in the U.S. that suggested that the cognitive development of children from advantaged families may be negatively affected by early entry into child care (Baydar & Brooks-Gunn, 1991). It seems that the home experiences of children with better educated parents may lead them to develop certain expectations from the environment, expectations that are not met by their experiences in FDC. It is not clear whether these expectations refer to the richness of the physical environment or to the availability of mediation offered by the caregiving adult.

Second, we found that mothers' attitudes to child care had almost no relation to the children's activities. Our data, therefore, do not support the conclusions of earlier research suggesting that mothers' feelings and attitudes toward child care affect the performance of their children (Hock, DeMeis, & McBride, 1988). It appears that it is mostly those attitudes that are related to mothers' conflicts vis-à-vis the use of child care and their maternal role that are related to children's behavior. Mothers in this study were fairly satisfied with their child-care arrangements, showed no obvious ambivalence concerning the use of child care, and their attitudes seemed to be irrelevant to the experiences of their children.

The relation found between maternal expectations and children's interaction with the environment is also contrary to what might have been expected. The results suggests that children may be using the FDC setting to complement aspects of the home environment, and that while in the day-care setting, they engage in those activities that are less expected of them and are less likely to be encouraged at home.

Our findings concerning the relation between family background and children's activities suggest this relation should be explored in terms of possible interactions between home and child-care influences. These interactions are explored in chapter 8.

The Influence of Child Characteristics

A hierarchical regression model was used to determine the extent to which variation in the children's performance was explained by the children's characteristics. As mothers' beliefs and attitudes contributed relatively little to the explanation of children's behavior, the following model examines the relative contribution of the children's individual characteristics and their life experience while controlling for the effects of family background.

Because social problems in the family correlated with parental level of education and showed similar correlations to other variables, a composite index of family SES was generated for this analysis to represent family influences on the children's experiences in FDC.

The discussion here is based on the beta coefficient of the final equation, where each effect is partialled out of the other effects.

As might have been expected our analysis (Table 6.4) shows that the children's age is the most powerful predictor of competence as it is expressed in the patterns described earlier. The children's positive engagement with peers, as well as their competence in the entire range of interactions observed, is significantly related to age.

TABLE 6.4
Hierarchical Regression of the Child's Behavior on the Child's Characteristics[a]

	Children's Personal Characteristics					Family Background	
	Age	Gender	Birth Order	Age Entry	Ease Separ.	Family SES	Final R-square
Active engagement							
Interaction with objects							
Fine motor	.11	.08	.11	.14	.14	−.22[†]	.12
Gross motor	−.05	−.03	−.13	−.21	−.13	−.42***	.24**
Competence:							
Mean play level	.27[†]	−.05	−.04	−.18	.05	−.28*	.12
Interaction with peers							
Positive inter'	.49***	.22[†]	−.20	−.05	.14	−.04	.22**
Agonistic inter'	−.04	−.28*	.02	.04	.01	.04	.07
Joint play	.06	.07	−.01	−.05	−.11	.36**	.14
Solitary context	−.19	−.10	.05	−.00	−.09	.06	.04
Competence:							
Play level 2–5	.36*	.12	−.07	.10	.25*	−.07	.19
Verbal communication	.30*	.26*	−.07	.10	.12	.16	.20*
Minimal engagement							
Aimless behavior	−.24	−.02	.07	−.01	.07	.45***	.23**
Emotional distress	−.20	−.12	−.18	.00	.11	−.23[†]	.14

[a]The table presents beta values from the final equation.
*$p < .05$. **$p < .01$. ***$p < .001$.

Like other studies (Maccoby & Jacklin, 1974), our data reveal some gender differences: girls communicate verbally more frequently than boys and are less likely, even at this young age, to engage in agonistic interaction. They were more likely to be seen in positive social interactions with peers.

It is interesting to note that the children's social experience with siblings or peers (birth order and age of entry into child care) was unrelated to any of their behaviors. Other studies have suggested that child-care experience may override the effect of social experience with siblings (Howes, 1988b; Phillips, 1987), yet our measure of child-care experience (age of entry) did not predict the children's performance. This finding differs from some studies (Vandell & Corasaniti, 1990) and is in agreement with others (Clarke-Stewart, 1987; Kontos, 1991; Phillips, McCartney, & Scarr, 1987). It could be that in this young age group the variability in age of entry was not sufficient for a strong association between the amount of social experience and the children's behavior. Differences may emerge at a later stage of development (Field, 1991). Alternatively, the potential effect of the children's length of social experience was possibly dampened by the fact that these were usually mixed-age groups, including children with varied amounts of social experience.

Contrary to expectations based on the research literature concerning the effects of age of entry into child care (Belsky & Rovine, 1988) and in support of others (Field et al., 1988; Phillips, McCartney, Scarr, & Howes, 1987), children who entered child care earlier did not display greater separation difficulties (r = .09). Although unrelated to any other aspect of their competence or engagement with the environment, children who found it easier to separate from their mothers were more competent in their interaction with peers. Our data suggest, therefore, that separation difficulties (as reported by mothers) are more likely to be associated with the children's experiences at home and with family factors such as SES rather than with the children's child-care history.

Thus, our analysis suggests that the children's experiences in child care reflect their competence and are strongly related to their age. It further proposes that even at this young age girls behave differently from boys. They spend less time in agonistic and more in verbal communication and positive social interaction with peers. The life experiences of children reflected in their birth order, age of entry into child care, and ease of separation from mother, bear almost no relation to their behavior in child care.

These findings indicate that children's age is an important factor to be examined in the exploration of the interactive effects of child, family, and child-care characteristics on their experiences in these settings (see chapter 8).

In conclusion, the children's behaviors described in this study depict the degree, quality, and competence of the children's engagement with the physical and peer social environment. They seem to represent, together with the children's interaction with the caregiver, the full spectrum of the children's experiences in the child-care setting.

The nature of the children's behavior observed in this study suggests that their overall experience in these FDC homes is positive and that individual differences in competence affect the type and quality of most of the children's engagements with the environment. Our data further suggest that FDC has a more positive current and future effect on young children who spend more time in a group context.

Furthermore, our findings support the "specificity hypothesis" in as much as the two domains of children's interaction with the environment, although related to the children's competence level, are explained differently by the children's personal and family characteristics.

Although these findings may be specific to this sample, they point at the need to examine the effects of the interface between child characteristics, home, and child-care environment at a level that is more subtle and complex than the simple "center selectivity" hypothesis may suggest. This analysis is pursued in chapter 8.

7

Family Day Care
as a Childrearing Setting

The way in which a child-care setting affects the daily experiences and development of a child depends to a great extent on the childrearing context it offers (Bronfenbrenner, 1979a; Dencik, 1989).

An ecological approach to the study of child development highlights the importance of studying the environmental circumstances of every child-care setting as a childrearing context, rather than narrow its interest to describing the developmental outcomes of the children's participation in one setting or another (Bronfenbrenner, 1979a; Cochran, 1977).

Although the child-care research literature has shifted its inquiries in recent years from asking whether child care is "good" or "bad" for children to exploring the effects of different kinds of child care (Clarke-Stewart, 1987a; Clarke-Stewart et al., 1994), it still demonstrates a consistent interest in mainly one aspect of the child-care setting. The one important dimension of this context, which has been shown to influence development, is the quality of care it provides (Clarke-Stewart & Gruber, 1984; Howes, 1988a; Howes & Olenick, 1986; Lamb et al.,1988; Phillips, McCartney, & Scarr, 1987; Roupp et al., 1979; Vandell et al., 1988). The quality of care and the related daily experiences of infants and toddlers in child care were found to be a more reliable predictor of children's development than any developmental test given at this early age (e.g., Carew, 1980). Furthermore, good quality care can serve as effective intervention for children from low-income families, leading to some positive long-term developmental outcomes (McCartney et al., 1985; Ramey & Haskins, 1981).

Thus, the analysis of the child-care environment remains closely linked to debates concerning its effects on contemporaneous and long-term developmental outcomes. This debate is of crucial importance in societies deliberating the extent of responsibility of public policy to provide support for quality child care to families with young children. Researchers in this field, especially in the United States, play an important role in providing policymakers with data. Their findings have demonstrated the important role played by day-care quality in determining long-term developmental outcomes (e.g., Carew, 1980; Golden et al., 1978; Vandell et al., 1988), or the pathways from regulatable aspects of child care (such as group size or teacher's educational level) to process indicators of quality (such as appropriate activities) and then to developmental outcomes such as social competence or free-play activities (Howes, Phillips, & Whitebook, 1992; Phillips, McCartney, & Scarr, 1987; Vandell & Powers, 1983).

However, the attempt to understand the relationship of child care, as a childrearing environment, to the behavior and development of children poses additional interesting research questions. First, research in recent years has drawn attention to the need to study the specific relation between specific aspects of the childrearing environment and specific dimensions of the children's performance (Wachs & Gruen, 1982; Wohlwill, 1983). Haskins' (1985) findings provide a dramatic manifestation of the importance of this approach. His study showed that although children who attended the high-quality, intellectually stimulating, program at the Frank Porter Graham Center were indeed significantly more intelligent they were also 13 times more aggressive than children who had not attended this program.

Second, the group context of a child-care environment generates conditions of socialization not present in a home setting, which enable the developmental researcher to explore areas of development that until recently have been under investigated.

The need for data concerning the effects of quality of care on child development drew attention to regulatable dimensions of the child-care environment and to those process variables that have been shown to have linear effects on the caregivers' behavior and the children's development (Howes & Olenick, 1986; Vandell & Powers, 1983). This need also led to an emphasis on a global definition of quality of care and to studies using a research tool such as the Harms and Clifford (1980, 1984) ECERS/DCHERS. As such, an attempt was made to demonstrate that "good things go together," and that a global index of quality can predict children's intellectual and social development (McCartney, 1984; Phillips, McCartney, & Scarr, 1987).

Recent work, however, has repeatedly challenged the assumption that different indices of quality care are intercorrelated (Kontos & Fiene, 1987) and arguments have been presented that a global index of quality care tends to mask effects of different components of a child-care setting on different aspects of development (Clarke-Stewart, 1987b). Furthermore, this emphasis led researchers to neglect structural variables that are irrelevant to the relation involved in this debate. Thus, for instance, although the child-care peer group context creates a laboratory rich with possibilities to investigate phenomena related to early social development, relatively little work is done on this subject as it is unrelated to issues of regulatable quality care. One possible example might be the investigation of the between-structural variables such as the gender or age mix of the children in the group, or process dimensions such as peer interaction, and outcomes such as frequency of joint peer play and social competence.

The work presented in this volume does not ignore the importance of investigating the relation between quality of care and children's behavior and development. It recognizes, however, that a child-care setting presents the child with a heterogeneous set of experiences. It, therefore, attempts to explore the nature of the different relation that various child-care characteristics may have with identified categories or domains of children's experiences.

THE CHARACTERISTICS OF FDC AS A CHILDREARING ENVIRONMENT

Although FDC always refers to a community arrangement wherein a local woman takes into her home a small group of children, the regulatable, or structural, characteristics of FDC can vary across countries, states or even between homes within a state, depending on the prevailing legislation concerning licensing and regulation.

The FDC system investigated in this study is a sponsored system in which most homes abide by an identical set of regulations. This results in great homogeneity among homes regarding most regulatable variables. Thus, in most groups there are five children under the age of 3 and one caregiver whose training and child-care experience are very brief.

This study focuses, therefore, on three major process dimensions of the child-care environment: the nature of the interaction between caregivers and children, the peer social context of the children, and the characteristics of the physical environment.

Caregivers' Interactions

The nature of the caregiver's interactions with the children is possibly the most important feature determining the quality of care offered in a FDC setting. Caregivers in high-quality centers are more invested and involved than caregivers in low-quality centers (Howes & Olenick, 1986; Kontos & Fiene, 1987). Children with involved and responsive caregivers displayed more exploratory behaviors, were more positive and emotionally secure with their caregivers, as well as more competent with their peers (Anderson, Nagel, Roberts, & Smith, 1981; Clarke-Stewart, 1987a; Goosens & van IJzendoorn, 1990; Howes & Hamilton, 1992; Howes, Phillips, & Whitebook, 1992).

Howes, Phillips, and Whitebook (1992) suggested a distinction between two dimensions of caregivers' behavior: "appropriate caregiving" and "developmentally appropriate activities." In our earlier discussion of caregivers' behaviors (chapter 4), we suggested a similar distinction between the caregivers' spontaneous interaction with the children and the educational program they provide. Both dimensions have also been shown by previous research to affect the development of infants and toddlers (e.g., McCartney et al., 1985).

The data presented in chapter 4 suggested that the spontaneous interactions of the caregivers in this study with their children was mostly positive and they used restrictions relatively infrequently. About one quarter of the daily program was given over to educational activities offered by the caregivers, which tends to be more frequent than that found in other FDC studies (Stallings & Porter, 1980).

The Caregivers' Childrearing Belief System

The findings presented in chapter 4 further suggested that the caregivers' behavior is related to their childrearing belief system. These beliefs may have both direct and indirect influence on the children's behavior. The following analysis, therefore, also examines the contribution of the caregivers' beliefs to an explanation of the experiences of the children in their care.

The Peer Group Context

The peer group context and the activity of other children in the same small group is also likely to influence the children's engagement with the environment. The competence level of a child's interaction with objects is expected to be higher in a group with predominantly older children (Whaley & Kantor, 1992). Similarly, the nature of the social interaction among the children may be related to the gender composition of the group. In this study we examined the effects of group characteristics such as the proportion of boys and girls in the group, the mean age or age mix of children in the group as well as the mean level of education of parents of children in the group.

The characteristics of the FDC groups were discussed in chapter 4 as aspects of the work environment of caregivers (see Table 4.1) and suggested sufficient variability among groups regarding these characteristics. In the context of this chapter they are examined as aspects of the children's social environment.

The Physical Environment

Characteristics of the physical environment can be discussed, as was done in chapter 4, in terms of the FDC caregivers' responsibility for the overall educational quality of the environment they offer in their homes.

This section examines instead the nature of three specific characteristics of the physical environment: the amount and variety of play materials, the amount of space (crowdedness), and the organization of space that allows children "space to be alone" (to be used freely by the children and that is different from time out used for disciplinary purposes). The ratings on our ERQ (chapter 2) indicate that homes tended to vary in these dimensions describing the physical environment.

Some of the characteristics of the child-care settings were intercorrelated. The discussion in chapter 4 already pointed out some of these relationships. Caregivers who engaged more frequently in positive interactions tended to engage less in group interaction with the children.

TABLE 7.1
Relation Between the Physical and Other Characteristics of the FDC Setting

	Play Materials	Space to be Alone	Crowdedness
Caregiver's interactions			
Positive interaction			
Restrictions	$-.26^\dagger$	$-.46^{**}$	
Group interaction		$-.38^{**}$	
Educational activities	$.44^{**}$	$.47^{**}$	$-.28^\dagger$
Peer group context			
Mean age	$.26^\dagger$		
Age mix			
Gender composition			
Mean parental education			$.27^\dagger$
Physical environment			
Play materials	xxxxxx	$.40^{**}$	$-.32^*$
Space to be alone	xxxxxx	xxxxxx	$-.46^{**}$
Crowdedness			xxxxxx

[a]Only $r > .25$ are presented.
$^\dagger p < .10.$ $^* p < .05.$ $^{**} p < .01.$ $^{***} p < .001.$

Similarly, greater age heterogeneity was found in groups with generally older children and in groups where the general level of parental education tended to be higher. Table 7.1 presents the interrelation among the different characteristics of the physical environment and their relation to the other aspects of the FDC setting. As could be expected from the earlier findings (chapter 4), all three characteristics of the physical environment were related to each other and to the frequency of educational activities.

This pattern implies that the quality of the educational environment was consistent within the different FDC homes. Some offered a "good" physical environment, with sufficient space and play materials, and some were crowded, with fewer toys or educational activities for children.

In addition, caregivers who arranged their home space so as to allow "shelter corners" for the children, were less likely to restrict the children, or to interact with them as a group. The fact that these caregivers also offered more educational activity and more play material suggests that these are "educationally minded" caregivers who allowed children more autonomy in general as well as in the choice to retreat from the group.

THE EFFECT OF THE FDC ENVIRONMENTAL SETTING ON THE CHILDREN'S BEHAVIOR

The analysis in chapter 4 showed that caregivers working with groups containing older children or with groups with a higher mean level of parental education provided more frequent educational activities. Thus, it is clear that the peer group context influenced the children's daily experiences. Therefore, the next question is: How do these contextual differences relate to the children's performance?

This section explores, therefore, the relation of specific behaviors of caregivers, and specific dimensions of the peer group context and of the physical environment with distinguished categories of children's activity.

We examined the effects of the child-care setting on the behavior of children by means of three sets of hierarchical regression analyses that examined the relative contribution of different aspects of (a) the nature of the caregivers' interactions with children, (b) the peer group context, and (c) the physical environment.

The Effects of the Caregivers' Beliefs and Interactions With Children

Cognitions such as childrearing beliefs appear to play an important role in shaping the interactions between socializing agents and children and may have long-term consequences for children's development (Miller, 1988; Sigel, 1985). As reported in chapter 4, caregivers' beliefs are related to their interactions with the children under their care (Kontos & Wells, 1986; Scott-Little & Holloway, 1991).

The research literature highlights the importance of the caregivers' involvement and responsiveness to children, their use of restrictions, and their general emotional tone in determining the quality of the daily experiences of children in child care as well as their intellectual and social development (e.g., Clarke-Stewart, 1987a; Golden et al., 1978; Howes, 1983; Phillips, McCartney, & Scarr, 1987; Roupp et al., 1979). Some studies suggested that educational experiences involving "verbal stimulation" or "language mastery" offered by the caregivers predicted children's performance on intelligence and language tests (Carew, 1980; McCartney, 1984). Clarke-Stewart's (1987b) Chicago study calls attention to the fact that although the overall amount of caregivers' interaction with children was unrelated to the children's competence, higher competence was associated with specific caregiving activities such as reading and providing children with choices. Others have identified specific dimensions, such as "appropriate caregiving" and "developmentally appropriate activity" as predictors of social development (Howes, Phillips, & Whitebook, 1992).

The educational philosophy guiding teachers (formal instruction vs. enrichment and discovery) has been shown to influence preschoolers' cognitively oriented play, but not social play (Johnson, Ershler, & Bell, 1980; Tizard, Philps, & Plewis, 1976)

Our analysis of the effects of caregiver's beliefs and activities on the children's performance proceeded in two stages. In the preliminary stage, we examined separately the effects of the caregivers' behaviors and their beliefs on the performance of children, while controlling for the effects of their education level. In the second stage, the relative contribution of caregiver's beliefs and behaviors was examined.

The results of the preliminary analyses suggest that, in contrast with the relatively low impact of maternal beliefs (chapter 6), caregivers' beliefs did have an effect on the behavior of children. Similarly, in contrast with the relatively consistent effect of parents' education on the child's behavior, caregivers' education level was, in general, unrelated to the performance of children. There was one exception to this generalization: Children in the homes of better educated caregivers tended to spend more time in a solitary rather than a group context ($\beta = .40$; $p < .001$). This result can be interpreted as a consequence of the preference of educated caregivers for individualized, rather than group, interaction with the children. The implications of the caregiver's preference for a given mode of interaction to the children's experiences in FDC are discussed later.

Caregivers' developmental expectations and their preferred disciplinary technique emerged from these analyses as the best predictors of children's behaviors. These behaviors were unrelated to the caregivers' attribution of influence.

The preliminary analyses that examined the relative influence of the caregivers' activities on the experiences of children showed that the caregivers' use of restrictions was generally unrelated to the children's behavior. However, children in the homes of caregivers who practiced frequent restrictions were emotionally distressed somewhat more often and tended to be less verbally communicative than children in other homes (both βs = .19; $p < .10$). It is interesting to note that this same pattern appears more frequently also among children from distressed families (chapter 6). This pattern might characterize children's general reaction to aversive interaction with their caregiving adults.

The caregivers' tendency to engage in spontaneous positive or group interactions with the children and the frequency with which they provided educational activities, emerged as the best predictors of the children's behavior.

The second stage of our analysis enabled us to examine the relative contribution of the caregivers' interactions with the children and their beliefs to the explanation of the children's experiences. The best predictors from among the caregivers' beliefs, and the best from among her behaviors, which emerged from the preliminary analysis, were entered into the following two-step hierarchical regression analysis. This analysis compared the relative influence on children, of caregivers' developmental expectations in the cognitive and social domains, and preferred disciplinary methods with that of their spontaneous interaction and planned educational activities (see Table 7.2).

Our analysis shows that the nature of both the caregivers' beliefs and activities influence all aspects of the children's engagement with their environment.

The results of the hierarchical regression analyses (see Table 7.2) suggest that the caregivers' developmental expectations had an important effect on the children. Children in the care of caregivers who expected them to attain cognitive skills earlier, spent more time in fine motor interaction with the physical environment and less time alone and emotionally distressed. They also tended to have fewer agonistic interactions with peers. This is in marked contrast to children of caregivers who expected early attainment of social skills. Contrary to what might have been expected (Holloway & Reichhart-Erickson, 1989), these children spent more time alone and in agonistic peer interaction. They also tended to be more often distressed and have less frequent positive interaction with peers.

TABLE 7.2

The Regression of Children's Behavior on Caregivers' Beliefs and Behaviors[a]

| | Caregiver's Belief System | | | | Caregiver's Behavior | | | | |
| | Dev. Expectation | | Severity | | | | | | |
	Cognit. Domain	Social Domain	Control Methods	Δ	Positive Inter.	Educat. Activity	Group Inter.	Δ	R_2
Active engagement									
Interaction with objects									
Fine motor	−.29*	.24	−.13	.15**	.16	.35**	.01	.17**	.30***
Gross motor	.21	.03	.16	.17**	.10	−.38**	−.08	.12**	.29***
Competence:									
Mean level of play	−.25	.23	−.08	.02	.29*	−.15	.29*	.12*	.14†
Interaction with peers									
Positive interaction	−.20	.27†	.06	.09†	.23*	.03	.37***	.15**	.23***
Agonist. interaction	.28†	−.39*	.25*	.04	−.21†	.31**	−.08	.09†	.13†
Joint play	.02	−.12	.32*	.12*	.06	−.08	.46***	.19***	.31***
Solitary context	.40**	−.57***	.26**	.16**	−.23**	.32**	−.39***	.20***	.36***
Social competence:									
Play Levels 2-5	−.05	.17	−.24*	.05	.05	−.10	.23*	.05	.10
Verbal communication	−.05	.09	−.23†	.05	.09	−.01	.20	.04	.09
Minimal engagement									
Aimless behavior	.08	−.30†	.19	.05	−.34**	.00	−.12	.10	.15†
Emotional distress	.39**	−.26⁶	−.12	.13**	−.01	−.10	−.21†	.04	.17*

[a]The table presents the beta values of each predictor variable as it appears in the final equation.
†$p < .10$. *$p < .05$. **$p < .01$. ***$p < .001$.

Children with caregivers who believed in using more authoritarian control techniques were observed more frequently alone, in agonistic interaction or in joint play with peers. These children showed a lower level of social competence.

Children in the homes of caregivers who engaged in frequent positive interactions with the children played more competently with objects, had more frequent positive interactions with peers and spent less time alone and in aimless activity. They also tended to engage in conflicts with peers less frequently. In a similar way, children in the homes of caregivers who engaged in frequent group interaction with the children played more competently with objects, had more frequent positive interactions with peers and spent less time alone. In addition, these children also showed greater competence in their interaction with peers, engaged more frequently in joint peer play, and tended to be less emotionally distressed.

The effects of the caregivers' providing educational activities seem to complement the effects of their spontaneous positive interaction and their tendency to interact with the children as a group: Although positive interaction and group interaction influence mostly the social behavior of children and their competence, the provision of educational activities influences mostly the frequency of the children's engagement with the physical environment. The fact that the frequent provision of educational activities is associated with the children's more frequent engagement in fine motor interaction with objects and less frequent gross motor activity, suggests that the caregivers' educational emphasis is on the development of fine motor, rather than gross motor, skills.

Second, we also found some negative effects: Children in groups with a larger proportion of educational activities spent more time in a solitary context and were likely to get involved more frequently in conflicts with each other.

A number of conclusions can be drawn from our analysis of the effects of the caregivers' beliefs and interaction with children on the children's engagement with the environment. First, contrary to the lack of effect of maternal expectations on the children's engagement with their environment (see chapter 6), the developmental expectations of the caregivers seem to be related more directly to the behavior of children. The relation found between expectation of early attainment of cognitive skills and frequent engagement in fine motor interaction with the physical environment and a general sense of well-being is in accordance with the research literature (Miller, 1988). However, expectation of early achievement of social skills seems to have a negative effect on the socioemotional behavior of these young children. It seems that because the caregiver's expectation was premature and not matched with the social abilities of these children, it led to a negative effect on their social interaction and well-being.

Second, it is interesting to note that, although the mothers' preference for power-assertive control methods had relatively little effect on the children's behavior, a similar preference on the part of the caregivers seemed to have, on the whole, a negative effect on the children's type and level of social interaction with peers. This preference, however, seems to have no effect on the children's interaction with the physical environment.

Third, the caregivers' tendency to engage in positive and group interaction with the children is associated with positive and competent social interaction with peers, as well as competent play with objects. In contrast, their frequent provision of educational activities, while leading to more fine and gross motor play with objects, results instead in more agonistic interaction among the children and more time spent in a solitary context. The children's performance suggests that these caregivers' educational emphasis is on fine motor interaction with objects and less on gross motor or social development.

Finally, contrary to the importance ascribed by educators to individual interactions between caregivers and children, our data suggest that the tendency of caregivers in an FDC setting to interact with the children as a group rather than individually, had some very positive effects on the children's experiences. The pattern of these relationships is consistent and should encourage educators to discuss the objectives and functions played by different types of adult–child interaction in this kind of child-care setting. It seems clear, therefore, that different aspects of the caregivers' functioning have a differential effect on specific behaviors of children. As such, all these aspects cannot be easily classified into a single dimension of quality of care.

The Peer Group Context

Older children are more competent in their interactions with their environments. Among others, they have more sustained sociable interchanges and engage at a higher level of social play (Sarafino, 1985). One would expect, therefore, that children in groups with higher mean age level will interact more competently with both the social and nonsocial environment.

Children in age-homogeneous groups behave differently from the same-age children in age-heterogenous groups. Bronson (1975) found that toddlers playing with same-age mates were more likely to show agonistic interaction than when playing with mates of different ages. Studies with preschool children have shown that younger children in mixed-age group settings can engage in more interactive and complex play with older peers (Howes & Farver, 1988). With the perspective of systems theory and based on Vygotskian notions that development is achieved through interaction with more competent peers and adults (Vygotsky, 1978), Whaley and Kantor (1992) argued that the opportunity to interact with children of different ages has benefits for both social and cognitive development of both younger and older children.

The gender composition of the group is also likely to affect social play. Preschoolers of both genders engaged more frequently in positive social interaction when playing with girls (Roopnarine, 1984). Because boy toddlers play more aggressively than girls (Fagot, 1980), more agonistic social interaction can be expected in groups with more boys than in groups with more girls.

As reported in chapter 6, our finding that children's family background has an effect on their performance in the child-care setting, is in agreement with other reports (Howes & Stewart, 1987; Phillips, McCartney, & Scarr, 1987). It is possible, therefore, that their engagement with the environment will be indirectly influenced by the background of other children in the group.

Thus, this study explores the effects of SES, age, and gender characteristics of the peer group on children's engagement with their social and nonsocial environment.

A multiple regression analysis, with the group's age and gender composition and parents' mean level of education as predictors, was used on each of the children's behaviors separately.

The regression analysis (see Table 7.3) shows that this equation explained relatively little of the variance in the children's engagement with their environment. As was expected, children in groups with higher mean age engage more frequently in positive interaction with peers and less in gross motor activity than children in younger groups.

It is interesting to note the effects of the group age heterogeneity on joint peer play. This form of peer interaction requires that more than two children will focus on a joint theme of activity. It is much more difficult to meet this requirement in small and highly heterogenous age groups of very young children.

The gender composition of the group did not affect the experiences of children, presumably because most of these small groups had children of both genders and a boy to girl ratio of 2:3 or vice versa is not sufficient to determine the nature of children's behavior in these groups.

TABLE 7.3
The Regression of Children's Behavior on the Peer Group Context[a]

	Mean Parent Educat.	Mean Age	Mean Gender	Age SD	R^2
Active engagement					
Interaction with objects					
Fine motor	.19	$.19^{\dagger}$	−.03	.20	$.10^{\dagger}$
Gross motor	−.51***	−.27**	.04	−.09	.30***
Competence:					
Mean level of play	.02	$.21^{\dagger}$	−.14	.15	.09
Interaction with peers					
Positive interaction	−.14	.36**	−.03	−.16	.11*
Agonistic interaction	.01	.12	−.15	−.18	.06
Joint play	.02	.12	.07	−.34**	$.11^{\dagger}$
Solitary context	.04	−.08	−.03	−.05	.02
Social competence:					
Play Levels 2–5	.02	$.21^{\dagger}$	.07	−.01	.05
Verbal communication	.12	.18	.02	−.12	.06
Minimal engagement					
Aimless behavior	$.23^{\dagger}$	−.13	.08	−.18	.16**
Emotional distress	−.04	−.11	−.01	.20	.04

[a]The table presents the beta values of each predictor variable.
$^{\dagger}p < .10$. $*p < .05$. $**p < .01$. $***p < .001$.

The effects of the mean level of parental education of the children in the group reflect the effects of the children 's own SES (chapter 6) on their performance, possibly because of the tendency of children of a given SES level to be put into groups with children of similar SES background.

The Physical Environment

Research has shown that neat, clean, and orderly physical settings that provide children with the opportunity to interact with varied toys and educational materials are related to children's higher level of competence (Clarke-Stewart, 1987a). Preschoolers in settings with more play material show more frequent gross motor activity, more interaction with materials, more social play, and less agonistic behavior (Johnson, 1935; Prescott, 1981). Although it is quite clear that the amount and variety of toys and play equipment encourage exploration and sensorimotor interaction with objects and cognitive development (Clarke-Stewart, 1987a; Yarrow, Rubenstein, & Pederson, 1975), their effect on social peer interaction among infants and toddlers is less clear and has in fact been the subject of some debate.

Although some researchers argue that the availability of toys and play material provides joint themes of attention for social exchanges among infants and toddlers, others claim that such material may distract a young child's attention from the peer to the object. Others still perceive play material as irrelevant to social exchanges among young peers (Eckerman & Whatley, 1977; Jacobson, 1981; Lewis, Young, Brocks, & Michalson, 1975; Mueller & Lucas, 1975; Mueller & Vandell, 1979; Vandell, Wilson, & Buchanan, 1980). It is unclear, therefore, how the availability of play material will be related to the peer social interaction in our FDC age-heterogeneous groups with very young children.

An important consideration regarding the physical setting in FDC is its crowdedness. Prescott (1981) reported that in conditions of high density preschool children were less involved in play. McGrew (1970) also reported that preschoolers in highly crowded settings spent less time in contact with each other. By contrast, Bates (1972) reported that in crowded conditions preschoolers tended to interact more frequently with each other but these tended to be rather agonistic interactions. Rohe and Patterson (1974), however, argued that sufficient amounts of play materials can alleviate the negative effects of high density. It seems reasonable to assume therefore, that crowdedness may have a dampening effect on interaction with objects and may result in more frequent agonistic interactions among children.

Space arrangement that allows children to have space to be alone is considered one of the variables defining "good space" by Prescott (1981), that is, space that contributes to positive interactions with both objects and peers. Others have stressed the importance of such "stimulus shelter" corners for sensorimotor development (Wachs, Francis, & McQuiston, 1979). However, these conclusions might not be generalizable to all age groups and for all care settings. Thus, for example, Legendre (1985) found that infants under the age of 21 months tended to stay in close proximity to the caregiver. Legendre implied that at that age infants are likely to avoid these stimulus shelter corners. It is not clear, therefore, what effects of space to be alone one should expect in FDC settings with infants and toddlers.

Multiple regression analyses with amount of play material, crowdedness, and availability of space to be alone as predictors were used to examine the effects of these aspects of the physical environment on the behavior of children.

The results of the regression analyses reported in Table 7.4 show that the physical setting affected both social and nonsocial interactions with the environment.

First, although as expected the availability of play material does indeed encourage children into more frequent fine motor interaction with the physical environment, contrary to expectations it was unrelated to gross motor activity or the children's competence in interacting with objects. The data support the claim of Lewis et al. (1975) that the availability of play material is irrelevant to social interaction among young children.

Second, our findings concerning the effects of crowdedness reflect to some extent what has been found by others (Prescott, 1981). Children in more crowded FDC homes engaged more frequently in aimless activity, and when they did engage in interaction with the physical environment they did it less competently. The limited space reduced even further their gross motor activities. At the same time, however, crowdedness brings children into closer contact with each other. Contrary to findings of previous research that suggested that this close contact is not conducive to positive peer interaction (Bates, 1972; McGrew, 1970), the young children in our FDC homes engaged more frequently in joint peer play, had more frequent verbal communication, and did not engage in more frequent agonistic

TABLE 7.4
The Regression of Children's Behavior on the Physical Environment[a]

	Play Material	Crowdedness	Space to be Alone	R^2
Active engagement				
Interaction with objects				
Fine motor	.36**	$-.20^\dagger$	.05	.25***
Gross motor	$-.09$	$-.33**$	$-.35**$	.14**
Competence:				
Mean level of play	.12	$-.22^\dagger$	$-.42**$	.12*
Interaction with peers				
Positive interaction	.14	.04	$-.27*$	.07
Agonistic interaction	$-.15$	.04	.28*	.06
Joint play	$-.05$	.33**	$-.28*$	.30***
Solitary context	$-.09$	.03	.47***	.18**
Social competence:				
Play Levels 2–5	$-.01$	.05	$-.14$	.03
Verbal communication	.00	$.23^\dagger$	.02	.05
Minimal engagement				
Aimless behavior	$-.20^\dagger$	.42***	.19	.20***
Emotional distress	$-.07$	$-.06$	.13	.02

[a]The table presents the beta values of each predictor variable.
$^\dagger p < .10.$ $*p < .05.$ $**p < .01.$ $***p < .001.$

exchanges with peers than children in other, less crowded homes. It could be that in a small group of very young children the sheer physical proximity to peers may facilitate social interaction among them (Mueller & Vandell, 1979). This proximity, however, was related to a group interaction such as joint peer play and not to positive peer interaction that is mostly dyadic.

A most interesting pattern of relationship was found concerning the effect of the availability of space to be alone or stimulus shelters.

Contrary to its description as a criterion of good space (Prescott, 1981), we find that infants and toddlers in FDC homes that offer such space arrangement spend more time in a solitary context, showing less frequent positive dyadic peer inter-action and joint play and when they do interact with the other children their interactions tend to be agonistic. Children in these homes tend to engage less often in gross motor activity and interact with object on a lower level than children in homes where such stimulus shelter corners are not available. The data seem to suggest that very young children, in a small setting such as FDC, do not benefit from such a space arrangement.

Our data show that the FDC as a childrearing setting has a definite effect on the behavior of the children attending it. The children's degree and type of engagement with the environment, as well as the competence demonstrated in this engagement, are affected.

Our expectation that specific aspects of the FDC environment will be found to be related to specific domains of the children's performance (Wachs & Gruen, 1982; Wohlwill & Heft, 1987) was confirmed. The specific relation were main-tained even when controlling for interdependency among some of the dimensions describing the FDC environment as well as for their relation to the children's background (M. Rosenthal, 1993)

Thus, as expected, we found that the caregivers' expectations of early attainment of cognitive abilities and the frequency of educational activities offered by the caregivers in this setting are related to the children's interaction with the physical environment. The latter, however, is related also to increased solitary play and agonistic peer interaction. The analysis clearly shows the caregivers' priorities in the educational interventions they offer (i.e., peer interaction is not defined as a goal in their choice of educational activities). Possibly because of the limited space in most homes, their choice of educational activities draws children more fre-quently into fine motor rather than gross motor activities. As expected, the avail-ability of play materials, like educational activities, has an effect on the children's interaction with the physical environment and not on their peer interaction.

Although Western-trained educators stress the importance of individual, rather than group, interaction with young children, our observations suggest a reconsid-eration of this generalization. Even though the better educated and more autono-mous caregivers in this sample demonstrated frequent positive interaction with the children, and tended to engage less frequently with the children as a group, those caregivers who prefer group to individual interaction ensured that a child is not left alone, or spends time in emotional distress. Furthermore, the group context of interaction seems to provide caregivers in this homelike setting with more opportunity to respond to the children; it also brings these very young children into close contact with each other, which may facilitate positive interaction among them and generate joint themes of activity. Moreover, the group context seems to generate experiences that enhance the children's competent engagement with both the social and physical environment.

Our findings question two accepted notions related to quality care. The first concerns the poor quality value attributed to group as opposed to individual interaction between caregivers and children. The other concerns the value of space to be alone as a component in good quality space organization. The first brings children into greater proximity to each other under the supervision of the caregiver, and the second distances the child from other children as well as from the watchful eye of the caregiver.

Our findings suggest, that in an FDC setting where a small group of infants and toddlers is cared for by only one adult, children seem to be better off when the space and interactions are organized to facilitate close proximity between the children, in the presence of a mediating adult. This proximity reduces children's distress, provides more opportunities for positive social interaction and encourages more competent play with objects.

When such proximity, however, results from overcrowding it is also likely to have negative effects such as increased aimless activity.

Contrary to our expectations, the peer group context did not contribute much to the explanation of children's behavior. It could be that the effects of this context interact with the effects of characteristics of the individual child. It could also be that the presence of children of varied levels of competence, or different degrees of age heterogeneity in the group, may have a different effect on the play of younger and older children (Brownell, 1982; Stallings & Porter, 1980). Chapter 8 examines how the children's behavior is affected by the interaction of children's personal characteristics and the nature of the child-care setting.

8

The Interface Between
Family, Child, and Child Care

A complete understanding of the development of children in child care, in any given
society, must take an ecological approach, whereby one studies the home and the
child-care environments, as well as the specific characteristics of the individual
child. The early research on child care tended to evaluate its socialization impact
on the child without taking into consideration the significant contribution of the
child's home. Recent work in this field, however, recognized the fact that childrearing in child care is not independent of the child's home but is in fact a collaborative
endeavor of the two environments.

Studies published in the early 1980s began to explore these complex relationships. One major and consistent finding is that certain child-care and family
characteristics are correlated, indicating that developmental outcomes cannot be
attributed exclusively to either environment. Some studies found that children from
poor and socially distressed families tended to be enrolled in poor quality child care
(Howes & Olenick, 1986; Howes & Stewart, 1987). Some argued, however, that
the specific nature of the correlations between home and child-care characteristics
may change according to cultural or social policy variations (Clarke-Stewart
1987b; Kontos, 1991). Child-care selectivity factors may thus be more typical of
societies where child-care provision is part of a free market economy rather than
part of a universal service available, on an equal basis, to all families.

As Holloway and Reichhart-Erickson (1989) pointed out, many of the early
studies that recognized the interdependence of home and child care focused on it
as a methodological handicap, thereby masking the effects of child care. Their main
goal was to examine the effects of variations in child-care quality while controlling
for family effects. They devised ways to partial out the effects of the home
environment from those of child care (Kontos, 1991; Phillips, McCartney, & Scarr,
1987). The results concerning the unique contribution of each environment are
inconsistent. Some studies have shown that when the effects of family characteristics such as parents' SES or childrearing values have been partialled out, the

104

effects of child care characteristics diminished considerably (Clarke-Stewart & Gruber, 1984; Kontos, 1987). Other researchers, however, proposed that even when controlling for the role of the home's influence one finds consistent, and sometimes substantial, effects of the quality of child care on children's development (McCartney, 1984; Phillips, McCartney, & Scarr, 1987; Scarr & Eisenberg, 1993). Others have suggested that specific aspects of children's behavior and development may be differentially sensitive to the different childrearing contexts of the two environments. Family background variables, for example, may be significant predictors of cognitive and language development, whereas child-care quality variables may be significant predictors only of social development (Kontos, 1991).

Phillips and Howes (1987) argued that the inconsistent results can be explained by the differences between the studies in the relative range of variation in the family variables and the child-care quality characteristics. When the range of characteristics of families in the sample is wider than the range of child care quality, family factors seem to be more influential and vice versa. This argument reflects suggestions made by others concerning the separate effects of each of these environments (Rutter, 1985; Scarr & Weinberg, 1978). Others argued that the disparate results may be attributed to the limitations of the outcome measures (Holloway & Reichhart-Erickson, 1989).

These findings, as well as theoretical considerations, have led researchers to go beyond the methodological concerns and to explore more carefully the rich intricacies of the combined and interdependent influences of these two socializing environments. At the present time, relatively little is known about how aspects of family life in conjunction with characteristics of the child-care setting actually contribute to the development of children. It has been suggested that their respective effects "may be additive; they may compensate for each other or some aspects of one may override aspects of the other in positive or negative ways" (Phillips & Howes, 1987, p. 11).

Some studies that examined the additive effects of the two environments showed that combined measures representing both home and child-care features are more predictive of developmental outcomes than analyses using measures that reflect only one of the environments (Howes & Olenick, 1986).

Child-care and home effects can compensate for each other. Thus, for example, infant–caregiver attachment seems to be independent of the nature of parent–child attachment. This means that even when infants are involved in insecure family attachments, they may still effect a secure attachment relationship to their caregivers. These attachments to caregivers have been reported by some researchers to be better predictors of the child's socioemotional development than attachment to parents (Goosens & van IJzendoorn, 1990; Oppenheim, Sagi, & Lamb, 1988).

Similarly, studies of compensatory programs for children from low-income families indicate that experiences in high-quality child-care programs may offset disadvantageous conditions in the home or community (Haskins, 1989; Lazar & Darlington, 1982). As suggested previously, a positive experience in one setting may override the effects of negative experience in the other. The impact of social experiences with their peers on children attending child care may override the effects of their social experiences with their siblings at home, thereby minimizing any effect that might be related to the number of children in the family (Howes, 1988b).

Some recent studies of the effects of child care qualify their conclusions by "it depends" (Clarke-Stewart, 1992), leading to the investigation of the interactive effects of structure and process variables in both the child's home and day-care settings. These studies found that children's development was influenced by an interaction of variables that include type of care setting, maternal marital status, and social interactions within the child-care setting. Presumably, family effects are mediated by the effects of child care (e.g., Cochran & Robinson, 1983). Thus, for example, it has been suggested that quality child care characterized by high educational stimulation has particularly strong effects on the intellectual development of children from lower class homes that provide less educational stimulation (Clarke-Stewart, 1987a; Ramey & Campbell, 1977; Ramey & Haskins, 1981).

Other investigators focused on maternal attitudes toward child care and its possible effect on the child's development. These studies suggested that working mothers whose children are enrolled in day-care centers were less concerned about the possible negative effects of maternal separation than working mothers whose children attended other forms of child care (Hock, DeMeis, & McBride, 1988). Everson et al. (1984) examined the way in which the impact of attending child care may vary depending on parental feelings and perceptions about appropriate childrearing practices. They found that children in child care whose mothers were uncomfortable about using it, as well as home-reared children whose mothers felt comfortable with the use of child care but were not using it, were easily frustrated and distressed at maternal separation as well as less compliant with teachers' requests. In the same vein, findings from a follow-up study 10 months later suggest that the effects of child care are influenced by the mother's positive or negative attitude toward the use of child care. Another analysis of such an interaction is provided by Holloway and Reichhart-Erickson (1989), who found that the effects of the quality of child care on the prosocial reasoning of children were stronger when their mothers held expectations for early development than when they did not.

The study of the interface between home and child-care effects on children's development is extremely complex; furthermore, recent research has suggested that yet another dimension must be added: the contribution of individual characteristics of children (Goelman & Pence, 1987; Vandell & Corasaniti, 1990). The same child-care arrangements may be experienced differently by different children; not all children are affected in the same way by the same child-care and family conditions. This line of inquiry suggests that discussions of the effects of the interaction of quality of care and family functioning should be qualified by certain individual characteristics. Thus, for instance, data coming out of Israel suggest that day-care attendance may have adverse effects on boys', but not on girls' intellectual development. Boys who attended day-care centers in the early years of life performed more poorly than boys in other forms of care (Auerbach, Lerner, Barasch, & Palti, 1992). In their review of child-care research, Gamble and Zigler (1986) concluded that the degree of risk from poor quality child care may vary with the characteristics of children and their families. Thus, poor child care is part of an additive model of stress influenced among others by the family's complex social problems and a child's gender (male). Another example is presented by Feagans (1992), who examined the interaction of factors related to child care, family environment, and children's illness and temperament on behavioral outcomes of children, such as peer relations and language development. Global concepts of quality care are modified by the notion of goodness of fit between child care, family background, and child characteristics (Kipp, 1992; Vandell & Corasaniti, 1990).

In a field that occasionally resembles an Escher drawing (Feagans, 1992), the interface between family, child, and child caregiver has shifted from being a background issue and has instead become a primary subject of the investigation. At present, there is no comprehensive theory relating to the behavior and development of children in child care. Therefore, it is difficult to construct specific hypotheses concerning which aspects of family background or family life are expected to interact with which elements in child care and with which individual characteristics of the child. Furthermore, the relationship between these mutual influences remains undefined. It is unclear as to which of these mutual influences are linear or direct, which are indirect, or possibly even circular. All research to date in this area has been exploratory. The ability to generalize from the findings is probably dependent on the specific culture or society, on the variability among the educational settings under investigation, and on the predictor and outcome measures employed.

Thus, recent research on the interface between home and child care has called attention to the contribution of family functioning, parental education, SES, economic and social resources, and stress (Clarke-Stewart & Gruber, 1984; Goelman & Pence, 1987; Howes & Olenick, 1986; Kontos, 1991; Vandell et al., 1988) as well as on parents' childrearing values and expectations (Holloway & Reichhart-Erickson, 1989; Kontos, 1991; Phillips, McCartney, & Scarr, 1987). Studies of this interface with the contribution of the characteristics of individual children focused on children's gender, age, or temperament as well as on aspects related to the children's life experiences (birth order, child-care history, age of entry into child care, and quality of attachment).

The nature of our investigation remains mostly exploratory due to the lack of a coherent theory about these intricate relations as well as the sparse and inconsistent evidence. Any finding must be carefully interpreted within the context of the specific constraints of the samples and the nature of the measures used in these studies.

In order to avoid the confusion typically generated when observing the total gestalt of an Escher drawing, investigators find it necessary to adopt a step-by-step strategy of data presentation, whereby each step focuses on a different perspective or research question related to these intricate relationships (Feagans, 1992; Holloway & Reichhart-Erickson, 1989).

Our presentation follows a similar process of untangling these relations: This chapter first assesses the association between family and child-care characteristics. This assessment explores all aspects of the two settings (see Fig. 2.1). The chapter then compares the relative impact of the childrearing beliefs of mothers and caregivers and the effects of differences between them (discontinuity) on the children's behavior.

The data analyzed in chapters 6 and 7 demonstrated some important contributions of child, family, and child-care characteristics to the nature of this engagement of children with their environment. Our analysis proceeds therefore, with an exploration of the unique contribution of child, family, and child-care characteristics to children's performance and the combination of variables representing these sources of influence that provides the best explanatory model of the children's behavior.

This chapter concludes with the examination of some interactions between child, family, and child-caregiver characteristics and their effect on the behavioral outcomes of children in the FDC setting. Our investigation followed the same empirical approach as previous analyses utilizing the same dimensions as significant predictors of children's performance. In addition, we have included those dimensions that might be relevant to parents' selection of child care or might interact with the effects of child care in another way. The child, family, and child-care variables included in these final analyses are presented in Fig. 8.1.

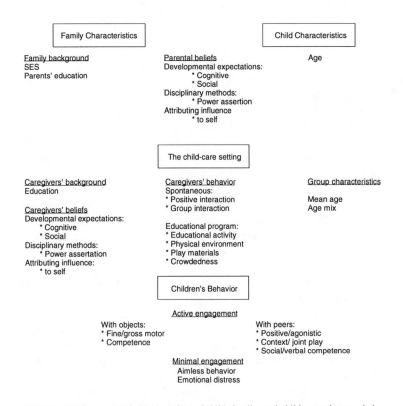

FIG. 8.1. Children in FDC: The interface of child, family, and child-care characteristics.

THE ASSOCIATION BETWEEN FAMILY
AND CHILD-CARE CHARACTERISTICS

We carried out a Pearson product moment correlation analysis to examine the association between all the different aspects of the two childrearing settings, as shown in Fig. 2.1. All family measures (demographic characteristics, childrearing beliefs, and attitudes to child care) were correlated with all child-care measures (caregivers' background, quality of the environment, the daily program, and that of caregiver–child interaction).

The findings of such an analysis should be regarded as very tentative, considering the large number of coefficients that were computed. The most impressive empirical result is the lack of significant correlations where these were expected and the relatively small number of statistically significant associations found.

Previous research in the United States found some of the multiple aspects of child care and some of the family characteristics to be correlated (Holloway & Reichart-Erickson, 1989; Howes & Olenick, 1986; Howes & Stewart, 1987). Parents were expected to place their children with caregivers who have a similar educational background, who share their childrearing beliefs (Long & Garduque, 1987; Nelson & Garduque, 1991), and who adhere to a similar style of interaction with their children (Howes & Olenick, 1986; Howes & Stewart, 1987). However, our data did not confirm these expectations. Instead, our findings suggest that one cannot predict the nature of the sponsored Israeli FDC homes from the available information concerning the children's families.

In general, our results suggest that when such associations are reported in the research literature, they are indeed related to some selectivity factors.

Coordinators interviewed in this study reported that as a matter of policy, they do not allow parents a choice among the list of sponsored caregivers, but rather assign, according to a fair share policy, the same number of children to all caregivers, allowing some flexibility with regard to geographic distance and transportation difficulties.

Therefore, in contrast to the United States where parents choose the specific child-care setting for their child, parents in our sample did not select the specific FDC home their children attended, but instead sent their children to the FDC home assigned to them by the local coordinator. This policy may explain why, unlike the U.S. researchers, we found very little association between child care and family characteristics. Thus, for example, with the exception of a low correlation between mothers' and caregivers' ages ($r = .25$; $p < .05$), no relation was found between family characteristics and the caregivers' education, training, or autonomy. In other words, mothers of different SES, different childrearing beliefs or attitudes to child care, do not select, and are not assigned to, FDC caregivers according to their education level, previous training, or the autonomy with which they run their FDC home.

Similarly, maternal beliefs had very little, if any, relation to the childrearing beliefs of caregivers or to the quality of care they offered in their FDC home. Of the 121 coefficients calculated, only a few reached statistical significance, but because these do not present a coherent pattern they have been dismissed as lacking empirical significance. In addition, very few of mothers' attitudes toward child care were found to be related to any other aspect of the FDC home. The only exception is that mothers, regardless of their educational background, were more satisfied with caregivers who interact positively with the children and use less frequent restrictions. Mothers were also more satisfied with caregivers who believe in less power-assertive control techniques, and who expect early achievement of cognitive skills and late achievement of independence. The mothers' satisfaction with their child-care arrangement seems to be a response to their experiences with the FDC caregiver rather than a criterion by which they select the home.

The paucity of consistent relations found between the two childrearing settings suggest some processes other than parents' selectivity. Our data shows that maternal level of education is not related to caregiver's education or training. Neither is it related to the overall quality of the FDC physical environment or the caregiver's use of restriction, although there is a relation to some important aspects of the FDC setting. Children of better educated mothers were more likely to be in FDC homes that are crowded and homogeneous age wise and these groups tend to have other children of better educated parents. In addition, the caregivers in these groups are more likely to interact positively with the children, provide frequent educational activities, and attribute a low degree of influence over the child's development to the mother.

This pattern is complemented by the finding that children of families with more social problems (although not necessarily lower education level), are found in the homes of caregivers who use more frequent restrictions in their interactions with the children and who offer less educational activities.

These findings suggest that more highly educated parents are better informed with regard to the quality of care offered in different homes. Consequently, they succeed in influencing the coordinator to assign them to a caregiver of their choice, regardless of the stated policy. Perhaps these parents are willing to compromise on the issue of crowdedness and to overlook the caregivers' lack of more formal qualifications. However, this interpretation does not fit most of the Pearson correlation coefficients.

An alternative explanation might be that parents tend to accept the FDC home to which they are assigned without exercising much choice provided it is within their neighborhood.

The correlation between parents' education levels, according to this interpretation, suggests that families of a given SES tend to live in neighborhoods with other families of similar SES and their children attend the local FDC homes. These homes are more crowded and more homogeneous age wise, which may reflect the tendency of coordinators to place children from lower SES families in what they consider to be better quality homes (i.e., less crowded and more age heterogeneous). The fact that caregivers in such homes interact positively with the children and provide more frequent educational activities can be explained by caregivers adapting themselves to assumed, or explicit, expectations of parents. Maternal satisfaction from the caregiver can further reinforce these behaviors.

It was noted that these caregivers tend to attribute to the mother only a low degree of influence over the child's development that may suggest a self-serving bias in an attempt to boost their sense of worth when compared with the more highly educated mothers. Furthermore, those caregivers whose clientele are children from multiproblem families tend to use more restriction and less frequent educational activities. One can understand this as a response to the behavior of the children and/or the caregiver's perception of the parenting style employed by their parents. This interpretation suggests, therefore, that some correspondence may be found between homes and child care as a result of policy decisions and of a process of mutual perception, evaluation, and adaptation between parents and caregivers.

We suggest that center selectivity is an important research variable in societies where child care is provided as part of a free market economy and where parents do select their child-care arrangement. However, in societies where child care is offered as part of a universally subsidized public service, and parents do not have many alternatives from which to choose, other processes that influence the association between home and child-care characteristics, such as adaptation to mutual expectations, should be examined.

GROWING UP IN THE CONTEXT OF TWO CHILDREARING BELIEF SYSTEMS

The data presented in chapter 5 suggest that, in spite of the similarities between the home and the FDC settings, caregivers in the latter hold somewhat different childrearing beliefs from those of mothers.

This finding raises two major questions when investigating the interface between these two childrearing settings. First, one should explore the extent to which the behavioral outcomes of children in FDC reflect the beliefs and expectations of their mothers, in contrast with the influence of the caregiver's beliefs and expectations. Are parents' beliefs so influential that even when in child care their children behave in accordance with the parents beliefs rather than those of the caregiver? Alternatively, could one demonstrate that children's behavior is situation specific and matches better the beliefs and expectations of the FDC caregiver than those of their parents?

A second issue is that of continuity, or discontinuity, between the two childrearing settings and its effect on the performance of children.

This section examines the differential effects of the beliefs of the two socializing agents as well as the effects of discontinuity between the two agents beliefs on the children's behaviors.

The Relative Contribution of the Belief Systems of Mothers and Caregivers to the Behavior of Children in FDC

An examination of this relative contribution can reveal the extent to which the children's activity in FDC is affected by the beliefs of the caregiver in this setting and to what extent it is affected by the beliefs and demonstrated by the mother at home.

Table 8.1 reviews the results reported in chapters 6 and 7 by presenting the standardized regression coefficients of each belief that explain each of the children's behaviors, while controlling for the differences in the agents' education level. Two beliefs that influence the child's development were chosen for this analysis: developmental expectations and preferred level of power assertion in disciplining children. The beta values in this table are derived from the separate regression analyses that in the case of the caregivers (see Table 7.2) also controlled for the effects of their interactions with the children.

In order to assess the statistical significance of the different contribution of the beliefs of the two agents, a test of difference (Cohen & Cohen, 1983) was performed on the beta values in the respective equations of mothers and caregivers.

Even though the Z scores in Table 8.1 suggest that only a few of the differences in the relative contribution of mothers' and caregivers' beliefs (6 out of 33) were statistically significant, the overall pattern of these differences is empirically meaningful and merits a discussion.

The comparison in Table 8.1 suggests that although mothers' beliefs had relatively little effect on the children's behavior in FDC, the caregivers' beliefs influenced a large number of these behaviors. Furthermore, the table reveals different patterns of relationship between children's actions and the beliefs of the two agents. The pattern of the relationship between the caregivers beliefs and the children's conduct is clear and coherent: Caregivers who expected early achievement of cognitive skills engaged the children in more frequent fine motor activities as a result of which the children spent less time in a solitary context or in emotional distress. These children, however, were somewhat more likely to enter into conflicts with each other, presumably over toys or other play materials offered by the caregiver. The caregivers' early expectations for achievement in the social area led them to assume that children could be left on their own to initiate positive social contacts, resolve conflicts and emotional distress, or to generally engage themselves with the environment. These unrealistic expectations were beyond the social capabilities of young children, resulting in aimless activity, emotional distress, and in the child being frequently alone or involved in agonistic instead of positive interaction with peers.

The pattern of relation between mothers' developmental expectations and children's conduct is completely different from that of the caregiver. Children whose mothers expected early achievement of cognitive skills engaged less frequently in fine motor play and more frequently in social peer interaction, whereas mothers with expectations of early achievement in the social area had children who engaged more frequently in fine motor play. Another aspect of the pattern echoes, although without statistical significance, the relation found for the caregivers between early social expectations and fewer peer interactions.

Similarly, although caregivers' preference for power-assertive disciplinary methods is associated with children's frequent agonistic interaction, joint peer play, time alone, and lower level of social competence, such maternal preference is not related to other behaviors of the children except for an association with somewhat more emotional distress.

TABLE 8.1
The Relative Contribution of the Beliefs of Caregivers and Mothers to the Children's Behavior[a]

| | Developmental Expectations | | | | | | Disciplinary Method | | |
| | Cognitive Skills | | | Social Skills | | | Mean Level Power Assertion | | |
	Caregiver	Mother	Z[b]	Caregiver	Mother	Z	Caregiver	Mother	Z
Active engagement									
Interaction with objects									
Fine motor	-.29*	.42*	-3.49		-.42*	3.39			
Gross motor									
Competence:									
Mean level of play									
Interaction with peers									
Positive interaction	.28†			.27*	.32†				
Agonist. interaction		-.41*		-.39*			.25*		
Joint play		-.37*			.32†		.32*		2.63
Solitary context	.40**			-.57***		-2.08	.26*		
Social competence:									
Play Levels 2-5							-.24*		
Verbal communication							-.23†		
Minimal engagement									
Aimless behavior	.39**			-.30†		-1.97			
Emotional distress				-.26†				.23†	-1.96

[a]The contribution of each agent is represented by the values of the standardized regression coefficients (betas) taken from the separate analysis of caregivers (chapter 7) and mothers (chapter 6).
[b]The Z scores assess the differences in the values of the regression coefficients of caregivers and mothers. Only $Z > 1.96$ ($p < .05$) are presented (Cohen & Cohen, 1983).
†$p < .10$. *$p < .05$. **$p < .01$. ***$p < .001$.

The overall comparison shows that children's performance, while in FDC, shows a closer, clearer, and more coherent relationship with the beliefs of caregivers than with those of mothers. It seems that when in this setting the behavior of children is responsive to the caregiver's expectation, which is presumably mediated by her interactions with the children and the environment she offers in her home. The possible interpretation of the relationship between mothers' beliefs and children's actions, while in FDC, is that children use their time in FDC to complement the experiences they have at home.

In general, our data suggests that even at this young age children are able to distinguish between the two childrearing environments with their different expectations, and to utilize the varied opportunities offered by each setting. This conclusion implies that the conduct of the same children when observed at home will show greater correspondence to the beliefs of their mothers rather than those of their caregivers. Unfortunately our studies have no data to test this hypothesis.

The Effects of Discontinuity

The issue of continuity versus discontinuity between childrearing contexts has been, and continues to be, of great concern to early childhood professionals. Thus, for example, much of the emphasis in early childhood programs on parent involvement (e.g., Powell, 1980) is related to the attempts to maintain as much continuity as possible between child care and home.

Earlier discussion (chapter 5) referred to a considerable body of research describing contextual differences between home and child care as childrearing environments. The findings reported in chapter 5 suggest that a certain measure of discontinuity is inherent in the contextual definitions of the two settings. Relatively little is known, however, about the implications of the differences in childrearing beliefs between mothers and caregivers that may affect the performance of children reared concurrently, in these two different contexts.

Lack of agreement or compatibility in beliefs concerning child development may lead to inconsistent expectations from the child and different patterns of adult involvement with the child. Incompatibility in the role perceptions of the two socializing agents may lead to competition and conflict between them with ensuing negative implications for the children. FDC has been a cause of special concern on this account, being suspect of causing greater confusion than other child-care settings because of its similarity to home in some of its contextual markers (Bryant, Harris, & Newton, 1984).

Data presented by Ispa and Thornburg (1993) suggest, however, that discontinuity between parents and FDC caregivers may not have many implications for child behavior. Although the children in their sample seemed to benefit from continuity of adult approval across the two settings, they adapted well to the differing discipline styles of mothers and caregivers. No other systematic effects of discontinuity were found.

This stage of the analysis explores, therefore, the impact of the discontinuity between the belief systems of mothers and caregivers on children's performance. Four main beliefs that were found in the previous analyses to influence children's behaviors were chosen for this analysis: expectations in the areas of cognitive and social development, preference for power-assertive disciplinary methods, and the agents' attribution of considerable influence over the children's development to themselves. The difference between the mother and caregiver scores on each of these beliefs was computed to generate measures of discontinuity. These discontinuity scores on the four beliefs were then entered as predictors in a series of regression analyses with the children's behavior as dependent variables.

Three major results emerged from this analysis. First, children's in FDC did not demonstrate any emotional distress or behavioral disorganization when their mothers and the caregivers had different beliefs. Differences in preference for power-assertive disciplinary methods were not related to any of the child's behaviors, suggesting that even at this young age children can adapt to such differences (Ispa & Thornburg, 1993).

Second, the analysis showed that differences in the agents' developmental expectations influenced the children's engagement with their environment. Children tended to engage more frequently in fine motor play when there was continuity in the agents' developmental expectations in the cognitive area ($\beta = -.50$; $p < .01$) and discontinuity in their expectations in the area of social development ($\beta = .52$; $p < .001$). Furthermore, discontinuity in the latter was associated with less frequent aimless activity ($\beta = -.36$; $p < .05$), and less time in a solitary context ($\beta = -.31$, $p < .06$).

It is interesting to note that although mother's expectations in the cognitive area had no effect on the child's engagement with objects (chapter 6), a discontinuity between her expectations and those of the caregiver in this area lowers the likelihood of fine motor play. The pattern associated with discontinuity of expectations in the social area suggests a dominant effect of the cases when caregivers expect late achievement and mothers expect early achievement of competence (chapters 6 and 7). It should further be noted that this is not a very frequent form of discontinuity because caregivers tended generally to have earlier expectations than mothers in the social area (chapter 5). We cannot offer a very clear interpretation of these results. Our main conclusion from this finding is that although discontinuity in agents' expectations did not result in increased emotional distress, it did have an effect on the children's behavior most relevant to these expectations.

Our third major finding is that emotional distress was observed only when the two agents share a similar attribution of influence to themselves. When both agents attribute to themselves a similar degree (either large or small) of influence over the children's development, children in FDC showed more emotional distress ($\beta = -.32$; $p < .01$). This distress could be either in response to conflicts between two socialization agents each attributing to herself significant influence over the child, or as a result of additive neglect by both agents who dismiss their responsibility to influence the child's development.

Although very little is known about the parameters determining the ease with which a child can negotiate the transitions between the discontinuous settings, common observations of children in child care suggest that most children negotiate them quite easily. Our data suggest that it is difficult to generalize from the effect of discontinuity in one set of beliefs on one set of behaviors to other beliefs and other behaviors. It seems that research into the contexts of childrearing may benefit from employing the specificity hypothesis as part of a more open approach to the issue of discontinuity. Instead of searching for the negative effects of discontinuity, one might study in a more systematic way the effects of varying degrees of discontinuity in different dimensions of the childrearing environment on different aspects of the child's performance.

It could be argued that clear markers of discontinuity between settings reduce the probability of interagent conflicts and in fact facilitate the children's adaptation to both. In some instances it might be detrimental to establish continuity between home and child care through the use of parent education as a means to encourage parents to adopt values, expectations, and practices held by the teachers. Beliefs and practices that facilitate the child's adaptation to the public context of child care may be quite unsuitable for the more intimate, emotionally involved context of home (Dencik, 1989). Some measure of discontinuity between settings might be important for the children's well-being and development (Lightfoot, 1975).

THE UNIQUE CONTRIBUTION OF CHILD, FAMILY, AND CHILD-CARE CHARACTERISTICS TO THE BEHAVIOR OF INFANTS AND TODDLERS IN FDC

The analyses in chapters 6 and 7 examined the contribution of each of the child, family, and FDC characteristics relative to all the other characteristics within each category.

The analysis presented in this section is designed to ascertain the relative importance of child and family variables when compared with variables describing the quality of the child-care setting. It does not include, however, the belief systems of mothers and caregivers that were discussed earlier. An attempt is made to describe what combination of child, family, and child-care variables provide the best model for predicting children's engagement with the environment.

Only the best predictors of the children's performance that emerged from our earlier analyses (chapters 6 and 7) were retained for this analysis (Fig. 8.1). These predictors were entered into a final series of regression analyses.

As can be seen in Table 8.2, only one of the children's behaviors, related to the child's competence, was explained mostly by variations in the children's family and personal background. Older children from higher SES backgrounds engage more frequently in verbal communication than younger children from lower SES families. None of the FDC characteristics affected this behavior. It is interesting to recognize that these relations were not uncovered by the earlier, separate analyses reported in chapter 6. It emerged only when controlling for other influences. This finding concurs with findings from other research in the field (Goelman & Pence, 1987).

It should be further noted that none of the other competence scores is adequately explained by this model. Although earlier analyses showed that the child's competence is related both to age as well as to various aspects of the child-care setting, these relations become insignificant when the analyses partial out their interdependent influences. This can be seen in the comparison of the coefficients of the zero-order correlations with the standardized regression coefficients.

TABLE 8.2
The Regression of Children's Behavior on Child, Family and Child Care Characteristics[a]

	Family SES	Child's Age	Δ	Group Inter.	Educat. Activity	Physical Environm	Mean Gp. Age	Δ	R_2
Active engagement									
Interaction with objects									
Fine motor	-.30**	.09	.12**	.04	.42**	.24†	-.11	.26***	.38***
Gross motor	-.29**	-.23†	.26***	.11	-.33*	.15	-.15	.09*	.34***
Competence:									
Mean level of play	-.13	.14	.08*	.20	-.11	.07	.09	.06	.14†
Interaction with peers									
Positive interaction	.10	.27*	.13**	.27*	.05	-.10	.05	.09*	.22**
Agonist. interaction	-.18	.07	.01	-.08	.30†	-.22	-.03	.05	.06
Joint play	.20*	.04	.11**	.45***	.25†	-.43***	-.08	.30***	.41***
Solitary context	-.08	-.23†	.05	-.45***	.18	.01	.07	.22***	.27***
Social competence:									
Play Levels 2-5	.13	.17	.06†	.12	-.12	-.09	.19	.07	.13
Verbal communication	.27*	.28*	.16***	.08	.02	-.17	.07	.03	.19**
Minimal engagement									
Aimless behavior	.31**	-.03	.13**	-.18	.06	-.44**	.13	.13*	.26***
Emotional distress	.02	-.44**	.10*	-.28*	-.25†	.15	.37*	.11*	.21**

[a]The table presents the beta values of each predictor variable as it appears in the final equation.
†$p < .10$. *$p < .05$. **$p < .01$. ***$p < .001$.

Similarly, we reported earlier on the effects of the groups' mean age on the activity of children. This factor was no longer statistically significant when controlling for the effect of the children's individual ages. Our investigation found that all other children's behaviors are affected by child and family variables as well as child-care characteristics. Their combined effect is greater than the effect of each one alone. Thus, the children's age together with the group interaction initiated by the caregiver explains more of the variance in the children's solitary play and positive peer interaction. Similarly, the children's engagement in aimless activity is explained both by their family SES and by quality of physical environment.

In some instances, however, the contribution of the child-care setting may be greater than that of the individual or family characteristics. This is especially evident in the nature of children's engagement with their peers, such as in joint peer play, an activity that occurs less frequently in the home setting. Therefore, it would seem to be clearly related to the caregiver's behavior the physical environment that create opportunities for this type of play. A caregiver's preference for power-assertive control, her positive spontaneous and group interactions with the children, the educational activities, and the space arrangement she offers in her home, contribute much more to the child's social interaction than any personal or family characteristics of the child.

A similar trend can be observed in the nature of fine motor play that, although influenced by the children's SES background, is influenced more by the availability of educational activities and a physical environment that encourages such play.

In conclusion, with the exception of children's verbal competence, the results of this analysis suggest that the type and frequency of children's engagement with the physical and peer environment are best explained by combining the effects of child, family, and child-care characteristics.

The fact that the child's social and play competence is not explained by this regression model, while it is related to the components included in the model (child's age, FDC environment) suggests that there might be an interaction between the effects of the different components of the model. The following section discusses this possibility.

THE INTERACTIONS BETWEEN CHILD, FAMILY, AND CHILD-CARE EFFECTS ON THE BEHAVIOR OF INFANTS AND TODDLERS IN FDC

The final stage in this analysis of the interface between child, home, and child care-setting explores the interactive effects of these three sources of influence.

The investigation of such interactive effects characterizes the more recent trend in child-care research. This approach presents the investigator with some interesting methodological questions the answers to which may determine the result of the investigation. One set of questions relates to the definition of the relevant characteristics to be explored. What are the relevant family characteristics that might interact with the effects of child care? In general, researchers have focused on factors that have been known to affect parenting and child development. Studies have employed a wide variety of variables: Parental involvement, social support network, quality of marital relationship, maternal separation anxiety, mother's role satisfaction (Hock et al., 1988; Howes & Olenick, 1986), SES, parental developmental expectations (Holloway & Reichart-Erickson, 1989), education, use of subsidy, social values, and an assessment of the home environment (Kontos, 1991) are only a few examples. One may wonder likewise as to the definition of child characteristics that are most likely to interact with family and child-care characteristics. Child's gender, illness, temperament, and child-care experience are some of the dimensions explored thus far (Feagans, 1992; Vandell & Corasaniti, 1990). Although there is general agreement that the child-care setting should be characterized by the quality of care it provides, it is not clear whether different definitions of *quality* are likely to lead to similar results. A definition, for instance, that is too global (e.g., the ECERS), or one that is too specific (e.g., amount of toys or free play activity) may lead to ambiguous results. Furthermore, some other characteristics that may be irrelevant to a particular definition of quality (e.g., age mix), are likely to interact with some child characteristic.

Another set of questions relates to the statistical analysis to be employed. Studies that use, for example, an interaction term, as a step in a regression analysis, are likely to overlook possible nonlinear trends in the relation between their dependent and independent variables.

Some of the recent data in this line of research (e.g., Kontos, 1991; McCartney, Rocheleau, Rosenthal, & Keefe, 1993; Vandell & Corasaniti, 1990), as well as our own study, should be examined, therefore, in the context of their choice of variables and statistical method. Such an examination may explain some of the inconsistencies among different reports and some puzzling findings, or lack of significant results.

The following presentation of our data should be treated with great caution and reservation. The limited size of our sample does not permit a statistical evaluation of any of the many relevant relationships under investigation. Our strategy, therefore, has been to investigate only a few of the possible interactions between child, family and child-care characteristic. The analysis focused on the relations that seemed interesting based on theory or previous research. In addition, our analysis dealt with only two dimensions at a time. The interpretation of our findings focuses on the overall pattern of results, rather than on their statistical significance.

Child and Child-Care Characteristics

The first set of hypotheses focus on the interaction between the child's age and the effects of the child-care setting. Several specific hypotheses are derived from previous research. These refer to the effects of age heterogeneity of the group on the performance of younger and older children as well as to the effects of the availability of toys on peer interaction among younger and older children in the age range under investigation.

Age Heterogeneity

The effect of age mix depends on the specific age of the child, whether the child is one of the younger or older children in the group, as well as on the type of behavior under investigation (Brownell, 1982). Clarke-Stewart's (1987b) data suggested that children in groups with older, more mature peers were more advanced in cognitive and social competence. Lougee, Grueneich, and Hartup (1977) reported, however, that although social interaction and verbal communication were less frequent in younger same-age dyads and intermediate in mixed-age dyads, they were most frequent in older same-age dyads. Stallings and Porter (1980) reported that although toddlers in FDC with more heterogeneous age groups exhibited more distress and spent more time alone, pre-schoolers in the same groups tended to interact more with other children, yet spent less time in educational activities. However, in homes where most of the children were infants, toddlers were more independent and spent more time in dramatic play and in interaction with the other children. At the same time, in homes with more toddlers, younger children spent less time in exploration of the physical environment, whereas older ones spent less time in agonistic social exchanges. Their findings concerning preschool children in heterogeneous age groups are similar to those reported by Fein and Clarke-Stewart (1973).

A two-way ANOVA was carried out to examine the interactive effects of the children's age and the age heterogeneity of the group on the children's actions. All children under the age of 2 were classified as "young" and those ages 2–3 as "old." Age mix was classified into three categories: "low," "medium," and "high" (when the difference between the youngest and oldest child in the group was greater than 17 months), to allow for exploration of possible nonlinear effects of age heterogeneity (Clarke-Stewart, 1987a).

Interaction between children's age and group age mix was found only for the children's engagement with the physical environment. Thus, although age heterogeneity of the group had no effect on fine motor play and mean level of play with objects of older children, younger children engaged in this behavior more frequently and showed a higher level of competence in their play with objects when in more heterogeneous groups. Although older children in this setting generally engage less frequently in gross motor activity than younger ones, they do it as frequently as young children when in highly heterogeneous groups.

The main effects of age heterogeneity were all linear and paralleled those reported in the regression analyses. Our data support, therefore, the findings of previous research that determined that age mix has a differential effect on different behaviors of younger and older children in a child-care setting. Age mix had no differential effect on the peer interaction of younger and older children. Although it appears beneficial for younger children age mix seems to cause no harm to older children in terms of their interaction with the physical environment, an interaction that is known to contribute to children's cognitive development.

Availability of Toys and Play Materials

There is an ongoing debate as to whether the availability of toys has a differential effect on the conduct of children of various ages. Mueller and Lucas (1975) and

Mueller and Vandell (1979) suggested that toddlers' first social interactions appear in the context of play around common objects whose availability encourages social exchanges such as giving, taking, resisting, or sharing. Longer peer interaction occurred for 14-month-old children when they played with a common object (Jacobson, 1981). Other researchers, however, argued that it is the nature of the peers' actions with the objects that is the major source of their attraction to other infants, rather than the objects themselves. Toys may be either competing with peers for the infants' attention or completely irrelevant to social play (Eckerman & Whatley, 1977; Lewis et al., 1975; Vandell et al., 1980).

We used a two-way ANOVA to elicit the effects of the availability of toys and play materials on peer interaction among children under and over the age of 2. Our data suggest that the amount of available play materials had no differential effect on any of the social behaviors of children of different ages.

Family SES and the Quality of Child Care

The second set of hypotheses concerns the interaction between parents' educational background and the effects of the child-care setting. Several specific hypotheses are derived from previous research. These refer to the effects of various aspects of the quality of care offered in the child-care setting on the performance of children of parents with high and low levels of education. A "high" level of education was defined in this analysis as "more than 13 years of education."

Intellectual Development. Research in this area suggested that high quality care has marked positive effects on the intellectual development of children from low SES background and may actually compensate for the presumably inadequate educational opportunities in the home environment of these children (Haskins, 1985; Phillips, 1987; Ramey et al., 1983).

Although our study does not measure intellectual development as such it allows us to assess the frequency and competence of the children's engagement with the physical environment that is at the core of such development. The results of our earlier analysis showed that children from lower SES were found to be more actively and competently engaged in interaction with the physical environment.

Our present analysis focuses, therefore, on the question of whether children of parents with different levels of education respond differently to those characteristics of the child-care environment that define its quality. Characteristics such as the nature of interaction with the caregiver, the frequency of educational activities and the quality of the physical environment were categorized into "high" and "low" quality and were entered into a two-way ANOVA where the second independent measure was parental level of education.

In general, the analysis failed to reveal any interactive effects between parents' education and child care characteristics on the children's engagement with the physical environment or on any of the measures of the children's competence. These findings suggest, therefore, that the differences in the competence of children of parents with different education levels indeed emerge from their different home experiences, regardless of the variations in the quality of care in this sample of FDC homes.

Social Development.   In a recent report McCartney, Rocheleau, Rosenthal, and Keefe (1993) investigated the social development of 720 children in 120 day-care centers located in three states in the United States. Their study examined the interaction between child and family characteristics. Only 2 out of the 36 interaction terms under investigation were found to be statistically significant.

Our study examined the interaction between child-care characteristics and parents' education with regard to their effect on the child's peer interaction. Two interesting interactions were found between aspects of the physical environment and parents' education on the children's social behavior. First, more frequent conflicts among children were observed either among children of parents with low education level who are in homes with a good quality physical environment and among children of better educated parents in homes that offered a poor quality physical environment. Second, the most frequent joint peer play was found among children of better educated parents who were in more crowded FDC homes.

In conclusion, this chapter has examined several aspects of the interface between child, family, and child-care characteristics. Such multidimensional analyses require a more comprehensive study with substantially larger samples. The nature of this interface, as well as the choice of dimensions to be examined may vary from one society to another and emphasizes the importance of cross-cultural investigation.

9

Summary of Results and Implications for Future Research

THE BEHAVIOR OF INFANTS AND TODDLERS IN FDC

This investigation of the experiences of children in FDC is based on the assumption that children's active engagement, exploration, and investigation of the environment contribute to (a) their current feelings of well-being resulting from self-perception of competence, and (b) their developing disposition and ability to negotiate the environment (Carew, 1980; Cassidy, 1986; Ruff et al., 1990). It is further assumed that in contrast to the effects of active engagement, the time the child spends in emotional distress or in aimless activity does not contribute to developing competence; nor is it associated with feelings of well-being (Vandell et al., 1988).

The analysis distinguishes two categories of interaction with the environment within "active engagement." The first refers to the children's interaction with objects, the physical, or nonsocial environment, and the second to the children's social interactions with peers.

On the basis of the specificity hypothesis (Wachs & Chan, 1986; Wachs & Gruen, 1982), we expected that active engagement with the physical environment was likely to facilitate the acquisition of motor skills, language, concepts of space and time relationships, and contribute to the child's intellectual development (e.g., Carew, 1980; Clarke-Stewart, 1973; Elardo et al., 1977). Similarly, it was expected that specific social interactions and social play with peers would facilitate the development of social competence and peer interaction skills that are important in later life (Garvey, 1977; Howes, 1987).

The study focuses, within each category, on the children's degree, quality, and type of engagement with the environment as developmentally valuable activities. Both theory and research have suggested that these have a potential contribution to children's future development and are indicators of their current feelings of well-being.

Patterns of Children's Activity

Two main conclusions can be derived from the data describing the children's experiences in FDC: First, the activities and experiences of the "average child" in FDC suggest a rather positive picture. For a lot of the time, most children are actively engaged in positive interactions with their physical and social environment. However, it is concerning that some children spent an average of 36.2% of the time in aimless, unoccupied behavior and that some spent as much as 75% of the time this way.

Another conclusion is that children's behaviors tend to be interrelated and can be described in three major patterns. The first pattern describes competent children. These children used language frequently, evidenced a higher level of play with both objects and peers, engaged more frequently in fine motor interaction with objects as well as in positive peer interactions and joint play, and were less likely to be seen in a solitary context. It is interesting to note that there was no relation between the frequency of interaction with objects and with peers. The second pattern describes children who spent much of the time in aimless activity. These children not only were observed more often in a solitary context and spent less time in active engagement with the physical environment, but also functioned at a lower level of competence in their interaction with both peers and objects. They were, however, just as verbally competent as the other children. A third pattern focuses on the children's peer interaction: More positive things happened to children who spent more time in a group rather than solitary context. These children were more likely to be seen in positive social interactions with peers, in joint play and less in agonistic peer interaction.

Factors Influencing the Behavior of Children

This summary highlights the major patterns of the relation between children's engagement with their physical and social environment and personal, family, and child-care characteristics.

Competent Versus Minimal Engagement
With the Environment

The analyses suggest that, without the effects of the FDC setting, children's competence is mostly related to their age: Older children interact more competently both with objects and with peers and use more verbal communication. Yet, in addition to the child's age, some features of the FDC setting also affect children's competence: First, children play more competently both with objects and with peers when the caregivers engage in frequent group interaction. Second, children display greater competence interacting with objects when they are in less crowded homes that have no space to be alone and where the caregivers engage with them mostly in positive interaction. Furthermore, younger infants, when in heterogeneous age groups, tend to display more competent play with objects. Third, children display lower levels of social competence in FDC homes in which caregivers prefer power-assertive control methods.

When child, family, and FDC effects are controlled simultaneously, the data suggest that verbal competence is related mostly to child and family characteristics such as age, gender, and family SES rather than to characteristics of the child-care setting.

Two categories of the children's activities were assumed to reflect minimal engagement with the environment: aimless behavior and the child's emotional distress.

Environmental factors affecting aimless behavior show a reversed pattern to those that influence competent engagement with objects: Children engage more frequently in aimless activity (a) when their caregivers expect early attainment of social skills, and do not engage in frequent positive interaction with them; (b) when the FDC homes are crowded and have fewer play materials; and (c) when their parents are older and better educated.

These findings as well as the correlation patterns previously described suggest that aimless behavior is more of an antithesis to the active engagement with the physical, rather than with the social, environment.

Children's emotional distress is related to personal, home, and child-care factors. We noted that the factors influencing the emotional distress of children resemble those that influence their negative social experiences rather than those that affect aimless behavior. Thus, children tend to display more frequent emotional distress while in FDC when they are younger, when their mothers are young and of low SES and attribute high influence to themselves and prefer power-assertive control methods. In addition, these young children show elevated levels of distress when in groups that have predominantly older children, and when in the homes of caregivers who expect early achievement of social competence and late achievement of cognitive abilities and who offer less frequent group interaction and educational activities.

In other words, children either bring their distress from their experiences in a stressful home environment or respond to the inadequate demands of a caregiver who on one hand expects them to negotiate social situations in a manner that is beyond their ability, and on the other hand does not offer sufficient cognitive challenges. Younger infants seem to have greater emotional difficulties coping with these stresses.

Active Engagement: Interaction With the Physical Environment

Infants and toddlers in the Israeli FDC homes engage much more in fine than in gross motor play with objects. Children who engage in frequent fine motor play tend to engage less frequently in gross motor play with objects and show a higher level of competence playing with objects than children who engage less frequently in fine motor activity.

The relative frequency of children's interaction with the physical environment is related to their parents' SES and developmental expectations and nature of the child-care setting more than to their personal characteristics. Thus, children of higher SES parents when in the FDC setting, tend to engage less often with the physical environment. The frequency of fine motor play is lower among children whose parents expect early cognitive and later social achievement. We have suggested that the children who are offered more challenging opportunities for fine motor activities at home, by their educated parents who expect early cognitive achievement, will engage in such activities less often when in FDC.

Children engage in frequent fine motor play when they are in FDC homes where the caregivers expect early cognitive competence, offer a well-equipped and less crowded environment with more educational activities. Also gross motor play occurs frequently in FDC homes that offer relatively more educational activities and are less crowded. Gross motor interaction with the physical environment is not related to any other aspect of the child-care setting.

The data suggest, therefore, that the educationally minded caregiver, in the Israeli FDC settings, does not regard gross motor play as important as fine motor play for the cognitive development of young children. Her choice of play materials and equipment mostly encourages fine motor, rather than gross motor, play. Therefore, children engage in gross motor play mostly when they are not engaged in fine motor play with the materials offered by the caregiver provided the environment is not too crowded.

Active Engagement: Interactions With Peers

Even at this young age, caregivers in the Israeli FDC setting tended to interact frequently with the children as a group. As a result, children in this study spent twice as much time in a group than in a solitary context. Most of the interactions among them were positive and agonistic interactions were rather rare. As noted earlier, different aspects of the children's social engagement with their peers were interrelated: Children who spent more time in a group context were more likely to engage in joint play and have frequent positive, and infrequent agonistic, interactions with their peers.

As may be expected from the contextual differences between home and child care and the fact that interaction with peers occurs mainly in the FDC setting, the relative frequency of children's involvement with peers is associated mostly with aspects of the FDC setting rather than with child or family characteristics. The same setting characteristics that result in children spending much time alone contribute also to elevated frequency of agonistic interaction (as well as to the emotional distress of children).

These include the caregiver's developmental beliefs, the way she organizes the space and daily program for the children, and the mode of her social interaction with them. Thus, we find children spending much time alone and in conflict with peers when in the care of caregivers who (a) expect early attainment of social skills but late achievement of cognitive skills; (b) prefer power-assertive control methods; and (c) do not have frequent positive interaction with the children, even though they emphasize educational activities and provide the children with space to be alone.

The child's personal characteristics have an effect as well. Whether or not children will spend much time alone in FDC depends on their own emerging motor and social skills that may enable them to join the other children. Young toddlers tend to spend more time alone than older toddlers. The child's gender is related, as may be expected to his or her agonistic interactions: Boys tend to engage more frequently in conflicts than girls.

The effect of the child's family background interacts with that of the quality of the physical environment. Children from different home environments react differently to the physical characteristics of the FDC home. More frequent conflicts occur when children from higher SES homes are frustrated by the poorer physical quality offered in the FDC, or when children from lower SES homes are offered a high-quality physical environment that they have difficulties sharing with the other children.

The positive interaction among peers is mostly related to characteristics of the child-care setting, but as in the case of agonistic interaction we found some influences of personal and family characteristics.

The child-care factors affecting positive peer interaction mirror to a great extent those that affect agonistic interaction. Thus, children engage in more frequent positive peer interaction in the homes of caregivers who expect later, rather than earlier, social competence, and who engage in more frequent positive interaction with the children, but do not necessarily offer frequent educational activities. Positive peer interaction is further facilitated by conditions that bring children into frequent contact with each other, under the watchful eye of the caregiver. Thus, positive peer interaction is more frequent in the homes of caregivers who do not provide space to be alone in their home and interact frequently with the children as a group. It is further facilitated by the presence of older children in the group.

In addition to these child-care influences, positive peer interaction is related to the child's age and emerging social competence. Thus, older children, in groups with other older children engage in more frequent positive peer interaction than younger children.

Positive peer interaction, unlike agonistic interaction, is directly related to mothers' expectations. Children engage in frequent positive interaction with peers when their mothers (like caregivers) expect later, rather than earlier, social competence and also expect early achievement of cognitive competence.

One notes, therefore, that the tendency to engage in positive interaction with peers is related to the child's and his or her peers' social skills, and to relaxed expectations of achievement of social skills. The most important role seems, however, to be played by the caregiver whose developmental beliefs, the way she organizes the space and daily program for the children, and the positive mode of her spontaneous social interaction with the children all have an effect on child behavior.

Children's joint peer play is an interesting phenomenon to observe at this young age. It bears no relationship to the children's personal characteristics but is strongly influenced by family and child-care characteristics. Joint peer play is generated by the children themselves. It is characterized by whole sequences of behavior that are copied by a group of children in some form of rhythmic repetition. In this way, the children have, on their own, organized a mutually shared frame of reference, or shared themes, in which the performance of a similar action glues the interaction together. These mutually understood themes are generated mostly by means of nonverbal communication and can be seen as precursors of more complex peer play that requires mutual understanding of shared themes as in the case of sociodramatic play (Brenner & Mueller, 1982; Budwig et al., 1986).

Even though children who tend to engage frequently in joint peer play show frequent positive peer interaction and a high level of verbal competence, they are not necessarily highly competent in peer interaction. These children are less likely to engage in interaction with the physical environment and more in aimless activity. Further, this behavior is affected by some factors that lead to elevated positive peer interaction as well as by others that increase the likelihood of agonistic interaction.

As in the case of positive peer play, children engage in frequent joint peer play in FDC where the caregivers offer no space to be alone and engage in frequent spontaneous positive and group interaction with the children and when their mothers expect early cognitive, but later social, competence. Yet, as in the case of agonistic interaction, joint peer play is more frequent in the FDC homes of caregivers who offer frequent educational activities, and prefer power-assertive control techniques. In addition, we find that joint peer play is more common among children of less distressed families with better educated parents, who attend FDC homes that are crowded and that are more age homogeneous. In fact, the highest frequency of joint play is found among children of better educated parents who attend more crowded FDC homes.

Joint peer play appears as a positive form of peer interaction among children who are at the stage of learning how to define shared themes of interest with their peers. This form of social play is facilitated by factors that bring children into close proximity with each other and factors that facilitate the establishment of shared frame of reference among young children: This is presumably why this form of peer play is more frequent in crowded FDC homes, without space to be alone, with a caregiver that brings them together by interacting with them as a group. It is also facilitated by the similar communication competence of children in age-homogeneous groups.

This form of play has a somewhat rebellious flavor, in as much as it occurs more frequently among children of better educated parents who do not find the FDC physical setting challenging enough and who seem to alternate between this form of play and aimless behavior rather than engage in the educational activities offered by an authoritarian caregiver.

This study suggests, therefore, that the daily experiences of children in FDC, and hence the effects of attending FDC on their development, are determined by the personal characteristics of children, their family background as well as the nature of the child-care setting.

Although children's age, and to some extent their gender, had a clear influence on their functioning while in FDC, other personal characteristics such as birth order, age of entry into child care, or difficulties separating from their mothers had relatively little, if any, influence.

Family factors such as parents' education and developmental beliefs, and to some extent the social stresses of the family, had a clear effect, other factors such as parental age, maternal employment, the use of financial support, or mothers' attitudes to child care, had little influence on the children's experiences and behavior in FDC.

The characteristics of the FDC setting, such as its space arrangement, some of the group characteristics, and the caregivers' beliefs and behaviors all had a substantial influence on most of the children's behavior. Only verbal competence was found, in the final analysis, to be affected by parents' SES, the child's gender, and age. The FDC setting had very little influence.

It is interesting to note that the children's engagement with the physical environment, which is seen as the experiential basis of their cognitive development, is directly related to the "educational" appropriateness of the setting rather than to the quality of the caregiver's spontaneous social interaction with the children. Thus, the caregiver's expectation of early cognitive development, her engagement in group interaction with the children while providing frequent educational activities, and sufficient amount and variety of play materials in an uncrowded environment, all contribute to the children's engagement with the physical environment.

The effect of the FDC setting on children's interaction with peers, which is seen as the experiential basis of their social development, is somewhat more complex mostly because different aspects of peer interaction are related differently to different dimensions of the FDC setting.

Generally, our findings concerning the factors that influence the social behaviors of children in FDC are reminiscent of the report of Phillips, McCartney, Scarr, and Howes (1987), who found that although social competence and considerate sociable behavior is related to caregivers' engagement in frequent positive social interaction with the children, children's social adjustment was actually related to poorer quality care. It seems that in Western societies there is a clear articulation of the relationship between goals of intellectual development and the educational processes required to reach these goals. In contrast, there is no clear articulation in these societies of either the goals set for social development nor the specific processes that lead to such goals. It is not clear whether our goals are of adjustment to the group, developing an ability to share, or the ability to resolve conflicts in a particular way. Nor is it clear what the processes in a child-care setting are that cause such results.

Furthermore, what may constitute an appropriate educational environment, supportive of cognitive development, may have actually negative implications for peer interaction and vice versa. Thus, the availability of educational activities that was found in our study to facilitate cognitive development also leads to elevated agonistic interaction and children spending more time in a solitary context. This kind of relationship may be at the basis of studies that found elevated level of aggression among children who attended high-quality day-care programs (Haskins, 1985).

Similarly, crowdedness is generally perceived as an indicator of poor quality care (Vandell & Powers, 1983), and was also found in this study to be associated with increased frequency of aimless behavior and low competence in playing with objects. However, crowdedness was found to facilitate joint peer play, seen as an important contributor to the child's emerging social skills at this age.

Hence, the definition of quality of care based on environmental conditions that facilitate cognitive development may not be very relevant or predictive of social development in child care (McCartney et al., 1993).

Our data further suggest that different children, with different family backgrounds, may react differently to similar characteristics of the FDC environment. Thus, older children may react differently to the age heterogeneity of the group than younger children. Children from higher SES homes may react differently to a given quality of the physical environment than children from lower SES homes. Similarly, children may react differently to various aspects of the child-care setting, and behave differently, depending on the developmental expectations of their parents as well as on the continuity, or discontinuity, between their parents' and the caregivers' expectations.

These findings raise some important questions concerning the definition of quality of care in the context of educational and social goals set for child care. These issues are discussed here. Altogether, this study has shown that specific aspects of the children's functioning are differentially sensitive to different aspects of their personal and family background as well as to different characteristics of the child-care setting.

Finally, a note of caution is needed. Although the pattern of our findings present a coherent ecological picture of child care, our specific conclusions are based on a relatively small sample, where multiple comparisons may increase the probability of spurious significant differences.

IMPLICATIONS FOR FUTURE RESEARCH

The findings of this study, as well as those that emerge from studies in other countries, raise some interesting issues concerning the cultural definition of the goals of child care and the match between these goals, the needs of different children, and the characteristics of the child-care setting. These issues raise questions concerning the definition of quality of care, and highlight different motivations and goals of child-care research with their implications for future research in this field.

Implications for the Definition of Quality of Care

Serious doubts about the adequacy of the current definitions of what constitutes quality care are raised by (a) the specificity of relationships between different aspects of the child-care environment and different developmental outcomes for children; and (b) the notion of a match between cultural goals, the specific needs of different children, and the characteristics of child-care settings.

A Global Definition of Quality of Care?

The data of this study argue against a global definition, or a monistic view, of *quality of care* and suggest that different environmental processes that define quality of care might be relatively independent of each other. Although there is a fairly high and positive correlation between the variables that describe a dimension of planned educational program, the relationship of this dimension to the more spontaneous aspects of the caregivers' interactions with the children is rather ambiguous. Furthermore, the different aspects of care are related differently to the caregivers' belief system and factors in her background and work environment.

The results lend further support to the argument against a global definition of quality of care by showing that the different aspects of the child-care environment bear specific relationships to various behavioral outcomes in children. Thus, the caregivers' expectations of early cognitive development, the play materials, and educational activities they offer are all related to children's increased engagement with objects (and intellectual development) but might have negative effects on their interaction with peers.

A similar reservation concerning the usefulness of a global definition of quality of care has been expressed by other researchers (Clarke-Stewart, 1987a; Howes, Phillips, & Whitebook, 1992).

We would like to suggest, however, that even a two-category description of the processes defining quality of care, such as proposed by Howes, Phillips, and Whitebook, (1992), may mask some important relation between cultural goals, social policy, the child-care environment, and children's development. This point is discussed later.

Defining Quality of Care in Terms of Structural and Process Variables

The present discussion of future research is concerned with the goals of child-care research and raises a few questions about the adequacy of the research strategy that incorporates both "structural" (or "regulatable") and "process" variables in the definition of quality of care. The validity of defining quality of care in terms of both structural and process aspects of the environment has been supported by ample research. Recent studies have shown clear relations between social policy and regulatable, or structural, criteria of quality on one hand and process variables and developmental outcomes on the other (Howes, Phillips, & Whitebook, 1992; Rosenthal, 1990).

This approach to the study of quality of care is extremely useful when the goal of research is to influence social policy by providing the policymaker with data about how certain policy decisions may affect children. Its ultimate purpose is to improve the quality of out-of-home care in a given society. It might be, however, a misleading research strategy when the purpose of the research is to expand our understanding of the impact of different childrearing conditions on children's development in general and to uncover the basic processes that occur in child care that lead to specific developmental outcomes.

Such research strategy may be misleading on two accounts. First, the ability to generalize from the results obtained by such a strategy, is limited to the society in which the investigation is conducted. Second, such a strategy may lead researchers to overlook important processes occurring in the child-care environment that have interesting developmental outcomes, but are deemed irrelevant to the particular regulatable variables under investigation.

The first culture-specific limitations of such research are demonstrated in the kind of regulatable variables that are selected for investigation in different societies, and that are found to have significant effects on child-care processes and children's developmental in these societies. The likelihood of finding sufficient variance among the child-care settings included in a given sample, on a particular structural variable depends on the child-care policy of the society in which the investigation takes place. Differences between samples in the relative range of variation in their predictor variables were suggested as a possible explanation for inconsistent results between studies within the same society (Phillips & Howes, 1987).

Lack of variability on a particular structural dimension may lead to a false conclusion that this dimension is not significant and therefore is unimportant. In this study, for instance, it was found that group size is not a significant predictor of either caregivers' or children's functioning, simply because the FDC homes in this sample almost all had exactly five children. This does not mean that group size is not an important structural variable that determines the quality of care. It is of great importance for researchers involved in influencing social policy in societies that value individualized care and where it is clear that regulating group size definitely improves the likelihood of individualized care and favorable developmental outcomes (Howes, Phillips, & Whitebook, 1992).

Besides its limitations on the variability of regulatable predictor variables, this strategy sets additional limitations to the generalizability of its findings by its choice of outcome measures. These tend to reflect the particular goals set by the society's child-care policy under investigation, or for that matter, the goals set for different child-care programs within the same society. Thus, if a society, or a specific program, considers improved intellectual achievement as its prime developmental goal for child care—the outcome measures will reflect this goal. The findings of such a study will be irrelevant to a society that considers "conformity to the peer group" as its main developmental goal for child care. The choice and different definitions of outcome measures may, in addition, lead to further inconsistencies in the results of child-care studies (Holloway & Reichhart-Erickson, 1989).

It is clear, therefore, that when our definition of quality of care is mostly empirically based, extracting its key components by means of factor analysis or other multiple variate procedures, our conclusions forever depend on the variability found in the given sample under investigation, within a given society, and the constraints of the goals it sets for its child care.

Children growing up simultaneously in two socializing worlds, is not only a social phenomenon, but also a natural experiment, with different experimental conditions occurring in different cultures. As such, it offers a very rich opportunity to expand our basic knowledge in an ecological framework of how different environments are related to different developmental outcomes.

A research strategy that overlooks aspects of the child-care setting and the behavioral outcomes that might be irrelevant to policy regulation in a given society, is likely to ignore some very important relationships between such "irrelevant" aspects of child care and child development. It may thus limit the scope of research into basic developmental processes.

This study, for instance, highlights some interesting relations between environmental aspects, such as space arrangement, and outcomes such as joint peer play. Overlooking such relations because they might be irrelevant to regulation of quality in some societies, may mean missing an opportunity to investigate some important aspects of early development of peer culture.

This discussion leads to two major conclusions. First, each society has its child-care policy that results in variability on specific structural dimensions as predictors and in outcome measures that reflect the developmental goals that society set for its child care. Caution is required, therefore, in any attempt to generalize from research results obtained in one particular society to the definition of quality care in other societies.

Second, quality of care should be defined in terms of process variables only, and these should be derived from our theories and general empirical knowledge about the relationship between environmental processes and different developmental outcomes. Structural, or regulatable, variables should be treated in future analyses as derivatives of the specific social policy under investigation, and its effect on child-care processes, but not as components in the definition of quality of care.

The Definition of Quality of Care in Reference to Developmental Goals

Future research on children in child care needs to define quality of care in reference to the cultural values and the developmental goals the society sets for its child care, as distinct from home care. The quality of care should be defined in terms of the underlying childrearing processes that both theory and research suggest are important for obtaining these developmental goals. The quality of care should then be evaluated in terms of the developmental outcomes that reflect these same goals.

We believe that such an approach will stimulate ecologically based research that will expand our basic knowledge concerning the effects of child care on children's development in the context of cultural values and goals.

Thus, for some culturally based developmental goals (e.g., attachment), a process of sensitive responsiveness by the caregiving adult may be an important component in the definition of quality of care. For other cultures, with different developmental goals (e.g., compliance with group goals or norms), a process of diverting bids for attention from caregiver to the peer group may be of greater value than sensitive responsiveness by the caregiver to each individual child (Tobin et al., 1989).

This study shows that processes such as positive spontaneous interaction between caregivers and children, the use of restrictions or of educational activities are all related to caregivers developmental expectations, control methods, and role perception. It is suggested, therefore, that our understanding of what constitutes quality care may be enriched if the processes that define quality of care include also the caregivers' cognitive structures concerning childrearing and role perception. Several studies have further suggested that these cognitive structures should be examined in the context of cultural values and goal of childrearing (Holloway et al., 1988; Winetsky, 1978).

The developmental goals set for child care can reflect, in addition to cultural values and social policy, the developmental needs of specific populations of children. An attempt to meet needs of different populations, within a society, may require setting different developmental goals for child care in accordance with these needs. The interaction found between aspects of the child-care environment and the children's personal or family characteristics suggests that what might constitute quality care for one child may not be such for the other. The definition of quality of care may thus have to vary with the different developmental goals set to meet the specific needs of different children using child care. Child care for children who might be delayed in their cognitive development may have different goals from that which serves, supposedly "spoiled," only children (Tobin et al., 1989). The data presented in this study suggest that even though the availability of space to be alone might be a positive feature of an environment designed for preschoolers in fairly large groups, it might be a negative feature of the quality of an environment of infants in a small group in a homelike setting. Similarly, our data suggest that what might be considered quality care for children from low SES families might not be adequate for children of parents with higher education level.

This discussion suggests that future child-care research examine its motivation. When the research motivation is to uncover environmental processes responsible for child-care outcomes, the definition of quality of care must rest on our general theoretical knowledge of the relation between environmental and developmental processes rather than on empirical analyses carried out in a specific society. The contribution of society-specific empirical findings will be enhanced if researchers clarify the relationship of their definition of quality care and their outcome measures to the culturally based developmental goals set for child care in that society. It is, therefore, suggested that such an approach may avert some culturally based methodological constraints that bias research findings and obscure some important research questions.

However, this does not mean that the empirical search for the relationship between society-specific regulatable and process variables should be dismissed. On the contrary, such research can be a powerful tool in influencing policy decisions. But the motivation for change and influencing policy decisions should not be confused with the motivation of uncovering basic environmental processes responsible for developmental outcomes among children attending child care.

McCartney et al. (1993) observed that although our investigation of the effects of child care is "informed by science," it is "guided by cultural and social values." Our suggestion is that these values become part of our scientific study and our guidance derived not from our social concerns but rather from our commutative scientific-based knowledge.

Peer Interaction Among Infants and Toddlers in Group Settings

In addition to our earlier argument that the definition of quality of care must be reviewed in the context of different social developmental goals, we wish to argue that the prevalence of group care for a growing number of infants and toddlers around the world, provides a precious natural laboratory to investigate a large number of issues pertaining to the early development of peer relations, or peer culture.

The issues to be investigated go beyond the potential harm of early separation from mother to the development of social competence. They even go beyond the investigation of the relationship between caregivers' responsiveness and the quality of peer interaction, or length of child-care experience and social competence. One can draw on the existing theory and research of the early social and cognitive development of infants and toddlers to investigate group processes, such as joint peer play, as precursors of the development of such social skills as forming joint themes of reference with peers. One can further investigate issues related to the establishing of leadership or friendship among these young children and examine the effects of specific dimensions in the child-care environment on this development.

The fact that different cultures have different values attached to the impact of peer culture, makes this yet another valuable area for cross-cultural investigation. Such an investigation should start by defining the particular cultural values that set the developmental goals for child care in the area of peer relations. It should then investigate the processes in the child-care setting that contribute to the achievement of the culture-specific goals and how these interact with family processes and individual characteristics of children attending child care.

Growing Up in Two Socializing Worlds

This study has only touched on a very limited aspect of this dual socialization. If one is to accept the fact that the next few generations of young children will be reared simultaneously in at least two socializing worlds, with different childrearing goals and contexts, one should shift from an examination of "which environment is better" or "which contributes more" to the child's development, to a systematic study of how this dual socialization affects children's future development as well as their current life and well-being (Dencik, 1989; Scarr & Eisenberg, 1993). Several implications for future research can be derived from our analysis.

Different Socialization Contexts

Acknowledging the fact that different socialization contexts may have different goals, structures, and childrearing practices, led us to the realization that not every dimension that contributes to quality care in the home is necessarily relevant to the definition of quality in the child-care setting. Because of contextual differences between the two environments, certain environmental features that are character-istic of a "good" home may have more ambiguous effects when they characterize a child-care setting (Rosenthal & Zur, 1993).

Observations made in Japan, for example, suggest that when the different goals of childrearing at home and in child care are clearly articulated, the differences in criteria for quality of care in the two environments are clarified as well. Thus, the criteria for a quality home environment may be defined in terms of the goal of establishing a nurturant and intimate relationship between mother and child. However, the criteria for child care may be defined in terms of it contribution to the child's adjustment to the group (Tobin et al., 1989).

A cross-cultural comparison of the lives of infants and toddlers moving back and forth between the socialization worlds of home and child care, is likely to contribute to our understanding of the relation between the goals, structure, and practices in the two childrearing settings in different cultures. Within such a research framework, one should also explore the childrearing beliefs of the two socialization agents in relation to the different goals assigned by the society to the two childrearing contexts.

We further conclude that a more articulated definition of the concept of a *childrearing context* is needed. Such a definition must transcend the dichotomy of *home* and *day care*. Our work in FDC alerted us to the possibility that the structure of childrearing contexts may differ along dimensions such as home versus institution like environment or along a dimension that defines the role of the caregiver varying from mother substitute to a professional educator. Thus, the sponsored FDC setting can be seen as a child-care context that is more homelike than a day-care center, yet more institutional than a family home. Our data showed that the beliefs of mothers and FDC caregivers differ as a result of differences in the childrearing contexts. The caregivers' beliefs can be described as occupying some middle point between those of mothers and those of a professional educator.

It is suggested, therefore, that future research explore the conceptual dimensions that will be useful in describing differences between various childrearing contexts.

The Relationship Between Home and Child Care

Our study touched on a number of issues related to this relation. It first deals with the correspondence between characteristics of the two settings. The data suggest that research into the relation between the two socializing worlds should go beyond uncovering, what might be society-specific, correlations between family and child-care characteristics. Thus, for example, the center-selectivity phenomenon does not seem to characterize the Israeli society. Very few associations were found, if any, between the quality of care in the FDC homes and families of children attending them.

The correspondence between home and child care may be a result not only of policy decisions but also of processes of mutual perception, evaluation, and adaptation between parents and caregivers in child care. Future research can explore such processes, and clarify the role of conflicts or of mutual adaptation between home and child care. Research can also examine how these may effect children's behavior in each context and/or their transitions between the different childrearing contexts.

Second, the study also relates to the similarity, or dissimilarity, between the two settings, comparing the childrearing beliefs of the two main agents and their implied values, goals, and practices. It further examines the implication of the degree of similarity to the question of continuity, or discontinuity, in the daily experiences of children moving back and forth between these settings. The data suggest that even in the case of FDC, where the two environments have some common features, the differences in contexts of care result in dissimilarity in their childrearing.

It has been suggested that discontinuity between these two socializing worlds is most likely inherent in the contextual differences between them. In spite of the discontinuity between the two settings, children's performance in FDC showed no sign of greater distress or disorganization when their mothers and the caregivers had different developmental expectations or held any other different beliefs. Although very little is known about the parameters determining the ease with which a child can negotiate the transitions between the discontinuous settings, common observations of children in child care suggest that most children negotiate them quite easily. Consequently, it is suggested that instead of searching for the impossible continuity or for the negative effects of discontinuity, one should begin to investigate in a more systematic way the processes that facilitate, or limit, the child's ability to negotiate the daily shifts between these worlds. For example, can clear "markers" of the two settings (specific clothing, ritualized routines) facilitate the transition and reduce potential confusion for the young child?

In general, our data suggests that even at this young age children distinguish between the two childrearing environments and their different expectations, and use to their advantage the different opportunities offered by each setting. Another line of investigation could thus focus on how children utilize the different experiences offered by each setting to their best developmental advantages. One example is the investigation of the development of secure attachment at home and in child care, and the ability of children to utilize a relationship with a responsive and sensitive caregiver to compensate for an insecure attachment with mother. Other examples include the way children utilize an enriched child-care setting to compensate for a disadvantaged home setting.

The Interface of Child, Family, and Child-Care Characteristics

There is a growing recognition that the study of children reared both at home and in child care should take into account the interface between the two environments and the personal characteristics of children.

There is no comprehensive theory of the behavior and development of children in child care from which one could derive specific hypotheses concerning which aspects of family life are expected to interact with which elements in child care and with which personal characteristics of children. Nor is there a theory as to which of these mutual influences are linear and direct, and which are indirect or possibly even circular. All research to date in this area has been exploratory and focused on the empirical identification of relevant predictors of developmental outcomes from among variables describing the child, the home, and the child-care setting.

Various studies may indeed uncover single best predictors or a very powerful combination of predictors, or find that a specific predictor explains more of the variance than other predictors. The ability to generalize from such findings, however, will remain specific to the society and population sampled, and the predictor and outcome measures employed. Their contribution may be important for the specific society in which the study is done and very relevant to policy negotiations in that society. But their contribution to our basic understanding of the

relationship between dimensions defining child-care quality and child development or the interrelatedness between child, family, and child-care effects, is limited.

It is much more likely, however, that this empirically based exploration may not
result in very powerful predictive multivariate equations because of some unknown
confounding effects of the interrelationships among the variables selected to
represent child, family, and child-care influences (McCartney, 1993; Scarr, 1993).

It is, therefore, suggested that future research shift from attempts to find "the
best predictor" or "the best combination of predictors" to a carefully planned,
systematic, and theoretically based, cross-cultural investigation of the interrelationship between child, family, child-care, and societal characteristics in their impact
on the development of children in child care.

10

Child-Care Policy

POLICY, STANDARDS, AND THE EXPERIENCES OF CHILDREN IN ISRAELI FDC

Child-care policy determines the standards most relevant to the quality of a child-care setting, and ultimately to the behavior and development of children. These relations are not always linear and may be at times interdependent and possibly even circular.

Our study investigated two major sets of regulatable standards that were directly determined, or indirectly influenced, by the social policy developed for the Israeli-sponsored FDC system. The first set refers to the required qualifications of the service providers: coordinators and caregivers. The second set refers to regulations that determine the caregivers' work environment. In the following section we summarize our findings that may be relevant to issues of child-care policy.

Standards Concerning the Qualification of the Service Providers

The FDC policy specifies the minimal level of education and preservice training required of caregivers. It also gives preference to more experienced caregivers. The data suggest that, as is the case in a number of other studies, the caregiver's experience in caring for her own, or other, children had very little relevance, if any, to the quality of care she provided in her home or to her childrearing beliefs.

The research literature suggests that in order for training to have an effect on the quality of care offered by caregivers it has to be more substantial and longer than the training required by the Israeli-sponsored FDC system (Arnett, 1989; Howes, Whitebook, & Phillips, 1992). Our data indeed show that altogether the short required training had relatively little impact on either beliefs or the quality of care.

139

However, this short training may have slightly improved the experiences of children in this setting. Even though individualized care seems to be a more frequent norm among the autonomous and better educated caregivers, it is the caregivers with more preservice training who seem to associate better quality care with group activities. We found that caregivers with somewhat longer training engaged more frequently with the children as a group and expected later development of social, but not cognitive, skills than the caregivers with less training. Children attending the homes of caregivers with such expectations and these modes of interaction, tended to play more competently with objects and have more positive exchanges with peers than children in the homes of caregivers with earlier expectation and less frequent group interaction.

Most caregivers in this study had between 8 and 12 years of formal education. It is interesting to note that even within this narrow range the better educated caregiver seem to have more internal locus of control, attributing less importance to maturation and more to environmental factors and influence over the child's development. She tends to be less restrictive and engages less frequently in group interaction with the children. However, the children in the care of caregivers with more years of education do not necessarily have better daily experiences than those in the care of less educated caregivers. This suggests that higher levels of education are required for caregivers' education to actually have an effect on children's experiences in child care.

Only nine coordinators participated in this study. Their professional backgrounds and experiences were quite varied, yet all of them had graduate studies related to early childhood. Because of their small number and great variability, it was not possible to conduct statistical analyses on the effects their backgrounds might have had on the daily experiences of children in the FDC programs that they operated. The data concerning the caregivers' work environment may help in formulating some conclusions concerning the coordinator's qualifications.

Standards Concerning the Caregivers' Work Environment

The FDC policy determined several aspects of the caregivers' work environment. The policy required the sponsoring agencies to provide supportive in-service supervision and allow caregivers a certain level of autonomy assured caregivers of a certain level of professional support. The child placement policy determined the group size, the ages of children in the group, and the SES background of their parents.

The caregiver's work environment had greater influence on her behavior and the quality of care she offered than on her beliefs.

The professional support given to the caregiver by the organization is related to the provision of a better physical environment, more varied toys, a better organized and less crowded space as well as a higher proportion of educational activities and more frequent positive interaction between caregivers and children (M. Rosenthal, 1990). Even though these caregivers, like the better educated ones, were less likely to engage in group interaction with the children, their behavior was related, on the whole, to positive daily experiences of children. It seems that the professional support and empowerment of the caregivers by their organization might have influenced their professional orientation (Jorde-Bloom, 1989) and thereby the quality of care they offered. Because of the great uniformity in caregivers' wages and duration of employment as an FDC provider, this study does not inform us as to their effects on professional satisfaction or burn-out.

In addition, the caregivers' behaviors were related to group characteristics such as the ages and family backgrounds of the children for whom they provided care. Because of the relatively uniform group size, this study does not allow any conclusion concerning optimal or maximal group size.

The best quality of interaction between caregivers and children is found in groups where the difference between youngest and oldest child is between 13 and 24 months (M. Rosenthal, 1990). When the group was fairly age homogeneous and the children were mostly less than 2 years old, the caregivers usually offered a poorer quality physical environment, fewer educationally oriented interactions, less frequent group interaction, and were more restrictive, than caregivers caring for children ages 2–3 in more age-heterogeneous groups. The children in these groups tended in turn to engage less frequently in fine motor play, have fewer positive peer interactions, and were somewhat more frequently emotionally distressed.

The parents' SES was also related to the caregivers' behavior. Caregivers caring for a group of predominantly higher SES children tended to provide more frequent educational activities, which supposedly counteracted some of the tendency of these children to engage in aimless activity and increased the likelihood of their engagement in joint peer play. The value of the general policy of creating SES-heterogeneous groups is highlighted by those cases where because of the demographic nature of some neighborhoods, the policy could not be implemented and groups were fairly homogeneous. A high percentage of children from socially distressed families had a detrimental effect on the quality of interaction between caregivers and children. The children in these groups spent more time in emotional distress (M. Rosenthal, 1990).

IMPLICATION FOR CHILD-CARE POLICY

The results of our analysis of the Israeli-sponsored FDC system suggest several regulatable conditions that may improve the quality of care provided in any child-care program.

The Qualifications of Caregivers and Coordinators

The data suggest that selection criteria need not refer to the caregivers' age, number of children, or experience in working with children in child care. As many North American studies found (e.g., Howes, Whitebook, & Phillips, 1992), the most important qualifications are the caregivers' education and training. Our findings imply, however, that for education and training to have a meaningful positive effect on the daily experiences of children in FDC, caregivers should have higher level of education and/or longer training. In addition, we suggest that both the content and structure of the caregivers' training should be examined. The training should provide them with a systematic knowledge base concerning child development and education and the skills they need in order to provide quality care in their homes. It should further address their childrearing belief system and match it with the values and goals set for child care in the society at large (Holloway et al., 1988).

The findings suggest that advanced knowledge of early childhood development and care, as well as supervisory skills, are mandatory for all coordinators of FDC programs so that they can provide the in-service supervision and support as well as enhance their ability to meet the specific needs of different children. This conclusion holds for any trainer or supervisor of teachers in any child-care system.

The Caregivers' Work Environment

It is suggested that a license to operate an FDC program should be given only to an organization that provides its caregivers with frequent, regular, and supportive supervision coupled with sufficient autonomy. Both these factors take into account and attribute importance to the professional identity of the caregivers and thus support them as responsible caregiving agents. Such support might be important for all caregivers in every child-care program, but seems essential for these basically untrained caregivers with a low education level.

In general, this study seems to show that quality of care may improve when a group has at least some higher SES children and some that are older toddlers. The findings concerning the effects of children's SES suggest that attention be given to SES heterogeneity of the group. An FDC group of five children with one caregiver should not include more than one child from a socially distressed family and should have parents of varied education levels. In addition, the findings suggest that caregivers need further guidance as to how to adapt their program to the developmental needs of children of parents of higher education level so as to allow for more active and competent engagement of these children with the environment she offers in her home.

The data also imply that the standard of mixed ages should be more carefully regulated especially when care is provided to very young children (Whaley & Kantor, 1992). The age mix should be moderate, of about 18 months between youngest and oldest child in the group. They further suggest that these caregivers may need more guidance in how to provide educationally valuable experiences to infants and toddlers under the age of 2.

CULTURAL VALUES AND CHILD-CARE POLICY

Child care in different countries has been designed to meet similar general needs such as facilitating maternal employment, or providing welfare and education. Cultural variations among child-care services reflect, however, basic differences in cultural values, social ideology, and attitudes (Lamb et al., 1992). A meaningful cross-cultural comparison of child care as well as a better understanding of the role of child care in any given society requires an articulation of the relations between political system, cultural beliefs and ideology, and child care (Sigel, 1992).

Our analysis points to some important differences in values and ideology, between the Israeli and North American cultures. Several investigators have proposed that it is the Anglo-Saxon valuation of individualism and individual freedom that may be at the base of the social belief that childrearing is the responsibility of the family. Countries such as the United States, Canada, and the United Kingdom are reluctant to create a national system of preschool or to provide the mechanism for universal support of such systems (Bronfenbrenner, 1992; Kamerman & Kahn, 1978).

The cultural values and beliefs at the basis of Israeli child-care policy, stand in contrast to those of the English-speaking countries. The commitment of the Israeli society to preschool education and to some extent also to its day-care system, reflect the overall goal of cultural survival and the value of community cohesion rather than the value of individualism. These values are at the basis of the belief in shared community responsibility for the rearing and education of its young.

The belief in community responsibility is reflected in the national system of preschool education and in the government's support of the establishment of a growing number of day-care facilities. This community responsibility has been interpreted differently in regard to the preschool and the day-care systems. The goal of "acculturation," however, with its clear educational implication, has been historically set for the preschool system only, whereas day care was seen as mostly providing family support. The main concern for day care, therefore, is to provide parents with a sufficient number of affordable public day-care facilities. Attention is given to pleasant physical settings, suitable equipment and play materials, nutrition, and elementary safety measures. There is relatively little awareness, however, on part of policymakers as well as parents, of what constitutes an appropriate program for infants and toddlers.

Furthermore, there are some interesting cultural differences in the attitudes of mothers to child care in the Israeli and North American societies. A majority of Israeli mothers of toddlers and many mothers of infants, opt to send their children into some form of group setting, in many cases, regardless of economic necessity or employment, suggests that they have little anxiety about the potential ill effects of early separation. The reasons mothers give for their decision to send their child into a group care setting suggest that they have no qualms about using child care to obtain some free time for their own needs. In addition, they believe that early group experience is important for the social development of the child. They seem to place a greater value on their child's independence and peer relation than on the attachment to mother. This attitude is more prevalent among mothers who were born, or reared, in Israel than among those who immigrated to Israel from other countries.

These attitudes of parents led to relatively little public concern for issues of regulatable standards that our study and worldwide research found related to the quality of care and to developmental outcome. Thus, even policymakers who expect day care to provide enrichment to socially underprivileged children, and contribute to their acculturation into the norms of the society, show no awareness of the fact that some minimal regulatable conditions, such as group size and caregiver training, must exist for such enrichment to occur.

Our analysis points to some serious gaps between some of the cultural values, goals set for early education and the Israeli child-care policy. We believe that such gaps occur in many other societies and should be understood in terms of conflicting values and inconsistent social goals.

This analysis has led us to two major conclusions. First, child-care policy must be consonant with the history, socioeconomic conditions, and social and educational goals of a given culture. Policymakers must, therefore, articulate the various social goals set for child care and design their child-care services and training of their caregivers accordingly. If the main goal is to provide affordable child care for every family, then the concern for quantity supersedes that of quality of care. In that case, educational goals and early intervention to overcome the effects of social disadvantage become a secondary concern. If, however, child care is to meet goals beyond that of family support, attention must be given to the quality of care issue in addition to the sheer availability of affordable out-of-home care. Whatever the goals are, the regulatable standards should match them, defining the key aspects of the quality of care offered in any given culture.

Second, regardless of the target needs that child care is designed to address, be it the educational needs of young children or maternal employment, the point of view of its policy should be systemic. The policy should consider the wider social support available to these children and their family. Considerations of the availability of early detection of developmental delay, of services for children with special needs, and the educationally oriented training of caregivers should be integrated into a child-care policy that attempts to meet the educational needs of young children. Similarly, consideration of the availability of paid or job-guaranteed maternity leave, unemployment benefits, and other family supports, should be integrated into a policy designed to meet the needs of families with young children (Scarr & Eisenberg, 1993). The policy should recognize the inherent contextual differences between childrearing at home and in child care and should enable children and families to utilize the best each setting can offer.

Finally, one last comment regarding the relationship between research and child-care policy. Our saddening experience with the attempt to modify policy decisions in the light of research has data taught us that the data can only be useful when it is consistent with the dominant cultural, social, or political goal of the policymaker. It can be harnessed to pull weight in arguments and debates over conflicting goals but cannot as such change these goals.

References

Anderson, C. W., Nagel, R. J., Roberts, W. A., & Smith, J. W. (1981). Attachment to substitute caregivers as a function of centre quality and caregiver involvement. *Child Development, 52,* 53–61.

Arnett, J. (1989). Caregivers in day care centers: Does training matter? *Journal of Applied Developmental Psychology, 10,* 541–552.

Auerbach, J., Lerner, Y., Barasch, M., & Palti, H. (1992). Maternal and environmental characteristics as predictors of child behavior problems and cognitive competence. *American Journal of Orthopsychiatry, 62*(3), 409–420.

Baer, H., & Marcus, Y. (1977). *Day care: A social service for mothers and children.* Jerusalem: Applied Social Research Institute.

Bates, B. C. (1972). *Effect of density on the behavior of nursery school children.* Eugene: University of Oregon Center for Environmental Research.

Baumrind, D. (1967). Child care practices anteceding three patterns of preschool behavior. *Genetic Psychology Monographs, 75,* 43–88.

Baumrind, D. (1971). Current patterns of parental authority. *Developmental Psychology Monograph, 4*(1), 1–103.

Baydar, N., & Brooks-Gunn, J. (1991). Effects of maternal employment and child-care arrangements on preschoolers' cognitive and behavioral outcomes: Evidence from the children of the National Longitudinal Survey of Youth. Special section data and analyses on developmental psychology. *Developmental Psychology, 27,* 932–945.

Belsky, J. (1984). Two waves of day-care research: Developmental effects and conditions of quality. In R. Ainslie (Ed.), *The child and the day-care setting: Qualitative variations and development* (pp. 1–34). New York: Praeger.

Belsky, J. (1986). Infant day care and socioemotional development: The U.S. *Journal of Child Psychology & Psychiatry, 29*(4), 397–406.

Belsky, J., & Rovine, M. (1988). Non-maternal care in the first year of life and infant–parent attachment security. *Child Development, 59,* 157–167.

Bentwich, J. S. (1965). *Education in Israel.* London: Routledge & Kegan.

Bergman, R. (1979). *Problems and needs of working women during and after maternity leave.* Tel Aviv: University of Tel Aviv.

Berk, L. (1985). Relationship of educational attainment, child oriented attitudes, job satisfaction, and career commitment to caregiver's behavior towards children. *Child Care Quarterly, 14,* 103–129.

145

Booth, A. E. (1992). *Child care in the 1990s: Trends and consequences.* Hillsdale, NJ: Lawrence Erlbaum Associates.

Brenner, J., & Mueller, E. (1982). Shared meaning in boy toddlers' peer relations. *Child Development, 53,* 380–391.

Bronfenbrenner, U. (1970). *Two worlds of childhood: U.S. and U.S.S.R.* New York: Russel Sage Foundation.

Bronfenbrenner, U. (1979a). Contexts of child rearing: Problems and prospects. *American Psychologist, 34,* 844–850.

Bronfenbrenner, U. (1979b). *The ecology of human development.* Cambridge MA: Harvard University Press.

Bronfenbrenner, U. (1992). Child care in the Anglo-Saxon mode. In M. E. Lamb, K. J. Sternberg, C. Hwang, & A. G. Broberg (Eds.), *Child care in context: Cross-cultural perspectives* (pp. 281–292). Hillsdale, NJ: Lawrence Erlbaum Associates.

Bronson, W. C. (1975). Peer–peer interactions in the second year of life. In M. Lewis & L.A. Rosenblum (Eds.), *Friendship and peer relations* (pp. 131–152). New York: Wiley.

Brownell, C. A. (1982). *Effects of age and age-mix on toddler peer interaction.* Paper presented at the International Conference on Infant Studies, Austin, TX.

Bryant, B., Harris, M., & Newton, D. (1984). *Children and minders.* Oxford: Grant McIntyre.

Budwig, N., Strage, A., & Bamberg, M. (1986). The construction of joint activities with an age-mate: The transition from caregiver–child to peer play. In J. Cook-Gumperz, J. Streeck, & W. A. Corsaro (Eds.), *Children's worlds and children's language* (pp. 83–108). New York: Monton de Gruyter.

Bugental, D. B., & Shennum, W. A. (1984). "Difficult" children as elicitors and targets of adult communication patterns: An attributional-behavioral transactional analysis. *Monographs of the Society for Research in Child Development, 49*(1) 205.

Carew, J. (1980). Experience and the development of intelligence. *Monographs of the Society for Research in Child Development, 45*(183), 1–2.

Cassidy, J. (1986). The ability to negotiate the environment: An aspect of infant competence as related to quality of attachment. *Child Development, 57,* 331–337.

Clarke-Stewart, K. A. (1973). Interactions between mothers and their young children: Characteristics and consequences. *Monographs of the Society for Research in Child Development, 38*(153).

Clarke-Stewart, K. A. (1987a). In search of consistencies in child care research. In D. Phillips (Ed.), *Quality in child care: What does research tell us?* (pp. 105–120). Washington, DC: NAEYC.

Clarke-Stewart, K. A. (1987b). Predicting child development from child care forms and features: The Chicago study. In D. Phillips (Ed.), *Quality in child care: What does research tell us?* (pp. 21–41). Washington, DC: NAEYC.

Clarke-Stewart, K. A. (1989). Infant day care: Maligned or malignant? *American Psychologist, 44,* 266–273.

Clarke-Stewart, K. A. (1992). Consequences of child care for children's development. In A. Booth (Ed.), *Child care in the 1990s: Trends and consequences* (pp. 63–82). Hillsdale, NJ: Lawrence Erlbaum Associates.

Clarke-Stewart, K. A., & Fein, G. G. (1983). Early childhood programs. In P. H. Mussen (Series Ed.) & M. Haith & J. Campos (Vol. Eds.), *Handbook of child psychology: Vol. 2. Infancy and developmental psychobiology* (pp. 917–999). New York: Wiley.

Clarke-Stewart, K. A., & Gruber, C. (1984). Day care forms and features. In R. Ainslie (Ed.), *The child and the day care setting: Qualitative variations and development* (pp. 35-62). New York: Praeger.

Clarke-Stewart, K. A., Gruber, C. P., & Fitzgerald, L. M. (1994). *Children at home and in day care.* Hillsdale, NJ: Lawrence Erlbaum Associates.

Cochran, M. (1977). A comparsion of group day care and family child rearing patterns in Sweden. *Child Development, 48,* 702–707.

Cochran, M. (1985). The parental empowerment process: Building on family strengths. In J. Harris (Ed.), *Child psychology in action: Linking research and practice* (pp. 12–33). London: Croom Helm.

Cochran, M. (1988). Parental empowerment in family matters: Lessons learned from a research program. In D. R. Powell (Ed.), *Parent education as early childhood intervention* (pp. 23–50). Norwood, NJ: Ablex.

Cochran, M. M., & Robinson, J. (1983). Day care, family circumstances and sex differences in children. In S. Kilmer (Ed.), *Advances in early education and day care* (Vol. 3, pp. 46–67). Greenwich, CT: JAI Press.

Cohen, J., & Cohen, P. (1983). *Applied multiple regression/correlation analysis for the behavioral sciences.* Hillsdale, NJ: Lawrence Erlbaum Associates.

Dencik, L. (1989). Growing up in the post-modern age: On the child's situation in the modern family, and on the position of the family in the modern Welfare state. *Acta Sociologica, 32*(2), 155–180.

Dencik, L., Langsted, O., & Sommer, D. (1989). Modern childhood in the Nordic countries: Material, social and cultural aspects. In B. Elgaard, O. Langsted & D. Sommer (Ed.), *Research on socialization of young children in the Nordic countries* (pp. 1–30). Aarhus, Denmark: Aarhus University Press.

Dix, T. H., & Grusec, J. (1985). Parent attribution processes in the socialization of children. In I. E. Sigel (Ed.), *Parental beliefs systems* (pp. 201–233). Hillsdale, NJ: Lawrence Erlbaum Associates.

Dubler, N. D. (1974). *Day care in Israel: The politics of playgrounds.* Unpublished report.

Eckerman, C. O., & Whatley, J. L. (1977). Toys and social interaction between infant peers. *Child Development, 48,* 1645–1650.

Elardo, R., Bradley, R., & Caldwell, B. (1977). A longitudinal study of the relationship. *Child Development, 48,* 593–603.

Emiliani, F., Zani, B., & Carugati, F. (1981). From staff interaction strategies to social representations of adults in a day nursery. In W. P. Robinson (Ed.), *Communication in development* (pp. 89–107). London: Academic Press.

Everson, M. D., Saranat, S. L., & Ambron S. R. (1984). Day care and early socialization: The role of maternal attitude. *The child and the day care setting: Qualitative variations and development* (pp. 63–97). New York: Praeger.

Fagot, B. (1980). *The maintenance of aggression in toddlers.* Paper presented at the meetings of the International Conference on Infant Studies, New Haven, CT.

Feagans, L. V. (Chairperson). (1992). *Infant daycare and developmental/behavioral outcomes: The effects of interaction among quality of care, family functioning, illness, and temperament.* Symposium at the eighth International Conference on Infant Studies, Miami Beach, FL.

Fein, G. G., & Clarke-Stewart, K. A. (1973). *Day care in context.* New York: Wiley.

Feldman, S. S., & Yirmiya, N. (1986). Perceptions of childrearing roles: A study of Israeli mothers and caregivers in town and kibbutz. *International Journal of Psychology, 21,* 153–166.

Field, T. (1991). Quality infant day care and grade school behavior and performance. *Child Development, 62,* 863–870.

Field, T., Masi, W., Goldstein, D., Perry, S., & Parl, S. (1988). Infant day-care facilitates pre-school behavior. *Early Childhood Research Quarterly, 55,* 1308–1316.

Frankel, D. G., & Roer-Bornstein, D. (1982). Traditional and modern contributions to changing infant-rearing ideologies of two ethnic communities. *Monographs of the Society for Research in Child Development, 47* (4, serial no.196).

Gamble, T. J., & Zigler, E. (1986). Effects of infant day care: another look at the evidence. *American Journal of Orthopsychiatry, 56,* 26–42.

Garvey, C. (1977). *Play.* Cambridge, MA: Harvard University Press.

Goelman, H., & Pence, A. (1987). Effects of child care, family and individual chracteristics on children's language development: The Victoria day care research project. In D. Phillips (Ed.), *Quality in child care: What does research tell us?* (pp. 89–104). Washington DC: NAEYC.

Goelman, H., Rosenthal, M. K., & Pence, A. R. (1990). Family day care in two countries: Parents, caregivers and children in Canada and Israel. *Child and Youth Care Quarterly, 14*(4), 251–270.

Golden, M., Rosenbluth, L., Grossi, M. T., & Freeman, H. (1978). *The New York City infant day care study.* New York: Medical and Health Research Association of New York.

Goodnow, J. J. (1984). Parents' ideas about parenting and development: A review of issues and recent work. In M. E. Lamb, A. L. Brown, B. Rogoff (Eds.), *Advances in developmental psychology* (Vol. 3, pp. 193–242). Hillsdale, NJ: Lawrence Erlbaum Associates.

Goodnow, J. J. (1988). Parents' ideas, actions, and feelings: Models and methods from developmental and social psychology. *Child Development, 59,* 286–320.

Goodnow, J. J., Cashmore, J., Cotton, S., & Knight, R. (1984). Mothers' developmental timetables in two cultural groups. *International Journal of Psychology, 19,* 193–205.

148

References

Greenberger, E., & O'Neil, R. (1992). Maternal employment and perceptions of young children: Bronfenbrenner et al. revisited. *Child Development, 63,* 431–448.

Gross, M. B. (1970). Israeli disadvantaged. *Teachers College Record, 72,* 105–110.

Harms, T., & Clifford, R. M. (1980). *Early childhood environment rating scale.* New York: Teachers College Press.

Harms, T., & Clifford, R. M. (1984). *The family day care rating scale.* New York: Teachers College Press.

Haskins, R. (1985). Public aggression among children with varying day-care experience. *Child Development, 57,* 698–703.

Haskins, R. (1989). Beyond metaphor: The efficacy of early childhood education. *American Psychologist, 44,* 274–282.

Henry, M. B. (1992). *An in-service program in family day care: Supporting the development of young children and their care providers.* Doctoral thesis presented to The University of Queensland, Brisbane, Australia.

Hess, R. D., Dickson, W. R., Price, G. G., & Leong, D. Y. (1979). Some contrasts between mothers and preschool teachers in interacting with four-year-old children. *American Educational Research Journal, 16,* 307–316.

Hess, R. D., Kashiwagi, K., Azuma, H., Park, G. G., & Dickson, W. P. (1980). Maternal expectations for mastery of developmental tasks in Japan and the USA. *International Journal of Psychology, 15,* 259–271.

Hess, R. D., Price, G. P., Dickson, W. R., & Conroy, M. (1981). Different roles for mothers and teachers: Contrasting styles of child care. In S. Kilmer (Ed.), *Advances in early education and day care* (Vol. 2, pp. 1–28). London: JAI Press.

Hock, E. (1984). The transition to day care: Effects of maternal separation anxiety on infant adjustment. In R. Ainslie (Ed.), *The child and the day care setting: Qualitative variations and development* (pp. 183–206). New York: Praeger.

Hock, E., DeMeis, D., & McBride, S. (1988). Maternal anxiety: Its role in the balance of employment and motherhood in mothers of infants. In A. E. Gottfried & A. W. Gottfried (Eds.), *Maternal employment and children's development: Longitudinal research* (pp. 192–212). New York: Plenum.

Hoffman, M. L. (1975). Moral internalization, parental power and the nature of parent–child interaction. *Developmental Psychology, 11,* 228–239.

Holloway, S. D., Gorman, K. S., & Fuller, B. (1988). Child rearing beliefs within diverse social structures: Mothers and day care providers in Mexico. *International Journal of Psychology, 23,* 303–317.

Holloway, S. D., & Reichart-Erickson, M. (1989). Child-care quality, family structure, and maternal expectations: Relationship to preschool children's peer relations. *Journal of Applied Developmental Psychology, 10,* 281–298.

Howes, C. (1980). Peer play scale as an index of complexity of peer interaction. *Developmental Psychology, 16,* 371–372.

Howes, C. (1983). Caregiver behavior in center and family day care. *Journal of Applied Developmental Psychology, 4,* 99–107.

Howes, C. (1986). *Keeping current in child care research: An annotated bibiliography.* Washington DC: National Association for the Education of Young Children.

Howes, C. (1987). Social competence with peers in young children: Developmental sequences. *Developmental Review, 7,* 252–272.

Howes, C. (1988a). Relations between early child care and schooling. *Developmental Psychology, 24,* 53–57.

Howes, C. (1988b). Peer interaction of young children. *Monographs of the Sociey for Research in Child Development, 53*(1, Serial No. 217).

Howes, C., & Farver, J. (1987). Toddler's responses to the distress of their peers. *Journal of Applied Developmental Psychology, 8,* 441–452.

Howes, C., & Hamilton, C. E. (1992). Children's relationships with caregivers: Mothers and child care teachers. *Child Development, 63,* 859–866.

Howes, C., & Olenick, M. (1986). Family and daycare influences on toddlers' compliance. *Child Development, 57,* 202–216.

Howes, C., Phillips, D. A., & Whitebook, M. (1992). Thresholds of quality: Implications for the social development of children in center-based child care. *Child Development, 63,* 449–460.

Howes, C., & Stewart, P. (1987). Child's play with adults, toys and peers: An examination of family and child care influences. *Developmental Psychology, 23,* 423–430.

Howes, C., Whitebook, M., & Phillips, D. (1992). Teacher characteristics and effective teaching in child care: Findings from the National Child Care Staffing Study. *Child and Youth Care Forum, 21*(6), 399–414.

Ispa, J. M., & Thornburg, K. R. (1993). *Continuity between parents and family child care providers: Does it matter?* Paper presented at the annual meeting of the Society for Research in Child Development, New Orleans, LA.

Israel Ministry of Education and Culture. (1974). *Report and recommendations of the Committee for Training Day Care Staff.* Jerusalem: Author.

Israel Ministry of Education and Culture. (1989). Administration of economics and budgets. *The Education System in the Mirror of Numbers (Hebrew).* Jerusalem: Author.

Israel Ministry of Labor and Social Affairs. (1987). *Children in Israel.* Jerusalem: Central Library of Social Work.

Israel Ministry of Labor and Social Affairs. (1989). *Women in the labor force.* Jerusalem: Author.

Jackson, B., & Jackson, S. (1979). *Childminder: A study in action research.* London: Routledge & Kegan Paul.

Jacobson, J. L. (1981). The role of inanimate objects in early peer interaction. *Child Development, 52,* 618–626.

Jaffe, E. D. (1982). *Child welfare in Israel.* New York: Praeger.

Jencks, C. (1972). *Inequality: A reassessment of the effect of family and schooling in America.* New York: Basic Books.

Johnson, J. E., Ershler, J., & Bell, C. (1980). Play behavior in a discovery-based and a formal education preschool program. *Child Development, 51,* 271–274.

Johnson, M. (1935). The effect on behavior of variation in amount of play equipment. *Child Development, 6,* 56–58.

Jorde-Bloom, P. (1989). Professional orientation: Individual and organizational perspectives. *Child and Youth Care Quarterly, 18*(4), 227–242.

Kahn, A. J., & Kamerman, S. B. (1987). *Child care: Facing the hard choices.* Dover, MA: Auburn House.

Kamerman, S. B., & Kahn, A. J. (1978). *Family policy: Government and families in fourteen countries.* New York: Columbia University Press.

Kaplan, M. G., & Conn, J. S. (1984). The effect of caregiver's training on classroom setting and caregiver performance in eight community day care centers. *Child Study Journal, 14,* 79–83.

Katz, L. (1980). Mothering and teaching: Some significant distinctions. In L. Katz (Ed.), *Current topics in early childhood education* (Vol. 3, pp. 47–63). Norwood, NJ: Ablex.

Kipp, E. K. (1992). *Illness and temperament as mediators of goodness of fit in infant daycare.* Paper presented at the International Conference on Infant Studies, Miami Beach, FL.

Kleinberger, A. F. (1969). *Society, schools and progress in Israel.* London: Pergamon Press.

Knight, R. A. & Goodnow, J. J. (1988). Parents' beliefs about influence over cognitive and social development. *International Journal of Behavioral Development, 11*(4), 517–527.

Kochanska, G. S., Radke-Yarrow, M., Kuczynski, L. & Friedman, S. L. (1987). Normal and affectively ill mothers' beliefs about their children. *American Journal of Orthopsychiatry, 57,* 345–350.

Kontos, S. (1984). Congruence of parent and early childhood staff perceptions of parenting. *Parenting Studies, 1,* 5–10.

Kontos, S. (1987). *Day care quality, family background and children's development.* Paper presented at the biennial meeting of the Society of Research in Child Development, Baltimore, MD.

Kontos, S., & Dunn, L. (1989). *Sensitivity of children's development to family and child care influences.* Paper presented at the meeting of the Society for Research in Child Development, Kansas City, MO.

Kontos, S., & Fiene, R. (1987). Child-care quality, compliance with regulations and children's development: The Pennsylvania study. In D. Phillips (Ed.), *Quality in child care: What does research tell us?* (pp. 57–79). Washington, DC: NAEYC.

Kontos, S., & Stremmel, A. J. (1988). Caregiver's perceptions of working conditions in child care environments. *Early Childhood Research Quarterly, 3,* 77–90.

Kontos, S., & Wells, W. (1986). Attitudes of caregivers and the day care experiences of families. *Early Childhood Research Quarterly, 1,* 47–67.

Kontos, S. J. (1991). Child care quality, family background and children's development. *Early Childhood Research Quarterly, 6,* 249–262.

Kraft, I. (1967). A "new man" in the Kibbutz? A review of recent writings on the Israel collective settlements. *Teachers College Record, 68,* 558–595.

Lamb, M. E., Sternberg, K. J., Hwang, C., & Broberg, A. G. (1992). *Child care in context: Cross-cultural perspectives.* Hillsdale, NJ: Lawrence Erlbaum Associates.

Lamb, M. E., Hwang, C., Bookstein, F. L., Broberg, A., Hult, G., & Frodi, M. (1988). Determinants of social competence in Swedish preschoolers. *Developmental Psychology, 24,* 58–70.

Lazar, I., & Darlington, R. (1982). Lasting effects of early childhood education: A report from the consortium for longitudinal studies. *Monographs of the Society for Research in Child Development, 47*(2-3, Serial No. 195).

Legendre, A. (1985). *Influence of spatial arrangement on young children's social behavior.* Paper presented at the 19th International Ethological Conference, Toulouse, France.

Levin, G. (1985). *Processes of change in communal early childhood education.* Kiriat Tivon: Oranim at Haifa Universiy.

Lewis, M., Young, G., Brocks, J., & Michalson, L. (1975). The beginning of friendship. In M. Lewis & L. A. Rosenblum (Eds.), *Friendship and peer relations* (pp. 27–66). New York: Wiley.

Lieberman, A. (1977). Preschoolers' competence with peer. *Child Development, 48,* 1277–1287.

Lightfoot, S. L. (1975). Families and schools: Creative conflict or negative dissonance. *Journal of Research and Development in Education, 9,* 34–44.

Livnat, Y. (1971). *Survey of day care centers.* Jerusalem: Prime Minister's Office.

Loeb, R. C. (1975). Concommitants of boys' locus of control examined in parent–child interactions. *Developmental Psychology, 11,* 353–358.

Lombard, A. D. (1973). Early Schooling in Israel. In N. D. Feshbach, J. I. Goodland, & A. Lombard (Eds.), *Early schooling in England and Israel* (pp. 63–102). New York: McGraw Hill.

Long, F., & Garduque, L. (1987). Continuity between home and family day care: Caregivers' and mothers' perceptions and children's social experience. In D. Peters & S. Kontos (Eds.), *Continuity and discontinuity of experience in child care.* Norwood, NJ: Ablex.

Long, R., Peters, D., & Garduque, L. (1985). Continuity between home and day care: A model for defining relevant dimensions of child care. In I. Sigel (Ed.), *Advances in applied developmental psychology* (Vol. 1). Norwood, NJ: Ablex.

Lougee, M. D., Grueneich, R., & Hartup, W. W. (1977). Social interaction in same- and mixed-age dyads of preschool children. *Child Development, 48,* 1353–1361.

Maccoby, E. E., & Jacklin, C. N. (1974). *The psychology of sex differences.* Stanford: Stanford University Press.

Maccoby, E. E., & Martin, J. P. (1983). Socialization in the context of the family: Parent–child interaction. In P. H. Mussen (Series Ed.) & E. M. Hetherington (Vol. Ed.), *Handbook of child psychology: Vol. 4. Socialization, personality, and social development* (4th ed., pp. 1–101). New York: Wiley.

Martin, B. (1975). Parent-child relations. In F. D. Horowitz (Ed.), Review of Child Development Research, Vol. 4. (pp. 463–540). Chicago, IL: University of Chicago Press.

McCartney, K. (1984). Effect of quality of day care environment upon children's language development. *Developmental Psychology, 20,* 244–260.

McCartney, K., Rocheleau, A., Rosenthal, S., & Keefe, N. (1993). *Social development in the context of center-based child care and family factors.* Paper presented at the meeting of the Society for Research in Child Development, New Orleans, LA.

McCartney, K., Scarr, S., Phillips, D., & Grajek, S. (1985). Day care as intervention: Comparisons of varying quality programs. *Journal of Applied Developmental Psychology, 6,* 247–260.

McGillicuddy-DeLisi, A. V. (1980). The role of parental beliefs in the family as a system of mutual influences. *Family Relations, 29,* 317–323.

McGillicuddy-DeLisi, A. V. (1982). Parental beliefs about developmental processes. *Human Development, 25,* 192–200.

McGrew, P. (1970). Social and spatial density effects on spacing behavior in preschool children. *Journal of Child Psychology and Psychiatry, 11,* 197–205.

Melhuish, E. C., & Moss, P. (1991). *Day care for young children: International perspectives.* London: Routledge.

Miller, S. A. (1988). Parents' beliefs about children's cognitive development. *Child Development, 59,* 259–285.

Moss, M. (1987). *A review of childminding research.* London: University of London Institute of Education.

Mueller, E., & Brenner, J. (1977). The origins of social skills and interaction among playgroup toddlers. *Child Development, 48,* 854–861.

Mueller, E., & Lucas, T. (1975). A developmental analysis of peer interaction among toddlers. In M. Lewis & L. A. Rosenblum (Eds.), *Friendship and peer relations* (pp. 223–258). New York: Wiley.

Mueller, E., & Vandell, D. (1979). Infant–infant interaction. In J. D. Osofsky (Ed.), *Handbook of infant development* (pp. 591–622). New York: Wiley.

Nelson, F., & Garduque, L. (1991). The experience and perception of continuity between home and day care from the perspectives of child, mother, and caregiver. *Early Child Development and Care, 68,* 99–111.

Neubauer, P. B. (Ed.). (1965). *Children in collectives, child-rearing aims and practices in the kibbutz.* Springfield, IL: C. C. Thomas.

Newson, J., & Newson, E. (1976). *Seven years old in the home environment.* Harmondsworth: Penguin.

Ninio, A. (1979). The naive theory of the infant and other maternal attitudes in two subgroups in Israel. *Child Development, 50,* 976–980.

Oppenheim, D., Sagi, A., & Lamb, M. (1988). Infant attachment at the kibbutz and their relation to socio-emotional development four years later. *Developmental Psychology, 24,* 427–434.

Pastor, D. (1981). The quality of mother–infant attachment and its relationship to toddlers' sociability with peers. *Developmental Psychology, 17,* 326–335.

Patterson, G. R. (1979). A performance theory for coercive family interaction. In R. B. Cairns (Ed.), *The analysis of social interactions: Methods, issues, and illustrations.* New York: Wiley.

Pence, A. R., & Goelman, H. (1987). Who cares for the child in day care? An examination of caregivers from three types of child care. *Early Childhood Research Quarterly, 2,* 315–334.

Peters, D. B., & Sutton, R. E. (1984). The effects of CDA training on the beliefs, attitudes, and behavior of Head Start personnel. *Child Care Quarterly, 13*(4), 251–261.

Pettygrove, W., Whitebook, M., & Weir, M. (1984). Beyond babysitting: Changing the treatment and image of child caregivers. *Young Children, 39,* 14–21.

Phillips, D., McCartney, K., & Scarr, S. (1987). Child care quality and children's social development. *Developmental Psychology, 23,* 537–543.

Phillips, D., McCartney, K., Scarr, S., & Howes, C. (1987). Selective review of infant day care research: A cause for concern! *Zero to Three, 7*(3), 18–21.

Phillips, D., & Whitebook, M. (1986). Who are child care workers: The search for answers. *Young Children, 41,* 14–20.

Phillips, D. A. (Ed.). (1987). *Quality in child care: What does research tell us?* Washington, DC: NAEYC.

Phillips, D. A., & Howes, C. (1987). Indicators of quality in child care: Review of research. In D. Phillips (Ed.), *Quality in child care: What does research tell us?* (pp. 1–20). Washington, DC: NAEYC.

Powell, R. D. (1980). Toward a socioecological perspective of relations between parents and child care programs. In S. Kilmer (Ed.), *Advances in early education and day care* (Vol. 1, pp. 203–226). Greenwich, CT: JAI Press.

Prescott, E. (1981). Relations between physical setting and adult/child behavior in day care. In S. Kilmer (Ed.), *Advances in early education and day care* (Vol. 2, pp. 129–158). London: JAI Press.

Prescott, E., Kritchevsky, S., & Jones, E. (1972). *The day care environment inventory.* Washington, DC: U.S. Department of Health, Education and Welfare.

Prime Minister's Committee on Children and Youth in Distress. (1973). *Final report* (2nd ed.). Jerusalem: Prime Minister's Office.

Ramey, C., & Campbell, F. (1977). The prevention of developmental retardation in high risk children. In P. Mittler (Ed.), *Research to practice in mental retardation* (Vol. 1, pp. 157–164). Baltimore, MD: University Park Press.

Ramey, C. T., & Haskins, R. (1981). The modification of intelligence through early experience. *Intelligence, 5,* 5–19.

Rogozin, A. (1980). Attachment behavior of day care children: naturalistic and laboratory observations. *Child Development, 51*, 409–415.

Rohe, W., & Patterson, A. H. (1974). The effects of varied level of resources and density on behavior in a day care center. In D. H. Carson (Ed.), *Man–environment interaction*. Milwaukee, WI: EDRA.

Roopnarine, J. L. (1994). Sex-typed socialization in mixed-age preschool classrooms. *Child Development, 55*, 1078–1084.

Rosenthal, D. A. (1984). Inter-generational conflict and culture: A study of immigrant and non-immigrant adolescents and their parents. *Genetic Psychology Monographs, 109*, 53–75.

Rosenthal, M. K. (1988). Child care in Israel: Current status and efforts toward change. *The Networker, 9*(3), 1–6.

Rosenthal, M. K. (1990). Social policy and its effects on the daily experiences of infants and toddlers in family day care in Israel. *Journal of Applied Developmental Psychology, 11*(1), 85–103.

Rosenthal, M. K. (1991a). Behaviors and beliefs of caregivers in family daycare: The effects of background and work environment. *Early Childhood Research Quarterly, 6*(2), 263–283.

Rosenthal, M. K. (1991b). Daily experiences of toddlers in three child care settings in Israel. *Child and Youth Care Forum, 20*(1), 39–60.

Rosenthal, M. K. (1992). Nonparental child care in Israel: A cultural and historical perspective. In M. Lamb, K. Sternberg, C-P. Hwang, & A. Broberg (Eds.), *Child care in context: Cross-cultural perspectives* (pp. 305–330). Hillsdale, NJ: Lawrence Erlbaum Associates.

Rosenthal, M. K. (1993). Social and non-social play of infants and toddlers in family day care. In H. Goelman & E. Jacobs (Eds.), *Children's play in child care settings* (pp. 163–192). Albany, NY: SUNY Press.

Rosenthal, M. K., Biderman, A., & Luppo, M. (1987). The day care standards committee. *Final report* (Hebrew). Jerusalem, Israel: Ministry of Labor and Social Welfare.

Rosenthal, M. K., & Zilkha, E. (1987). Mothers and caregivers as partners in socializing the young child. In L. Shamgar-Handelman & R. Palomba (Eds.), *Alternative patterns of family life in modern societies* (pp. 119–131). Rome: IRP.

Rosenthal, M. K., & Zur, H. (1993). *The relationship between caregivers' interventions during peer interaction and toddlers' expression of concern for others*. Paper presented at the Society for Research in Child Development, New Orleans, LA.

Rotter, J. B. (1966). Generalized expectancies for internal versus external control of reinforcement. *Psychological Monographs, 80*(1, Whole No. 609).

Roupp, R., Travers, J., Glantz, F., & Coelen, C. (1979). *Children at the center*. Cambridge MA: ABT Associates.

Roupp, R. R., & Travers, J. (1982). Janus faces day care: Perspectives on quality and cost. In E. F. Zigler & E. W. Gordon (Eds.), *Day care: Scientific and social policy issues* (pp. 72–101). Boston: Auburn House.

Rubenstein, J. L., & Howes, C. (1979). Caregiving and infant behavior in day care and in homes. *Developmental Psychology, 15*, 1–24.

Ruff, H. A., Lawson, K. A., Parrinello, R., & Weissberg, R. (1990). Long term stability of individual differences in sustained attention in the early years. *Child Development, 61*, 60–75.

Rutter, M. (1985). Family and school influences on cognitive development. *Journal of Child Psychology and Psychiatry, 26*, 683–704.

Sarafino, E. P. (1985). Peer–peer interaction among infants and toddlers with extensive daycare experience. *Journal of Applied Developmental Psychology, 6*, 17–29.

Scarr, S., & Eisenberg, M. (1993). Child care research: Issues, perspectives, and results. *Annual Review of Psychology, 44*, 613–644.

Scarr, S., Phillips, D. A., & McCartney, K. (1990). Facts, fantasies, and the future of child care in the United States. *Psychological Science, 1*, 26–35.

Scarr, S., & Weinberg, R. A. (1978). The influence of "family background" on intellectual attainment. *American Sociological Review, 43*, 674–692.

Schindler, P. J., Moely, B. E., & Frank, A. L. (1987). Time in daycare and social participation of young children. *Developmental Psychology, 23*, 255–261.

Scott-Little, M. C., & Holloway, S. D. (1991). *Caregiver causal attributions regarding child misbehaviors: Relationship to caregiver behavioral responses*. Paper presented at the biennial meeting of the Society for Research in Child Development, Seattle, WA.

Shinman, S. (1981). *A choice for every child? Access and response to pre-school provision*. London: Tavistock.

Sigel, I. E. (Ed.). (1985). *Parental belief systems: The psychological consequences for children*. Hillsdale, NJ: Lawrence Erlbaum Associates.

Sigel, I. E. (1992). A political-cultural perspective on day care in the Netherlands, Italy and Sweden. In K. J. Sternberg, C. Hwang, A. G. Broberg, & M. E. Lamb (Eds.), *Child care in context: Cross-cultural perspectives* (pp. 119–134). Hillsdale, NJ: Lawrence Erlbaum Associates.

Smilansky, M., & Smilansky, S. (1967). Intellectual advancement of culturally disadvantaged children: An Israeli approach for research and action. *International Review of Education, 13*, 410–428.

Smilansky, M., Weintraub, S., & Hanegbi, Y. (1960). *Child and youth welfare in Israel*. Jerusalem: The Szold Institute.

Smilansky, S. (1968). *The effects of sociodramatic play on disadvantaged preschool children*. New York: Wiley.

Spodek, B., Saracho, O. N., & Peters, D. L. (Eds.). (1988). *Professionalism and the early childhood practitioner*. New York: Teachers College Press.

Stallings, J., & Porter, A. (1980). *National day care home study: Observation component*. Washington DC: DHEW.

Steinberg, L., & Green, C. (1979). *How parents may mediate the effects of day care*. Paper presented at the biennial meeting of the Society for Research in Child Development, San Francisco.

Super, C. M., & Harkness, S. (1986). The developmental niche: A conceptualization at the interface of child and culture. *International Journal of Behavioral Development, 9*, 545–569.

Tizard, B. (1974). Do social relationships affect language development? In J. Connolly & J. Bruner (Eds.), *The growth of competence* (pp. 227–237). New York: Academic Press.

Tizard, B., Philps, J., & Plewis, I. (1976). I. Play in preschool centers, II. effects on play of the child's social class and of the educational orientation of the center. *Journal of Child Psychology and Psychiatry, 17*, 265–274.

Tobin, J., Vu, D., & Davidson, D. (1989). *Preschool in three cultures*. New Haven, CT: Yale University Press.

Tulkin, S. R., & Cohler, B. J. (1973). Child rearing attitudes and mother child interaction in the first year of life. *Merril-Palmer Quarterly, 19*, 95–106.

Vandell, D. L., & Corasaniti, M. A. (1990). Child care and the family: Complex contributors to child development. In K. McCartney (Ed.), *New directions in child development research* (pp. 23–37). San Francisco: Jossey-Bass.

Vandell, D. L., Henderson, V. K., & Wilson, K. S. (1988). A longitudinal study of children with varying quality day care experiences. *Child Development, 59*, 1286–1292.

Vandell, D. L., & Powers, C. (1983). Day care quality and children's free play activities. *American Journal of Orthopsychiatry, 53*, 493–500.

Vandell, D. L., Wilson, K. S., & Buchanan, N. R. (1980). Peer interaction in the first year of life: An examination of its structure, content, and sensitivity to toys. *Child Development, 51*, 481–488.

Vygotsky, L. S. (1978). *Mind in society: The development of higher psychological processes*. Cambridge, MA: Harvard University Press.

Wachs, T., & Chan, A. (1986). Specificity of environmental action, as seen in environmental correlates of infants' communication performance. *Child Development, 57*, 1464–1474.

Wachs, T., & Gruen, G. (1982). *Early experience and human devlopment*. New York: Plenum.

Wachs, T. D., Francis, J., & McQuiston, S. (1979). Psychological dimensions of the infant's physical environment. *Infant Behavior and Development, 2*, 155–161.

Waters, E., Wippman, J., & Sroufe, A. (1979). Attachment, positive affect and competence in the peer group. *Child Development, 50*, 821–829.

Whaley, K. L., & Kantor, R. (1992). Mixed-age grouping in infant/toddler child care: Enhancing developmental processes. *Child and Youth Care Forum, 21*(6), 369–384.

White, R. W. (1959). Motivation reconsidered: The concept of competence. *Psychological Review, 66*, 297–333.

154   References

Whitebook, M., Howes, C., & Phillips, D. A. (1990). *Who cares? Child care teachers and the quality of care in America* (The National Child Care Staffing Study). Oakland, CA: Child Care Employee Project.
Winetsky, D. P. (1978). Comparisons of the expectations of parents and teachers for the behavior of preschool children. *Child Development, 49,* 1146–1154.
Wohlwill, J., & Heft, H. (1987). The physical environment and development of the child. In D. Stokols & I. Altman (Eds.), *Handbook of environmental psychology.* New York: Wiley.
Wohlwill, J. F. (1983). Physical and social environment as factors in development. In D. Magnusson & U. L. Allen (Eds.), *Human development: An interactional perspective* (pp. 111–129). New York: Academic Press.
Yarrow, L. J., Rubenstein, J. L., & Pederson, F. A. (1975). *Infant and environment: Early cognitive and motivational development.* New York: Wiley.

Author Index

Subject Index